WOMEN
BUILDING PEACE

WOMEN BUILDING PEACE

WHAT THEY DO, WHY IT MATTERS

WITHDRAWN

Sanam Naraghi Anderlini

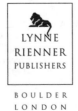

LYNNE
RIENNER
PUBLISHERS

BOULDER
LONDON

Published in the United States of America in 2007 by
Lynne Rienner Publishers, Inc.
1800 30th Street, Boulder, Colorado 80301
www.rienner.com

and in the United Kingdom by
Lynne Rienner Publishers, Inc.
3 Henrietta Street, Covent Garden, London WC2E 8LU

Library of Congress Cataloging-in-Publication Data
Anderlini, Sanam Naraghi.
    Women building peace : what they do, why it matters / by
Sanam Naraghi Anderlini.
      p.   cm.
    Includes bibliographical references and index.
    ISBN-13: 978-1-58826-536-4 (hardcover : alk. paper)
    ISBN-13: 978-1-58826-512-8 (pbk. : alk. paper)
1. Women and peace. 2. Peace-building. I. Title.
JZ5578.A63 2007
327.1'72082—dc22   2007011092

British Cataloguing in Publication Data
A Cataloguing in Publication record for this book
is available from the British Library.

Printed and bound in the United States of America

The paper used in this publication meets the requirements
∞ of the American National Standard for Permanence of
Paper for Printed Library Materials Z39.48-1992.

5 4 3 2 1

For Lydy and Sol-Sol,
Thank you for being mine

In loving memory of Daie Joon,
Dr. Sabbar Farman Farmaian

Contents

Acknowledgments

For over a decade I have worked as an advocate, researcher, trainer, and writer on peacebuilding and conflict prevention. I have met women from Rwanda, Sri Lanka, Somalia, Nepal, Uganda, Iraq, Afghanistan, Bosnia, South Africa, Colombia, and Palestine—women from all walks of life. These are women whose lives have been ripped apart by violence and war; whose children have been kidnapped, raped, or killed; whose fathers and brothers, or they themselves, have been victims of acts that are beyond the imagination. Yet they go on, not in anger or shame, not in revenge and hatred, but with a will to survive and to seek out humanity amid the violence.

In times when brute force holds sway, when we dehumanize the other so that killing is guilt-free, these women—and there are thousands of them everywhere—have a different answer. They recognize that wars make victims of everyone, on all sides. They know that the "enemy" is not simply skin color, religion, or ethnicity, but also poverty, oppression, and ignorance, often manipulated by politicians to sow fear and distrust. These women recognize that fear and distrust are complex and layered, fueled by every act of violence or retaliation. But they also know that in the end the killing must stop. Life must prevail. Away from the spotlight, without airtime or accolades, they focus on a vision of a better future, of normalcy and coexistence, and of building a genuine, just peace. It is an honor to work with such extraordinarily courageous women and a privilege to call so many friends. Without them, this book would not be possible. They are an immense source of inspiration, and I hope I have done them justice.

In writing about women, my intention is not to discount the peace efforts of men. Nor is it to understate the trauma and victimization of

women. Rather, it is to draw attention to their agency and dignity, experiences and contributions. I also reflect on my own experiences in
bridging the chasm between the reality of women's lives and work on
the ground, and the world of international policymakers and institutions
based in London, Washington, New York, Brussels, and elsewhere. It is
a privilege to be involved in this field and witness the changes taking
place.

As I look back over the years, I am also grateful to colleagues and
mentors who paved this path ahead of me. Ndeye Sow of International
Alert initiated some of the most important work on women's networking and conflict resolution in Burundi, at a time when thousands were
dying every year. Eugenia Piza Lopez had the vision to think big and
aim for the Security Council. Her grasp of international policy knows
no bounds. Ancil Adrian Paul, my friend and former colleague, has
waged a steady campaign, building international coalitions and influencing policies. The late Angela King walked the talk, setting a precedent during her time at the UN and in South Africa.

In 2000, I was privileged to work alongside Felicity Hill, Isha Dyfan,
Maha Muna, Ramina Johal, Florence Martin, Betty Reardon, and Cora
Weiss in our efforts toward the goal of what was to be UN Security Council Resolution 1325. Mahnaz Ispahani, then at the Ford Foundation, had
the faith and stamina to support our work. Ambassador Anuwral
Chowdhury of Bangladesh took the first and most difficult step by
embracing the issues at the Security Council during his presidency and
paving the way for future efforts. He showed us how business as usual
can be changed, if there is a will to do so. Aina Iyambo, then of the
Namibian mission, and Beatrice Maillé of the Canadian mission carried
the baton forward, and Ambassador Patricia Durrant of Jamaica was a
staunch supporter.

In the context of the US policy environment, the Initiative for Inclusive Security (IIS), formerly known as Women Waging Peace, and its
parent organization, the Hunt Alternatives Fund, must be given much
credit. IIS has been a consistent and prominent voice of support for
women's inclusion in peace processes. I thank Swanee Hunt and Judith
Kurland, who gave me the opportunity to establish and direct the
Women Waging Peace Policy Commission from 2002 to 2005. It was a
privilege to work with them and the most extraordinary team of
researchers. Together we produced groundbreaking field-based case
studies and the *Inclusive Security, Sustainable Peace* toolkit. This material has made a significant contribution to our collective understanding
of women's roles in the peace process. We used the findings to success-

fully reach out to the mainstream policy community and show that women make a positive difference to the promotion of peace and security in every arena. IIS has also led the effort to bring the voices of women peace activists—Afghans, Iraqis, Sudanese, Colombians, Israelis, Palestinians, and Liberians—to the international community at critical junctures. In my colleagues there, particularly Miki Jacevic, Camille Pampell Conaway, Elizabeth Powley, and Victoria Stanski, I witnessed a passion and commitment that are humbling.

Since 2005 I have had the opportunity to work more closely with colleagues within international agencies. I have learned a great deal from this experience and have immense appreciation for the efforts of many individuals who are supporting the women, peace, and security agenda from the inside. I thank Kanchan Paser, Laura Layton, Sherrill Whittington, Sahir Abdul Hadi of the UN Population Fund, and colleagues at the UN Office for the Coordination of Humanitarian Affairs, the UN Development Programme, the UN Development Fund for Women, the World Bank, and the UK's Department for International Development.

For their faith in my work and for encouraging me to write, I thank Jane Mansbridge of the Kennedy School and my mother, Khorshid F. F. Vickers. At Lynne Rienner Publishers, I am grateful to Lynne Rienner, Marilyn Grobschmidt, Karen Williams, and Beth Partin; their patience and support have been boundless. Books are not produced by one person alone. I have drawn upon the works of Julie Mertus, Rita Manchanda, Catalina Rojas, Pumla Gobodo Madikezela, Laura McGrew, and others; and I am thankful for the opportunity to have worked with these women at the policy commission. I am immensely grateful to Sarah Maguire for her willingness to discuss key points and read pieces; to Astrid Hieberg, Ramina Johal, Marcia Greenberg, Visaka Dharmadasa, Asha Elmi, Don Steinberg, and Vanessa Farr for sharing their observations; and particularly to Miki Jacevic, Sattareh Farman Farmaian, Julissa Mantilla, Dyan Mazurana, Jolynn Shoemaker, Victoria Stanski, John Tirman, and Cora Weiss for reading sections of the manuscript and being gentle but constructive in their criticism.

Finding the time to write would have been impossible without help at home. For this I thank my husband, Luca, who kept daily life and dinner going; and Julianne Ruckdeschel and Julia Wagner, who were immensely supportive and loving in their care for my daughters. As for the girls themselves, Lydia Leila and Soleh Banou, in their humor, love, empathy, and curiosity, they are a daily reminder of all that is good and why we have a responsibility to work for peace. I also take this opportunity to remember my uncle, Sabbar Farman Farmaian—"Daie Joon."

In his life and work, his love, his compassion, and his humor, he was and will always remain a source of inspiration. His death in Tehran during the writing of this book brought profound sadness to all of us who knew and loved him.

I recall that, in 1999, UNIFEM's executive director Noeleen Heyzer said, "It takes many hands to beat the drums." There are many hands now. The bandwagon of women in peace and security that started then is now a full-fledged convoy on a bumpy road. And there is still much we have to do. In 2007, the violence is raging in Iraq and Darfur. The Middle East is a tinderbox. What follows is a momentary pause to review, collate, and reflect on how far we've come and how far we have to go.

WOMEN
BUILDING PEACE

one

Introduction

I feel compelled to narrate that side of peace which standard textbooks of history and political science tend to ignore—a personal account of one player and the human dimension of an impersonal process. While the fate of nations and the course of global politics are generally perceived in abstractions and sweeping moves, something remains to be said about the view from within.
—Hanan Mikhail Ashrawi, *This Side of Peace* (1995)

New York City, March 2006: Across the street from the imposing United Nations building, on the second floor of the Church Center, known for its snail-paced elevators and myriad peace and justice organizations, pictures and stories of a thousand women hang side by side along the walls of a large meeting room. Collectively, they are the 2005 Nobel Prize nominees of the 1,000 women peace activists' campaign. They come from all walks of life and every corner of the globe. Some are teachers, doctors, lawyers, and environmentalists; others are antimilitarists and peace activists, promoting reconciliation and social justice. Many also devote themselves to women's rights and children's rights. They have given voice to the voiceless—children trapped in child-labor rings, women abused in sex trafficking, the elderly, the maimed, the sick, the disappeared. These 1,000 women are just the tip of the iceberg. For every one recognized, countless others remain unnamed. The breadth of their work is at once overwhelming and simple to understand; they are fighting for rights and equality, security of their people and communities, and dignity. But they remain steadfast in their commitment to nonviolence and coexistence. They are the very essence of peace.

The exhibit came to New York in time for the annual UN Commission on the Status of Women (CSW) meetings and the virtual pilgrimage of hundreds of women from around the world to the United Nations headquarters. Each year they come to follow the proceedings of the CSW, a typical UN body whose purpose and functions are barely understood outside the confines of the UN system and the organizations that follow it. But like other UN bodies, the CSW has significance. It is the organ within the UN system that follows the status and progress of women worldwide. In 2005, some 3,000 women came to mark the tenth anniversary of the Beijing Platform for Action. Human rights activists, educators, politicians, representatives of civil society organizations, peace activists, they all came to deal with serious issues of life and death. Yet their issues (or, more accurately, their perspective on the key issues facing the world) and their experiences at the front lines of many of the battles—from HIV/AIDS to poverty and war—were barely covered by the mainstream press.

Two parallel universes are at play. In one, women are active, vocal, and present in every sphere. In the other, they have been invisible, with limited roles in the management of power or the direction of their own lives. This book examines how women are striving to bridge the divide. It focuses on the contributions of women to peacebuilding and security, primarily in the context of transnational and civil wars since the end of the Cold War. It draws on international frameworks and explores women's contributions to pressing issues facing the global community, namely the prevention of violent conflict, peace negotiations, and peacebuilding at war's end.

The international community, dominated by multilateral bureaucracies and major industrial countries, has begun to take notice of women but seems incapable of addressing the complex reality of their experiences. The pendulum swings to extremes. On the one hand, women are vulnerable, passive, unable to protect themselves, inevitable victims of physical and sexual abuse, and in need of protection. On the other hand, women are the panacea, the internal bulwark against extremism; their political participation is the solution to all evils—particularly those of religious militancy.

Regardless of the view taken, the political rhetoric, amplified through speeches and policy statements, goes further than any action to support women. Sexual abuse, a known quantity in camps for the internally displaced and refugees, is still not prevented adequately. Peacekeepers, both military and civilian, continue to be implicated (publicly or privately) in the sexual abuse of precisely those populations they are sent to protect. Talk of engaging with women's peace organizations, ensuring their participation in peacebuilding, remains largely talk. The practice is at best ad hoc.

Arguments suggesting that women have a right to be present at forums where their future is discussed still hold little sway. Implicitly and often explicitly, decisionmakers want proof that the inclusion of women in peacemaking or recovery will make a positive difference. Yet, regardless of the proof that is provided and the failures of existing processes, bureaucracies and their technocrats are slow to budge. "Business as usual," says one former ambassador to the UN, is the root of inertia.

To be fair, the gap between the two worlds is not entirely the fault of the international actors. Veterans of the international women's movement regard the mainstream with a mix of frustration, disillusionment, and anger. For too long, activists have tried, and the system has not complied. The disdain for existing systems—including the political and diplomatic processes that often result in amnesty for perpetrators of war, the lack of real justice for victims, and the preservation of the ruling elite—has pushed many women away from the formal political arena. Unwilling to give up their beliefs and morals, too many women remain outside the institutions and structures in which decisions are made.

In reality, resolving conflicts and building peace, particularly in situations of internal war, are too complex and messy to be left to any one sector. The international community and those in the formal political sector need to understand the work of women, what impact it has, and what potential it could have if supported and sustained. Women active in peace and security issues also need to engage more fully with the processes that exist. Business as usual will not change unless it is forced to change.

This book is about those women who are working for peace and striving to engage in the formal processes. It is about those who bring new perspectives and commitment to issues of conflict prevention, peacemaking, and reconstruction, and the differences they are making. It is neither a denial nor a dilution of women's inalienable right to be present and active in decisionmaking that affects their world, countries, communities, and families. Regardless of whether women have a positive or negative impact, they, like men, have a right to participation; it is a given.

This book is not about what rights women should have. The discrimination, obstacles, and exclusion facing women are addressed, and certainly many of the activities or issues that women bring forth relate to women's inequality, but the book is not primarily about those issues. There are countless articles, reports, and books written on this aspect of the subject. Nor is this book a treatise on how the international community must use peace processes to promote women's rights. I take that as a given, for three reasons. First, supporting women's full and active participation in decisionmaking, particularly in countries emerging from conflict, is a key indicator of a shift away from the status quo that, in many instances, catalyzed the conflict. Second, as 50 percent or more of the population, women are an important resource. Overlooking their capacities and commitment to peacebuilding is an indication of bad planning. Third, respect for and promotion of women's rights are mandated by international law. The problem is implementation or political will, and the lack thereof.

Instead, here I seek to bridge the chasm between the work of women and the efforts of international players. The central question addressed is not so much what peace processes can or should do for women, but what do women do for peace processes, which by definition benefit society as a whole. It is about examining women's actions within the framework and set of priorities already identified by the international community, demonstrating how and why they make a positive difference, and what limits and challenges they still face.

This book does not attempt to deny women's extensive experiences of victimhood and the debilitating effects of war. The direct and deliberate targeting of women, the use of their bodies—through rape, forced impregnation, sexual torture—as literally the front lines of the battlefield, cannot be overlooked. The loss of livelihoods and social networks and the violence, isolation, and hardship that result from forced displacement are overwhelming and extend far into the future for many. Yet, in acknowledging women's experiences of violence, we cannot overlook or ignore their resilience, sense of self-dignity, desire for survival, and struggle to move beyond passive victimhood. In the words of one United Nations officer, "in crisis situations, the women are the best humanitarian workers."[1] They are also among the most committed peacebuilders. We must recognize, respect, and support their efforts.

Discussions about women's participation in peace and security inevitably lead to the question of "which women?" Detractors often point to Margaret Thatcher, Condoleezza Rice, or the new crop of women suicide bombers as the antithesis to the arguments being presented. Women's roles in sustaining war and perpetuating violence are also not in question in this book. Women, like men, can spread fear and mistrust, commit atrocities, and send armies of young men and women to kill and be killed. As politicians, they can be as hawkish as men. I do not suggest that all women are inherently more competent and skilled than men at negotiations or that they are more naturally peace loving. Inevitably, as individuals, both men and women can exert positive and negative influences in war and peacemaking. Clearly, women are not homogeneous. But for every Thatcher or Rice there is an Aung San Suu Kyi, Jody Williams, or Wangari Maathai, women who have waged peace through nonviolence, the destruction of weapons, and care for the environment. Thus, while we cannot ignore women who take up arms, we cannot brush aside the thousands of women who proactively pursue peace through nonviolent means.

Is this activism a new phenomenon? Yes and no. History has much to say about women's activism in the political sphere, of women calling for peace, prior to and during World War I, or of women being depicted as the wagers of peace—albeit using unorthodox methods—as in the Greek play *Lysistrata*. There is also an implicit and unconscious expectation that women are not naturally violent. Why else is there such shock when young women (or worse, mothers) strap explosives to their bodies and blow themselves up? The same shock is rarely, if ever, expressed about young men or fathers. Yet the expectation that women are less violent or more peaceful than men is rarely translated into an acknowledgment of how women can be effective in promoting peace. On the contrary, a common reason given for the exclusion of women from peace talks is that they were not "waging the war." To borrow from Carl von Clausewitz, peace negotiations are, in effect, an extension of war by other means. Experience and skills in building trust, alleviating fear, and making compromises—essential ingredients of peacemaking—are often ignored when peace or power is up for grabs.

In part, however, contemporary women's peace activism, particularly in its ubiquitous presence across the world, is indeed a new phenomenon: it is intricately tied to the changing nature of warfare, the blurring of lines between battlefield and community, victim and perpetrator, enemy and neighbor. It is both highly localized in nature and increasingly a global movement with its own characteristics, linked to the UN and the system of international conferences and networks that have emerged since the early 1990s. As wars (particularly civil wars) destroy the social taboos and mores that protected women, so women themselves are taking a stand and saying enough is enough.

Where the Local Meets the Global

The United Nations–sponsored Fourth World Conference on Women, held in Beijing in 1995, had much to do with catalyzing women's activism in peace and security. The focus on women's experiences in war, articulated in Chapter E (Women and Armed Conflict) of the Platform for Action (PFA), was a new addition to the broader agenda of women and development. In 1995, a year after the genocide in Rwanda and the rape camps of Bosnia, the ugly reality of civil war and its impact on women's lives needed to be addressed head-on. Chapter E does not just dwell on women's victimization. It addresses women's agency in promoting peace and calls for the increased involvement of women in the resolution of conflicts. Such demands seem out of step and time, except for the conference participation of Israeli and Palestinian women, Northern Irish women, survivors of the Rwandan genocide and Bosnian war, and veteran activists from South Africa. These women had experienced war in their homes and their lives but had chosen to resist the violence and work for peace. They had crossed the invisible lines of conflict to embrace the "other" and search for solutions together. In 1995, in Northern Ireland and the Middle East particularly, these women had made strides, mobilizing public support and giving voice to the silent majority that wanted peace.

The conference delegates, both governmental and nongovernmental, who drafted the language of Chapter E could not have known that their words were launching a global revolution—inspiring women to step into the realm of global peace and security, challenging perhaps the last bastion of male-dominated decisionmaking. Beijing and the PFA were a turning point—a call to action and an inspiration for many women experiencing violent conflict firsthand.

In the years that followed, local, national, and international women's activism in peacemaking and security-related issues grew exponentially, with regional and international networks taking shape. The spontaneity and seemingly unrelated and discrete nature of the initiatives that emerged are in part deceptive. How is it that women across the world were standing up to the status quo and saying "enough" to violence and conflict? In reality, it was a convergence of factors. In some instances, as in Liberia and Sierra Leone, women took a stand against the encroachment of war into their daily lives and were later supported by the international community, beginning with a handful of nongovernmental organizations (NGOs). In other cases, donors—including the Ford Foundation, bilateral aid agencies, and the UN Development Fund for Women (UNIFEM)—supported women's leadership, recognizing that women were not simply passive victims of war, but rather had specific capacities and potentials for the promotion of peace. Invariably, the support provided by such organizations was internally driven by a handful of visionary and committed women.

As activism in conflict-affected countries evolved at the international level, the demand for formal political inclusion of women's rights in peace and security issues also gathered momentum. In 2000, at the fifth anniversary review conference of the Beijing declaration (Beijing +5), a group of NGOs launched a global appeal for a Security Council resolution that would formally recognize women's rights to participation in peace and security issues and protection in conflict zones. Forging new partnerships with governments and UN agencies, the NGOs—initially known as the Ad Hoc Working Group on Women, Peace, and Security[2]—reached out to their extensive networks of civil society organizations to generate consensus and a constituency for the resolution. Working with the governments of Bangladesh, Jamaica, Canada, Namibia—all of whom had temporary seats on the Security Council—and eventually the United Kingdom, they built a coalition.

Bangladesh cracked opened the door to the Security Council in March 2000. Under the leadership of Ambassador Anwarul Chowdhury, a formal presidential statement was issued that recognized both women's need for protection and contributions to peacebuilding. Namibia pushed it open even further. In May 2000, the government hosted a high-level seminar, "Mainstreaming a Gender Perspective in Multidimensional Peace Support Operations," and issued a formal plan of action known as the Windhoek Declaration.[3] In subsequent months, as the key pillars of a possible resolution became more concrete, the link between women's peace and security demands and peace support operations (clearly a purview of the Security Council) added weight and helped legitimize the discussions at the council. Finally, on October 31, 2000, under Namibia's presidency, the Security Council passed Resolution 1325 on women, peace, and security. For the first time in its fifty-year history, the council recognized that women had a right to protection and a role to play in maintaining peace and security. The chamber was filled, and the audience applauded.

This resolution marked a watershed. It provides a critical legal and political framework through which, for the first time in history, women worldwide can claim their space and voice their views on peace and security matters. It also marks a turning point in the relationship between civil society, especially women's organizations, and the international system, particularly the Security Council. Each October, since the passing of 1325, the NGO community has pressed for and succeeded in obtaining a review of progress on the implementation of the resolution's key provisions. Upon the first anniversary, in 2001, the council members expressed surprise. "Other resolutions don't have anniversaries," they said, to which the NGOs replied, "Other resolutions don't have a global constituency."

Perhaps most importantly, 1325 has become a tool for empowering women, enabling them to mobilize on a global scale to assert their demands for a place at the table when issues of war and peace are addressed and resolved. Since 2000, women's advocacy has increased.

A brief overview of activities in early 2007 reveals a wealth of initiatives under way. Among grassroots activists in Nepal and Somalia, international NGOs, bilateral donors, the UN, and academia, attention to sexual and gender-based violence in conflict-affected societies is increasing. The status of female ex-combatants is appearing on the agenda of international policymakers. Women's political participation is being debated in Kabul and Kigali. Transitional justice processes are more amenable to women. The discourse on women in the security sector and in peacekeeping is gaining ground.[4] Traditional activism also continues. From Bogotá to Baghdad, women are on the front lines of providing services, heading households, caring for the sick and the elderly, and sustaining and ensuring the survival of their families. Even in refugee camps, women shoulder the responsibilities of others. Despite the traumas and victimization they experience, particularly where sexual assault of women is a strategy of warfare, they are initiating peacemaking efforts. It is often women who first give voice to civilians silenced by atrocities. And long after international support has ended, women are left to handle the trauma and violence that come home with men whose lives have been devastated by war. Such women provide the continuity that enables families and communities to heal and move forward. Increasingly, they are claiming their place as major stakeholders and active agents in resisting war, building peace, and defining security on their terms.

This book spotlights these women and their experiences. It does not deny the hardship and trauma that come with peace activism. The burnout rate is high among local and international players. Neither does it deny the ambivalence that women often feel in taking on the new burdens. Working for an end to war is not a choice for many; it is a necessity for survival. Once a crisis is over, many are compelled to return to their daily lives and jobs. Countless others remain committed to the slow and painful work of rebuilding their communities, healing the trauma, and taking a stand in their respective nations' political process.

Perhaps most important, this is not a book about the exceptional few, the "superwomen" of our age. Rather it is about ordinary women—teachers, social workers, doctors, mothers, actors, dancers, lawyers, politicians, fighters—who find themselves caught in extraordinary times and take action to bring normalcy back to their lives.

Just as there is no homogeneity among women at large, there is no single ideology, approach, or even motivation that defines this growing sector, which veteran activist Cora Weiss calls "peace women." Many are intellectuals or academics rooted firmly in antimilitarist feminism. Others are emerging from armed forces—state or opposition groups—

motivated by a desire for equality, justice, and an end to discrimination. As much as they find common ground, they are also challenged by the myriad women who are active at the grassroots, often oblivious to the intellectual discourse of feminism or equality, but driven by the harsh realities of their own existence. As the lines of warfare have become more blurred and civilians have become the primary targets, more women are emerging from grassroots and rural communities to resist the violence. Too many have seen their children kidnapped or killed and found strength in their identities as mothers to speak out. From Sri Lanka to Uganda, they enter the political fray, demanding accountability and justice. Others, in Sierra Leone, Liberia, and elsewhere, themselves both victims and forced perpetrators of violence, are seeking justice and raising their voices. Once free, they take on the mantle of reintegrating former combatants, encouraging trust and reconciliation in communities that barely exist anymore. Of the elite or from the grassroots, educated or not, these women play a transformative role in peacemaking in their societies, through civil society and in official governmental processes.

Although their motivations and ideologies may differ, their vision and demands for the future often converge. Peace is seen as freedom from violence; access to safe housing, employment, and education; equality in the eyes of law and society; the right to property ownership; a return to normalcy. They seek to bring the voices of the marginalized and the unrepresented into the political arena. They advocate a policy of inclusion, equality, freedom, and plurality. They emphasize a holistic notion of peace, defined not just in military security and political terms but also in terms of human security, rooted in a combination of political, economic, personal, community, and environmental factors.[5] In effect, these women—be they antimilitarists, former fighters, the elite, or grassroots actors—come together through their commitment to social justice, fairness, and equality for all.

Claiming a Space Within the Policy Discourse[6]

Within academia, this emerging field of women, peace, and security studies has not found a permanent home yet. A growing body of literature has contributed to the evolution of the discourse on many levels. Ann Tickner, Cynthia Enloe, Betty Reardon, Jacklyn Cock, and others have brought a feminist lens to the study of international relations and the intersections of militarism and peace.[7] Simona Sharoni writing on the Middle East; the works of Sheila Meintjes and Anu Pillay, and Meredith Turshen and

Clotilde Twagiramariya on Africa; Cynthia Cockburn on the Balkans
and Cyprus; and Rita Manchanda on South Asia all have contributed to
the feminist traditions and have drawn attention to the regional experiences of women in war and peacemaking.[8] Caroline Moser's work as
scholar and practitioner has defined new links between gender and
political violence. *Arms to Fight, Arms to Protect: Women Speak Out
About Conflict* (1995), an edited volume of women's testimonies, has
given space to the experiences of ordinary women in war. Susan McKay
and Dyan Mazurana's *Women and Peacebuilding* (1999), together with
my own *Women at the Peacetable: Making a Difference* (2000) and conference reports by International Alert and other NGOs, have drawn specific attention to women's agency and personal experiences in peacemaking. *Women, War, and Peace,* an independent evaluation conducted
by Ellen Johnson-Sirleaf and Elizabeth Rehn for UNIFEM in 2002,
together with the UN Secretary-General's study on *Women, Peace, and
Security,* have also helped frame much of the debate. A complete literature survey is beyond the scope of this book, particularly given that so
much that has contributed to our collective understanding comes from
outside the boundaries of academia or traditional texts. International
and national NGOs that document the voices and experiences of women
at conferences and workshops, alongside the UN and research and policy institutions, are at the forefront of this growing discourse.

The field itself continues to expand. Activists and academics are
turning their attention to peacekeeping, disarmament, and broader security sector issues. The discourse about women and transitional justice
is evolving, as is that on postconflict governance. The issue of violence
against women has also gained significant traction within academia and
the activist and policy communities. In effect, the field of women, peace,
and security is interdisciplinary, straddling anthropology, security studies, international relations, women's studies, political science, and development economics; it is firmly rooted in the reality of women's lives,
which cannot be artificially delineated.

For the purposes of advocacy, the activist community often emphasizes three key issues: participation, protection, and prevention. Participation relates to the need to include women in peace- and security-
related decisionmaking at the local, national, and international levels.
Protection addresses women's needs and the provision of assistance
during and after crises and conflicts. Prevention is discussed broadly
with regard to avoiding violence and transforming conflict peacefully,
and specifically in terms of stopping violence against women in conflict
situations.[9] At a conceptual level, however, this field draws from and is
influencing four key areas of discourse related to peace and security: the

human security framework, conflict transformation discourse, humanitarian accountability issues, and women's rights.

Human Security

Articulated in the 1990s by the UN Development Programme (UNDP) and adopted by the Canadian government, the human security framework challenges the traditional notion of state-based (and by extension militarized) security. It places people's security first. In the immediate aftermath of the Cold War, insecurity within state borders—caused by economic decline, bad governance, health epidemics (notably HIV/AIDS), environmental degradation, and the pervasive presence of small arms, criminal activities, and organized crime—became more widely recognized as a threat to the state and its people. Moreover, the increased prominence of nonstate, substate, and transnational actors continues to challenge notions of national and international security. (For a more in-depth discussion of human security, see Chapter 7.)

In 2000, then UN Secretary-General Kofi Annan distilled and defined human security as "freedom from want and freedom from fear,"[10] addressed through four key components: critical and pervasive threats, human rights, protection, and building on people's strengths.

Critical and pervasive threats are elements within the physical or social environment that could have destructive effects over long periods of time, undermining people's ability to recover from shocks and disasters. For example, economic deprivation, pervasive corruption, and long-term mismanagement of resources, leading to shoddy infrastructure, bad roads, and substandard health care and education, can have an exponential impact on the number of people affected if natural disaster strikes. Similarly, corruption and repression foment anger and increase the vulnerability of young people—oftentimes men—to recruitment by militias. Proponents of human security advocate for attention to the needs of the people and redressing underlying factors that fuel the sense of insecurity in a society.

Human rights are central to the human security discourse. Human rights law comes together with international humanitarian law in the context of armed conflict, environmental security, and other issues. The human security framework also draws attention to the rights of groups that are not specifically addressed in international humanitarian law, notably the elderly, internally displaced persons, the disabled, minorities, and others. Human security also makes human rights (i.e., people's rights) central to state security. Implicitly, the argument is that human rights violations are often catalysts for the emergence of armed opposition groups that in turn threaten state security. It counters the tendencies of many states to withhold, curtail, or withdraw civil and human rights in the name of state security.

Protection is also a central theme, particularly in the context of emergency situations. Human security advocates argue that people's basic human rights must be protected at all stages of armed conflict and human or natural disasters. They cannot be left until later, after the political deals have been made. Finally, by placing people at the center, the human security paradigm recognizes and encourages the strengths and potential that individuals can use to create positive change.

As noted above and discussed in later chapters, women peace activists are often natural proponents of the human security paradigm, simply because their notion of security is derived from their lived experiences. They know and cope with the consequences of basic insecurity—the lack of education, health care, and sanitation and the fear of violence—but they also draw on their own strengths and position in society to bring greater security for themselves and their dependents.

Conflict Transformation

The conflict transformation or coexistence framework that has emerged and evolved since the late 1980s has also been a key source of influence for the women, peace, and security discourse. In the context of intergroup communal violence or civil war, specialists in this field focus their attention on the need to abolish the cyclical nature of violence. Conflict, they argue, is a natural and often positive expression of social dynamism; the challenge is to avoid the emergence of violence by creating an environment in which conflict can be addressed constructively. The notion of transformation embraces traditional elements of conflict resolution, such as mediation, dialogue, and negotiation. It also goes beyond tradition to draw attention to issues of rights and justice, promoting inclusive decisionmaking and participation, addressing the welfare and survival needs of people, strengthening civil society, encouraging social and economic reconstruction, and promoting reconciliation.

A defining feature of this discourse is the notion that—particularly in the context of civil wars—multiple actors from a cross section of society, nationally and internationally, are needed to bring peace and rebuild the trust and fabric of society. Much of women's peace activism fits into this framework. They live with the consequences of failure and are thus motivated to take action. Many recognize that women—not only as half the population, but also as the sector that tries to maintain elements of peace and normalcy in their homes and communities in the midst of raging war—have something to offer, whereas political and military leaders' commitment to peace may be less than certain.

As victims of violence and as a cross section of society that experiences exclusion and discrimination systematically, women activists focus their efforts on changing entrenched attitudes and practices by finding their own entry points and building on their social ties. It is not surprising, therefore, that women often work through their socially accepted identities as elderly women and mothers, or their personal affiliations—as daughters, wives, sisters—to engage in informal and behind-the-scenes mediation.

Humanitarian Accountability

A key element of the women, peace, and security discourse arises from basic protection needs in emergency and civil war situations. It draws from and has sought to influence the theory and practice of humanitarian work. In the early 1990s, humanitarian agencies sought to clarify the basic principles on which they conducted their work in emergency and crisis situations. They recognized that their short-term planning, misunderstanding of local dynamics, and lack of coordination at times fueled conflict inadvertently. From the standpoint of women, many projects were criticized for ignoring women's roles and needs. In some instances, interventions caused greater harm to women, for example, by escalating sexual exploitation and abuse. Oftentimes, ignorance of social and gender dynamics led to the perpetuation of discrimination and the abuse of women. Throughout the 1990s, key entities within the humanitarian community developed a range of guidelines and codes of conduct to enable the principles to be implemented effectively. Yet for some time, the "tyranny of the urgent" claim overshadowed demands for gender awareness and sensitivity to women in particular. With interventions by organizations such as the Women's Commission for Refugee Women and Children in the late 1990s, recognition of the urgency and centrality of women's basic needs gained ground. The issue of protection from and, most important, prevention of violations against women is therefore a key feature of the field of women, peace, and security.

Women's Rights

Clearly, the women, peace, and security discourse is also linked to the world of women's rights activism, which is itself an offshoot and integral aspect of human rights. The Universal Declaration of Human Rights (UDHR) is the home of many of the issues and concepts that remain unaddressed. Yet, even though the UDHR takes a holistic approach to human rights, the field of human rights that evolved during the Cold War years was largely limited to political and civil issues. Consequently, violations against women that occurred in homes and communities as a result of cultural and traditional practices were overlooked. This oversight resulted in women's activists' demands for specific attention to women's rights. In 1975, the First World Conference on Women was held in Mexico; it was a catalyst for a global movement that has strengthened and diversified since then. The Convention on the Elimination of All Forms of Discrimination Against Women (CEDAW), which emerged in 1979, is seen as the international bill of rights for women. By 2006, 182 states—over 90 percent of the UN's membership—had ratified it. Many countries, including Uganda, South Africa, Brazil, and Australia, have incorporated CEDAW provisions into their constitutions and national legislation.

Twenty years after the Mexico conference, the Fourth World Conference on Women in Beijing set a new milestone. The Platform for Action outlines twelve critical areas concerning women's lives: poverty, education, health care, violence, armed conflict, unequal access to resources, power and decisionmaking structures, lack of mechanisms to promote women effectively, inadequate respect for and promotion of women's human rights, stereotyping and inequality in communications and the media, environmental concerns, and discrimination against the girl-child.

Beijing gave women the opportunity to come together and raise the specter of armed conflict collectively under the framework of women's rights. The ensuing UN-sponsored conferences on women continue to provide activists with the chance to meet and exchange views, to evaluate where they stand, and to draw others into the realm of peace and security. The rubric of women's rights is a comfortable zone, one that provides sustenance and encouragement most naturally. In reality, however, women peace activists are not just women's rights activists. They embrace and embody a complex array of values and approaches emerging from the conceptual frameworks discussed above. Therefore, they face a dual challenge.

On the one hand, there is an ongoing effort to bring the complexity of war and peace and the need for engagement in these issues firmly into the work of traditional women's rights and development actors. On the other hand, even as the fields of human security and conflict transformation claim to promote inclusivity and participation, there is still a tendency for women to be rendered invisible. For women peace activists, this struggle to bring "conflict sensitivity to women's rights" and "women's peace activism and protection needs to conflict and security people" is in itself a formidable but necessary task. With the former, there is the difficulty of drawing attention to yet another range of issues, much of it outside the domain of women's traditional activism. With the latter, there is a combined task of bringing visibility and volume to women's experiences and demonstrating the actual and potential contributions of women that can enhance these fields.

The Structure of the Book

In writing this book, I draw and build upon recent and ongoing research in the field of women, peace, and security, with a close eye on the policies and practices of the international community. Much of the material quoted comes from the findings of the Women Waging Peace Policy Commission, which I directed. The commission produced field-based case studies across Africa, Asia, Europe, and Latin America with a focus on women's contributions to different pillars of peace and security: (1) conflict prevention; (2) peace negotiations; (3) postconflict disarmament, demobilization, and reintegration; (4) governance; and (5) transitional justice. These same five themes make up the chapters of this book. The chapters are put in a particular order for ease of reading, not because the process itself is always linear. I deliberately chose to place women's activism within the framework of the international policy community to show how women engage in, contribute to, and often make a critical difference to the issues that continue to challenge international actors.

The peace and security world is complex and ever-expanding. There are countless macro- and microfactors to consider, and much lies beyond the scope of this book. The countries, groups, and individuals I mention in many ways characterize and exemplify the nature of women's activism and approaches across the world. But for every case mentioned, there are others that fit the bill. Much of the discussion focuses on contemporary events that occurred in the course of writing this book. Inevitably, there will be setbacks or progress in the field, within international entities and in the countries mentioned. I have tried to keep up-to-date with events. Where women have had a more profound impact, their experiences are discussed across various chapters.

Chapter 2 addresses conflict prevention practice, with a specific focus on the early prevention of violence and the nonviolent transformation of conflict (not escalation or postconflict resurgence). It offers examples of women's activism, its effects and limitations, as well as a discussion of how and why information from and about women can enhance conflict early warning processes. It also highlights the ongoing dilemmas that the international community faces in tackling the rise of insecurity within state borders.

Chapter 3 discusses women's mobilization for peace during war and attempts to address the formal negotiation processes. It highlights the strategies and tactics that women adopt to get their voices heard at local, national, and international levels. Drawing on the handful of instances where women made it to the formal negotiations process, it analyzes the qualities they bring to the process and substance of peace talks.

Chapter 4 is an examination of disarmament, demobilization, and reintegration (DDR) processes as a thin slice of more complex security-related interventions. Reflecting on El Salvador, Sierra Leone, and elsewhere, it draws attention to the challenges that women face in gaining access to such programs. It further explores how women, as civilians and as fighters and supporters of armed groups, contribute to DDR. In doing so, it critiques existing practices that tend to exclude women.

Chapter 5 looks at women's contributions to postconflict governance processes. Drawing on a range of cases, including Rwanda, Cambodia, and Afghanistan, it highlights how women contribute to key aspects of good governance by promoting cooperative working practices, addressing corruption, and representing fresh perspectives in the immediate postwar years.

Chapter 6 delves into the difficult and delicate world of justice and reconciliation. It compares and contrasts women's roles in international criminal tribunals and truth and reconciliation commissions. In highlighting the contributions they make, it also points to significant gaps in the treatment and rehabilitation of victims.

Chapter 7 takes a different turn, presenting a discussion and assessment of the international community—individual countries, the UN system, and others—that are engaged in peace and security efforts worldwide. It examines how the rhetoric on women's inclusion and rights is matched (or unmatched) in reality. It identifies constraints and bottlenecks, normative and institutional factors that have resulted in slow and limited support for and attention to women from the international community.

My goal in addressing these issues through the lens of women's contributions is not to suggest that they alone have all the answers. Nor is it to attribute strength to women's activism in areas where they are struggling and where the tides of today easily wash away the progress of yesterday. Rather it is to bring to light peace activism, as limited or extensive as it may be in each country and under different circumstances, to demonstrate its value and its need for support, resources, and recognition. By looking through the lens of women's experiences, this book also reveals flaws and gaps in the existing peace and security paradigm. Although it does not pretend to have solutions for the problems that are noted, it raises questions that need to be addressed. It also challenges the institutions and political leaders who bask in the rhetoric of gender equality or Security Council Resolution 1325 but have demonstrated insufficient commitment to overhauling existing practices to ensure its full implementation.

Finally, I would like to pause to address the words *gender* and *women*. Too often the terms are conflated and used interchangeably. This book is first and foremost about women and the transformative nature of women's peace activism. *Gender* will be used specifically in circumstances where the discussions address either the differential needs and experiences of women and men or the links to power and decision-making that affect men and women differently. Throughout the text, I provide definitions of specific terms that have been developed and used by the mainstream global peace and security community.

Notes

1. Discussion with the author, Cambridge, Massachusetts, 2007.

2. The founding members of the working group were International Alert, the Women's Commission for Refugee Women and Children, Amnesty International, the Hague Appeal for Peace, and the Women's International League for Peace and Freedom. The group has since formalized and grown to twelve members and remains active at the UN level.

3. Windhoek Declaration, available at http://www.un.org.

4. Women's International League for Peace and Freedom, "2007: Challenges and Opportunities for Implementing 1325," *1325 PeaceWomen's E-news,* issue 85, January 31, 2007, available at http://www.peacewomen.org/news/1325 News/Issue85.pdf.

5. See Lloyd Axworthy, *Safety for People in a Changing World* (Ottawa: Canadian Ministry of Foreign Affairs, 1999).

6. This section replicates and summarizes parts of Sanam Naraghi Anderlini and Judy El-Bushra, "The Conceptual Framework: Security, Peace, Accountability and Rights," in *Inclusive Security, Sustainable Peace: A Toolkit for Advocacy and Action* (Washington, DC: International Alert, Hunt Alternatives Fund: 2004), pp. 5–13.

7. The full references are included in the bibliography.

8. The full references are included in the bibliography.

9. Security Council Working Roundtable, background paper, January 27, 2004, available at http://www.international-alert.org/pdfs/SC_roundtable_three _p.pdf.

10. Kofi Annan, *In Larger Freedom: Towards Security, Development and Human Rights for All* (New York: United Nations, 2005).

two

Preventing and Transforming Conflict Nonviolently

Could we have managed [the threat of Saddam Hussein] by means other than a direct military intervention? Well, maybe we could have.
—Richard Perle, former chair of the Pentagon's Defense Policy Board, November 2006[1]

Just people cannot follow unjust laws. . . . We seem to be the only people bravely standing in the street, owning the street, commanding it. . . . And so they [the police] felt they had to trample upon us much harder. . . . But we have a slogan: "Strike a woman and you strike a rock." We are not going to be deterred.
—Jenni Williams, founder, WOZA, 2005[2]

In 2002, a US-led war against Saddam Hussein's regime in Iraq was inevitable in the minds of most people. In Washington and London, discussions among policy pundits and analysts had moved beyond the prevention of war into the realm of possible scenarios in the aftermath and detailed plans and recommendations for "winning the peace."[3] In the midst of this, a group of women in shades of pink took a different stand. Calling themselves "Code Pink" in response to the Bush administration's color-coded warnings against the threat of terror, the US-based group defined itself as "a women-led and women-initiated grassroots peace and social justice movement dedicated to stopping the war in Iraq, preventing future wars and redirecting our country's resources into life-affirming activities: education, health care, veteran's benefits and social services."[4]

Code Pink led protests, mobilized women and men, opened chapters across the United States and internationally, and became an organized movement. In the same year, in Zimbabwe, the government-induced economic crisis and descent into mass poverty were accelerating. In response, Women of Zimbabwe Arise (WOZA), officially formed in 2003, also started peaceful but noisy public protests against the government. In its first demonstration, WOZA took to pot banging on the streets of Harare, protesting violence against women. At its second gathering, the women, representing a cross section of Zimbabwean society, protested the increasingly harsh government policies by handing out roses to symbolize love. "We challenge the love of power, with the power of love," says WOZA founder Jenni Williams, veteran of twenty-five arrests.[5]

Across the world in Venezuela, the pot-banging tactic has also been at work. Protesting President Hugo Chavez's encroachment on democratic freedoms from 2000 to 2005, women in Venezuela adopted nonviolent strategies to protest his actions. Firmly identifying themselves as women, mothers, sisters, daughters, and grandmothers, they joined the broader resistance movement and adopted three strategies: protest and persuasion, noncooperation, and intervention.[6] They initiated community meetings to discuss nonviolent strategies for protest and mobilized to collect signatures for a referendum in 2004. Waving flags and blowing whistles, banging pots and shouting slogans, they often accounted for over 50 percent of the protesters.

Code Pink did not succeed in preventing the onset of the Iraq War. Will WOZA or the women of Venezuela succeed in bringing about change nonviolently? Difficult to predict; for every attempt at a Czech-like Velvet Revolution, there are countless other instances where nonviolent demands for change have ended with state-sponsored and even communal violence. That is ironic. The need to prevent violent expression of conflict is an easy concept to grasp. Yet avoiding overt violent conflict remains a critical challenge for most societies struggling for peaceful transition from oppression to coexistence and democracy.

No society wants violence, so much so that the tolerance threshold for oppression, poverty, fear, and abuse is extremely high in most instances. The horrors and unpredictability of war are too well-known, and violence is not the route that most people wish to follow. Yet preventing violent conflict and civil wars is proving to be an elusive challenge.[7]

Even in the case of the US war on Iraq, those opposing the war could offer no viable alternative way of dealing with Saddam Hussein. Some argued for the maintenance of international sanctions and isolation, which had hardened the regime's grip on the country. But in taking that stance they were implicitly willing to leave the Iraqi people at the mercy of the Hussein regime for a further indeterminate period. Talk of lifting the sanctions or exploring alternative long-term solutions was either limited or never fully aired. The space for deliberations was heavily circumscribed by the political class and the media. The mass public demonstrations had no effect. By the time the Iraq invasion began in March 2003, the trajectory of violence was not a surprise. Like the wars in Kosovo and the Democratic Republic of Congo in 1998, we watched as the inevitable became reality.

Throughout the late 1990s, the idea of conflict prevention—particularly in the context of intrastate conflicts—captured the imagination and pockets of many European nations and through them the European Commission. The term *conflict prevention* became internationally accepted shorthand for describing the prevention of the outbreak, escalation, or resurgence of *armed* conflict.[8] In the United States, the Carnegie Commission on Preventing Deadly Conflict (1994–1999) made distinctions between direct (short-term) conflict prevention that aims to halt the rise of violence and structural (long-term) prevention that seeks to address the root political, social, and economic causes of conflict so that it can be resolved and transformed nonviolently.[9] In practice, however, much of the developments in the field of conflict prevention have focused on the direct/short-term approach in situations of state fragility or collapse, with a primary focus on the actions of international agencies or actors rather than the capacities and potential of national actors or civil society.

The international nongovernmental community also continued its efforts and activism. The establishment of the International Criminal Court (ICC) as a means of prosecuting and preventing war crimes and crimes against humanity was a key mechanism of the broader discourse of conflict prevention. The September 11, 2001, attacks in the United States shocked the Western world into registering the threat posed by nonstate actors, within and across national borders. The knee-jerk reaction in the United States was to beef up military responses and define virtually all nonstate armed groups as "terrorists." But the 9/11 attacks also provoked a significant shift in thinking about "nontraditional" security threats, the nature of violent conflicts, and the range of actors involved.[10]

The concept of conflict prevention, which in the mid-1990s was absent from the lexicon of international policymakers, is not only widely used but has spawned an ever-evolving field of study, policy, and practice. In the process it has become increasingly nebulous and all-encompassing. As a concept, it is everything to everybody: violence prevention, prevention of escalation, prevention of resurgence that merges with postconflict reconstruction and even nation building. All for good reason: successful peacebuilding is effective conflict prevention. Increased attention to "fragile states" is also an important development, but the dilemma remains of addressing seemingly strong states, where governments not only have a monopoly over the use of violence but also are not shy about using oppressive measures to quell dissent. Political sensitivity, together with a conflation of terms, has led to oversight of cases where the state is strong but conflict with society is rife, where violence has not erupted but a sociopolitical pressure cooker is evident, and where state-sponsored aggression is rampant. Iraq a decade ago, Zimbabwe today, perhaps Iran tomorrow: the outstanding challenge is how to resolve the conflict that exists, without violence and without suppressing the legitimate grievances of all parties. Who should and could be involved?

In this chapter I consider early or structural prevention and nonviolent transformation, with a particular focus on the contributions, pertinence, and limitations of women's activism. I begin with a discussion of the international context in which conflict prevention has emerged, then consider the limitations of the United Nations. The focus then turns to the relevance of gendered conflict indicators and analysis of country situations. This is followed by an overview of women's actual activism and its strengths and weaknesses. The chapter concludes with a reflection on the existing gaps relating not only to the prevention of violence but the necessary links to peaceful transformation of conflict.

The International Context: Developments in Conflict Prevention

The prevention of war and preservation of international peace and security are the guiding principles and rationales for the existence of the United Nations. Despite the onset of the Cold War, the international community made significant advances since World War II in promoting cooperation, managing competition between nations, and many a time preventing potential wars. Largely done through quiet diplomacy hidden from the eyes of the media, cross-border disputes have been settled, compromises reached, and conflagrations prevented. The European Union (EU), for example, despite its many detractors and its less than stellar performance in the Balkans crisis, has been the single most successful conflict prevention mechanism worldwide since its founding in the aftermath of World War II. So much so that the idea of its member states waging war against each other is no longer within the realm of the possible in the thoughts and minds of its citizens. The history of the EU is beyond the scope of this chapter, but the strategies that European governments adopted were based on economic interdependence. Cooperation within the coal and steel industries (the producers of weaponry) was the first key step. Over time the economic partnerships evolved into increased political collaboration.

The Conference on Security and Cooperation in Europe (CSCE)—later the Organization for Security and Cooperation in Europe (OSCE)—and particularly the high commissioner for minorities during the early years after the Cold War, played a pivotal role in mitigating tensions and resolving disputes in former Soviet republics such as Estonia and Latvia.

Certainly, the United Nations, the global peace and security institution, has played its role. By definition, preventive diplomacy is discreet, so we hear only of the failures that result in conflict. The diversity of its members, however—major powers and lesser ones, the rich and the poor, too often pursuing their national interests at the expense of the institution—has resulted in an uneven record. The 1980–1988 Iran-Iraq War, the 1994 genocide in Rwanda, the 2003 invasion of Iraq, the devastation of Darfur, and the 2006 bombing of Lebanon by Israel are among the institution's bleakest moments.

The end of the Cold War and the demise of the Soviet Union as a superpower led in part to the onslaught of violent conflict within states and across state boundaries, often perceived to be artificially drawn by former colonial rulers. Existing global institutions, driven by member states guarding their sovereignty and sensitive to external intervention, have struggled to prevent, avert, and respond to such conflicts effectively. Nonetheless, the 2005 *Human Security Report* indicates that from 1991 to 2004, despite conventional wisdom, 28 armed struggles for self-determination started or restarted, while 43 were contained or ended. There has been a decline not only in international but also internal conflicts.[11] The end of colonialism, a decline in proxy wars, growing economic interdependence and democratization, and a growing aversion to war are contributing factors, but the UN is also credited. There has been "a dramatic increase in preventive diplomacy and peacemaking,"[12] the report says. Statistics tell the story more clearly. From the late 1980s to the early 2000s, the UN became more involved in peacemaking (stopping ongoing wars), increasing the number of its interventions from four to fifteen; its postconflict peace operations rose from seven to sixteen.[13]

Member states' support for the UN's peace efforts has also increased, says the report. In 1990 there were four contact (or friends) groups made up of UN member states with interests in specific conflicts; by 2003, there were twenty-eight. These figures are indicative of the stage at which conflict prevention practice is most widely embraced, notably postwar. The World Bank estimates that countries emerging from war have an average 44 percent chance of relapse in the first five years of peace.[14] Given that just World Bank assistance to postconflict states increased from 16 to 25 percent of its lending budget from 1998 to 2003 (when it reached $18.5 billion), it is not surprising that resurgence is a primary concern.[15] Since the wars in Afghanistan and Iraq, the elusive and misguided goal of "winning the peace" has become the mantra of international agencies.

It is the number of preventive missions (prior to the outbreak of conflict) that indicate the difficulty that still exists. From 1990 to 2002, UN-led preventive missions increased from one to six.[16] The UN Preventive Deployment Mission to Macedonia (UNPREDEP), established in 1995, is among the six. But information about discreet UN diplomatic and political initiatives that prevented potential conflicts elsewhere, between states or within states, is not readily available.

The Limits of the UN

Particularly in matters of peace and security, the UN, as an organization of member states, has no independent decisionmaking authority outside its membership. Despite the changing nature of warfare, the institution remains severely restricted in its ability to intervene in the internal affairs of a sovereign state. In 1992, then UN Secretary-General Boutros Boutros-Ghali published the groundbreaking *Agenda for Peace,* challenging the international community to address the phenomenon of internal conflict through the application of conflict prevention policies to prevent the outbreak and emergence of violence, stop the spread of violence, and deter the resurgence/reemergence of violence in situations where cease-fires or peace had been reached.[17]

The idea was seductive, the practice ineffectual. Two years later, as Yugoslavia splintered, bled, and burned and Rwanda exploded, the world watched and the Security Council debated the applicability of the term *genocide* to the ongoing slaughter of some 800,000 people in the tiny African country. The decision to avoid the use of the term *genocide* freed the international community of its obligation to intervene.

In this vacuum of silence, civil society organizations, ranging from traditional human rights groups to newly minted conflict resolution entities, found a space and a common voice. They drew attention to the changed nature of warfare and an end to the familiar boundaries of battleground versus civilian community. Civil wars, they said, are fought in homes and villages. Civilians make up 90 percent of the dead and injured. Trust and security are ripped aside in civil war, and peace cannot be made solely by military and political leaders. They advocated for a broader inclusion of civil society in the prevention and resolution of intrastate violent conflicts. They also called for increased and earlier intervention on the part of the international community. Others, notably Francis Deng, the former UN special representative for internally displaced persons (IDPs), tackled the question of state sovereignty from a different angle, suggesting that sovereignty came with the responsibility to protect citizens, not the right to oppress them.[18]

In the case of stronger states particularly, however, the impasse remains. Unless a state itself is willing to acknowledge its potential for internal violence and the need for structural change, typically involving the sharing or relinquishing of power, there is limited opportunity for the international community to act. More often, when internal forces threaten a state's legitimacy it grows more defensive and resistant to external intervention. Zimbabwe is a case in point. In 2005, the security situation deteriorated as some 3 million people reached the point of starvation, 80 percent of its population was unemployed, and massive crackdowns against civil society in all sectors were under way. In an ideal world, the international community would be at hand to acknowledge and limit the state's excesses and support efforts to transform the existing social, economic, and political conflict nonviolently, in a timely manner. But when is the time right?

In Zimbabwe, as elsewhere, the trends were evident years in advance. But beyond some rudimentary steps—criticism of electoral procedures, targeted sanctions against the government, expulsion from the Commonwealth, verbal condemnation by UN Secretary-General Kofi Annan in late 2005, limited efforts at dialogue between opposition and government supports, and isolation from the world stage—the international community has done little to prevent the escalation of state-sponsored violence and the public descent into despair. In 2007, reflecting on Tony Blair's decade-long premiership, for example, writer Msekiwa Makwanya points to the isolation of Zimbabwe, and Blair's unwillingness to engage diplomatically with President Mugabe, as a key foreign policy failure. Makwanya points to various actions that the UK could have initiated, given its long history with Zimbabwe, including fulfilling its long-standing promise to compensate white farmers for lost land. "Zimbabwe," writes Makwanya, "could be a different place. We will never know just how much Britain maintaining its leverage on Zimbabwe's political situation would have achieved, because Blair missed the opportunity."[19] The policies of isolation adopted by major powers are often compensated by the provision of emergency assistance through aid agencies, which can indirectly prop up the very governments inflicting the crisis. This paralysis at the international level leaves national actors, typically those in civil society (human rights groups, political dissidents, organizations like WOZA, and others) who are themselves targeted and undermined, to confront the state.

Iran is another example, especially following the election of Mahmoud Ahmadinejad as president in 2005. Politically, the defeat of the "reformist" camp after eight years of struggle within the state apparatus brought extreme conservatives to the fore. They, in turn, have maintained control through a complex state-sponsored security apparatus, which for the time being can instill fear and maintain a monopoly on violence. Conflict between the state and society has intensified and is evident in the political and social realms as well as economically. Human rights organizations and others working on civil rights issues are under intense government pressure to curb their activities. Activists are being pursued, forcing them either to flee the country or limit their work. A clampdown on social interactions, particularly among urban youth, has generated further resentment. The economy is stagnant, with most businesses taking a "wait-and-see" approach as the president's interactions with the international community, particularly the United States and Israel, become more vitriolic and bombastic. The downward economic spiral has resulted in increased poverty and unemployment, particularly among the majority youth population.[20] The state is by no means collapsing, and wide-scale violent conflict is not imminent. But for many Iran watchers in 2007, the country is in political turmoil. Like their Zimbabwean counterparts, dissident political activists, human rights groups, and increasingly women's groups are at the front lines, with little support from the outside world.

The international community still has limited ability to prevent the outbreak of intrastate violence by creating alternative peaceful means through which social and political conflict can be addressed and resolved. There is also a significant chasm between the fields of conflict prevention (which at times seems to result in quick-fix solutions bordering on suppression rather than attempts at tackling root causes) and nonviolent conflict transformation.

Notwithstanding these gaps, the international community continues to grapple with the issues. A discourse of coexistence and interdependence is also gaining credence within multilateral institutions and major donors. Conflict resolution programming, including the provision of a safe space for dialogue among multiple stakeholders, is on the rise. International agencies and donors are paying significant attention to the development and tracking of conflict indicators and frameworks for monitoring and analyzing situations with a view to identifying opportunities for intervention and avoidance of violence.

Gendered Indicators and Early Warning

From an analytical standpoint, the evolution and use of conflict early warning indicators is among the more developed aspects of the field. Such indicators cover a range of security, political, economic, and sociocultural issues. They can be divided into three categories. First, structural indicators provide an assessment of the baseline state of a country, ranging from its political nature to economic conditions, the historic role of the military, and sociocultural traditions. Second, proximate indicators relate to noticeable trends or changes that emerge. For example, if military spending has been stagnant for an extended period of time but begins to increase in a recognizable trend, it can be viewed as a proximate indicator. Similarly, changes in the status or treatment of minority groups or sectors of society are proximate indicators. Finally, there are triggers or indicators that, when viewed in the wider context of the structural and proximate developments, can be identified as catalysts for violence. For example, a state of perpetual bad governance, overlaid with a political crisis and accusations of electoral fraud, can erupt into public violence as it did in the Solomon Islands in 2006. Ideally, of course, those monitoring and analyzing the situation should be able to predict the escalation and put in place mechanisms to avert the violence. In practice, more often than not, the international community is still reacting. Sometimes it is caught off guard, as in the case of Timor Leste, where violence erupted in the spring of 2006, only a year after the UN's peacekeeping mission ended and was replaced by a small political office. Other times, the UN is unable to take early enough action because the sovereign state is unwilling to concede that there is trouble brewing.

The field of conflict early warning, like other aspects of peace and security work, has largely neglected consideration of what happens to women and the integration of women's experiences as indicators and potential warning signs in the monitoring and analysis of conflict. To be fair, much of the early work done on conflict indicators and analysis is indifferent to the direct experiences of women *and* men.[21] In effect, issues relating to gender dynamics, either as variables of analysis or as the basis for early warning indicators, are poorly considered. To a large extent gender relations should be considered in sociocultural analysis. But there is a gap. Such analyses overlook the role of men and women within a society, their access to and control of power and resources, forms of discrimination, the opportunities available to them and the constraints on them, and socially sanctioned notions of masculinity and femininity that often play into conflict. The indicators that do appear relate to broader developmental issues—literacy, maternal mortality, employment—rather than in relation to conflict dynamics, as part of the trends or triggers of conflict.

In 2001 Eugenia Piza-Lopez and Susanne Schmeidl published the earliest hypotheses about the relevance of gender analysis as a variable for conflict early warning.[22] To date, much of this thinking has not yet entered the frameworks for analysis and assessment that international agencies use.

Canaries in the Coal Mine

Their first argument is analogous to the canary in the coal mine metaphor.[23] Deterioration or changes in the status of men or women can be the earliest signs of conflict trends that might lead to violence. For example, one of the earliest signs of the spread of less tolerant forms of Islam is the noticeable increase in Muslim women wearing head scarves in public and the decrease in their participation in public affairs. In France, the spread of extremist Islamism and the crisis brewing in the Parisian suburbs that ignited in riots in 2006 were preceded by an increase in "honor killings" and violence against women in immigrant North African communities.[24] In Iraq, the US invasion helped unleash religious fervor and crime, and among the first casualties was the status of women. Women's increased use of the hijab (Islamic covering) and the absence of girls and young women from schools indicated growing insecurity and intolerance.

The targeting of women is not limited to any one country. Too often women's roles and position in society are among the first to be circumscribed. Their employment, their freedom of movement, their dress, and legislation governing their citizenship, as well as a rise in sexual violence and parallel decline in prosecution of such crimes, are among the earliest indicators of increased social and political intolerance. That was the case among Serbian women, says Sarah Maguire, human rights lawyer and adviser to the UK's Department for International Development (DFID). "Domestic violence spiked as the Balkans conflict escalated in the 1990s, yet the authorities did not heed the calls coming into domestic violence hotlines."[25]

On the same basis, what women know is also important. In Sierra Leone in the late 1990s, women watched as arms were shipped in overnight along the river. Interviewed in 2001 for a UN study, one spoke of wanting to alert the international peacekeeping forces of the buildup to another attack, but she had no means of gaining access to the relevant officials.[26] In 2006, in the Solomon Islands, women's groups predicted an outbreak of violence based on corruption in the run-up to the parliamentary elections. Again, they had no access or direct mechanism to communicate with the regional peacekeeping authorities.[27]

Ignorance of gender dynamics can also lead to oversight of fundamental causes of conflict. For example, the promotion of hypermasculinity or perceptions of manhood as being intrinsically related to violence can be indicative of social forces influencing men. Prior to the outbreak of war in the Balkans, the situation and activities of young men should have been a warning of the emerging threat and nature of violence that ensued. Many unemployed and disenfranchised were readily recruited by hypernationalists into "soccer teams" and indoctrinated with ethnic hatred. According to some experts, many of the teams fed into the militias and armed gangs that terrorized the region as the war spread.[28]

Such oversight can also result in a lack of understanding of the gendered impact of conflict. An increase in violence against women, for example, impedes their ability to engage in development-related activities, reduces productivity, and affects their levels of employment. Restrictions on movement and random arrests of men have direct and indirect consequences for men and women. The situation in Palestine following the collapse of the Oslo process in 2000 illustrates this point. In 2004 over 50 percent of Palestinian men were unemployed.[29] The implications for the men—ranging from depression to increased inclination or propensity to engage in violence against Israel—are significant. Coupled with the direct and indirect impact on women—increased economic burden, greater risk of domestic violence due to the frustration, humiliation, and presence of men in closed spaces—this situation creates new and complex social dynamics that need to be addressed if the goal is to prevent the escalation of violent conflict.

Piza-Lopez and Schmeidl argue that watching the trends, patterns of behavior, and conditions of men and women can alert the international community to potential conflict at an earlier stage ("early" early warning), and provide opportunities for addressing the tensions long before they heighten, ignite, and spread.[30]

The argument can be extended further: being mindful of the changing circumstances or portrayal of men and women can be indicative of the type of violence that might arise. Where there is a marked increase in sexual violence against women, it is likely that such violence will characterize any emerging conflict. Yet internationally, the use of indicators relating to the changed status of men and women is limited and ad hoc. Within the UN system, for example, an increase in sexual violence is among the signs monitored in the context of genocide prevention, but it does not feature particularly in other areas of analysis.

Knowledge of the relationship between genocide and sexual violence has much to do with the history of Rwanda's descent into genocide. Reflecting on the buildup to the 1994 genocide, Elizabeth Powley notes the deliberate attack on women by extremist Hutu propaganda.[31] "One popular tract, the 'Hutu Ten Commandments,' was circulated widely and read aloud at public meetings," she writes.

> It portrayed Tutsi women as deceitful "temptresses" and urged Hutu women to protect Hutu men from treacherous influences. Three of the commandments addressed gender relations:
>   1. Each Hutu man must know that the Tutsi woman, no matter whom, works in solidarity with her Tutsi ethnicity. In consequence, every Hutu man is a traitor: who marries a Tutsi woman; who makes a Tutsi woman his concubine; who makes a Tutsi woman his secretary or protégé.
>   2. Every Hutu man must know that our Hutu girls are more dignified and more conscientious in their roles as woman, wife, and mother. Aren't they pretty, good secretaries and more honest!
>   3. Hutu women, be vigilant; bring your husbands, brothers, and sons to reason![32]

These indicators were particularly blatant, and in retrospect, it is clear that the propaganda would very likely lead to sexual violence against women. As the genocide unfolded in April 1994, Tutsi women, particularly the educated and the young, were among the key victims. The violence they endured was deliberately sexual, including rape and torture, breast oblations, and forced incest and pregnancy. As in Bosnia, Darfur, and elsewhere, the sexual nature of the attacks is a particularly cruel means of attempting to destroy family ties and the very notion of ethnicity through forced pregnancies. In societies where men's honor is bound by their ability to protect their family, sexual attacks on women are also a means of bringing shame and dishonor to men. In effect, men communicate with each other through attacks on women: thus women's bodies are literally the front lines and battlefields of many contemporary wars.

Indicators relating to women can also be used to monitor potentially positive trends. In Iran, since the 1979 revolution that brought the Islamic government to power, women have been the barometers of society, as the regime systematically sought to curtail their rights. Their presence and activities in the public sphere, education, and political participation have signaled the extent to which the government is adhering to its extremist ideology. In turn women have used their physical appearance, including the Islamic dress codified by law, to resist the state's control. The long, dark-colored overcoats *(manteaux)* of the early 1980s have long been relinquished in favor of shorter, tighter, lighter, more colorful fabrics. Head scarves are worn with flourish. Makeup, once severely restricted and monitored by black-hooded women patrolling the streets, is evident throughout the cities. Women have also fought against legislative restrictions. Educational courses in the scientific fields closed to them in the 1980s have, through intense pressure, been opened. By 2004, women—who had once been threatened with exclusion from the university—represented over 60 percent of the undergraduate population. Even birthrates have dropped from an average high of 8.1 children to below 2 births per woman in 2005.[33]

From the intellectual elite to the taxi drivers of Tehran, there is resounding agreement that the changing role of women indicates a societal transformation on a mass scale. When speaking of women's roles in society, terms such as *an unstoppable river* and *a torrent* are often used.[34] Given that the status of women and even their dress has been a defining feature of the Islamic republic, it could be argued that change in women's legislative status, or an end to the compulsory hijab, would signal a significant transformation of the regime. In the words of a leading male political activist in 2004, "Before the 1979 Islamic Revolution, girls in traditional families were not attending university or working outside the home. Now they are all expected to get degrees and have jobs. They are demanding rights and want modern lives."[35]

Another key political figure noted, "The more the state pushes for the implementation of hijab, the more women will resist. The hijab became a symbol of struggle against the state's policies. Today, after 25 years, everybody knows that the compulsory hijab will not work in Iran. On the contrary, it backfired and it will rebound more."[36] Yet the reform-minded leadership that controlled much of Iranian politics from 1997 to

2004 squandered the opportunity afforded by a focus on women's rights
to transform the political landscape. Their cultural biases and inherent
patriarchy kept male leaders—seemingly educated and sensitive to issues
of oppression—from acknowledging openly that women could be of
such significance politically. By contrast, among the hard-liners and
those controlling the state, the threat posed by women was recognized
early on, and the response, particularly since their ascendance to power
in 2005, has been swift, oppressive, and increasingly violent.

Do No Harm

Piza-Lopez and Schmeidl's second hypothesis is that if gender issues
are excluded from situation analyses, there is a danger of compounding
existing discriminations, particularly against women. By including gender issues in the analysis and response options, they argue, international
actors can help ensure that discriminatory policies are not perpetuated
in emergency and postconflict situations. For example, in Afghanistan
under the Taliban (1995–2001), women were severely repressed—unable to leave their homes unless escorted by a male relative. Yet by many
counts, women represented a majority (60 percent) of the population,
and many were either widows or running households.[37] The absence of a
gendered analysis of the Afghan situation led to programs that perpetuated the hardship they endured. Religious leaders issued fatwas to re-
strict the movement of women in camps. "It helped the men feel secure
about their women and safe in the knowledge that they were not out in-
teracting with other men," reflects researcher Saba Kattak.[38] The women
were trapped in their temporary homes, isolated, depressed, and traumatized. Ignorant of their needs or the structures of Afghan society, the
international community exacerbated the problem. Even though women
made up the majority of refugees, job creation projects were not available or culturally acceptable for them. Kattak says that there was "a perception that Afghan women should not be touched, that they [did] not
want waged work. The jobs that were created were road and canal-
building positions. Afghan men, the Pakistani government, and donors
were respecting each other's boundaries, but women were ignored."[39]

Without a profound understanding of the social constraints and gender dynamics in society, even interventions directed at women and girls
can fail. For example, understanding the need for women's clinics is
commendable, but if the clinic is built at a distance that is deemed too
far for women to walk to alone, it can be ineffective and, worse, counterproductive. Women may not use it, which could be easily interpreted

as the project "failing" or the clinic being unnecessary. Practitioners must be aware of the constraints that women face in order to target their intervention effectively. In the case of the clinic, for example, the provision of mobile clinics is one solution.

Finally, understanding the gendered implications of a situation should in theory lead to political and humanitarian interventions that address the vulnerabilities specific to women and men. In Darfur's camps, displaced women are at daily risk of sexual assault and rape, particularly when they leave designated camp areas to search for firewood. This is not a new phenomenon; it is reality in many situations where women are forced into displacement. In practice, however, interventions to help prevent the extent of rape (either through the provision of alternative forms of cooking and heating material, better security, or otherwise) have been delayed and limited. Rape prevention should be a priority for all international actors. But it isn't. Rather, within the international community, there remains a culture of reaction and seeming acceptance of the inevitability of such attacks, characterized by the scramble to provide emergency kits (for the care of rape victims).[40] There is rarely consultation with women themselves to garner their views and opinions about the threats they face and possible solutions. Instead, as in the case of Darfur, the men or tribal leaders (often self-nominated) are consulted.[41]

In sum, indicators that highlight men's and women's experiences can enhance international efforts to prevent violence and ensure more effective and better-timed responses in political, humanitarian, and developmental terms. Consultations with men and women themselves are critical. First, they can show aid agencies which actions are acceptable. Second, those consulted may have alternative strategies and capacities that could be drawn upon and strengthened.

Women's Activism: Preventing War, Promoting Change

The early warning discourse focusing on how women are affected has often overshadowed women's agency and activism when faced with oppression and potential violent conflict. Like men, women suffer under repressive regimes and respond to the call to arms to fight for liberation. From Kashmir to Colombia, El Salvador to Sri Lanka, particularly where identity, freedom, or self-determination fuels warfare, women have been involved in prewar propaganda, inciting violence, encouraging revenge, and taking up arms themselves. Nonetheless women's activism for peace broadly is often more prevalent, but also less visible. They are often at the front lines of resisting war, as well as engaging in longer-term efforts to challenge oppression and push for a transformation of state-society relations and the promotion of social justice.

Resisting Violence and War

In terms of explicit conflict prevention, more often than not, women are among the first to speak out collectively against war and to try to prevent escalation. That is evident globally. In October 1984 in Sri Lanka, as the conflict between the government and the Liberation Tamil Tigers of Eelam (LTTE) intensified, some 100 feminist activists formed Women for Peace, and launched a signature campaign to call for a negotiated solution. They collected 10,000 signatures and took their campaign into communities across the country. In October 1991, as war in the Balkans gained steam, Women in Black launched its antiwar campaign in Serbia. For years they stood dressed in black protesting the war and militarization of their society. The campaign spread across the Balkans and to the Middle East. In Palestine, despite media stereotypes of militant Palestinian mothers sending their sons to their death, many take measures to prevent their children's involvement in violence, including marrying them off early.[42]

In Burundi in 1995, as the threat of a genocide like that in neighboring Rwanda loomed closer, national and international NGOs took action to prevent the spread of violence on a national scale. Sabine Sabimbona was among the many women who tried to stop the escalation. Speaking at high schools in Bujumbura, she and colleagues warned young Hutu and Tutsi men against the deliberate manipulation of ethnicity by political leaders. Others, such as journalist Agnes Nindorera, put themselves on the line as they wrote and spoke out against the government's propaganda. NGOs such as International Alert and Search for Common Ground arrived in 1996 with programs directed at the political leadership, the media, youth, and women. They worked with Burundians to launch radio shows promoting dialogue and reconciliation and trained hundreds of men and women in conflict resolution, mediation, and peacemaking skills. In partnership with existing women's NGOs, they established women's peace centers and a nationwide network of women skilled in mediation. There was impact; in communities where women were active, the levels of violence were significantly lower, according to some observers.[43]

In Fiji, where tensions between Indo-Fijians and indigenous Fijians culminated in coups d'état in 2000 and 2006, women have been the voice and conscience of the public. They launched a multiethnic women's movement called the Blue Ribbon Campaign and a peace and prayer vigil in the midst of the 2000 coup and hostage taking in the parliament. In describing their intervention, the movement states, "In organizing daily prayer vigils, women came together, in a natural response, unified as wives, mothers and daughters of Fiji. They gave life to shared values at a time when many social and religious institutions were silent. They communicated a vision of peace, unity, justice and reconciliation for their country."[44] In 2006, as the war of words between military and political leaders escalated, leading activists such as Sharon Bhagwan Rolls warned against the inevitability of another coup. Reflecting on the developments in November 2006, she wrote, "I have once again become mindful . . . of how the military speaks such a different language from the civilian sector and this remains a long term struggle for our transformation from a very militarized society to a more peaceful and integrated society, including women's participation in any security sector reform. . . . [T]here is a serious need for us not just to react to the words, but to listen and understand deeply what is being said, by all players in this current impasse."[45]

By and large, though, the public activism is not enough. Often it comes too late, when the path to violence or war is inevitable. Even when they raise concerns early enough, the activists are not involved in the political and decisionmaking processes. Their efforts are valiant, the desire to prevent the outbreak of war beyond reproach, and the incremental impact worth noting, but it is not enough to counter the political and military drive to war. The propaganda machines used by states are too powerful and more prepared than women, who are often stepping into the fray for the first time. National security, typically defined within a military discourse, is not a domain in which women civil society activists feel comfortable. It is seen and presented as an area where expertise and knowledge of hard security issues are needed. In the United States, as in many other countries, it is an exclusive club where the opinions and views of ordinary citizens are easily sidelined. Often identity issues are used too, be they religion, race, ethnicity, or nationality, to deepen divisions in society. That makes it doubly difficult for those advocating for peace and compromise, as they are perceived as being traitors to their own.

Against this tide, women's message can seem incomplete. They may call for diplomatic initiatives or negotiations, but neither side in a conflict is listening. Even if they offer a realistic alternative path to transform the paradigm of war and address the source of the conflict, they are not influential where it counts. They operate outside the confines of politics and power, and they have limited access. The rhetoric of extremism is louder, tougher, and seemingly more decisive. That is not just women's dilemma. As proved by discussions across the world in the run-up to the Iraq War, the momentum of the war machine drowned out all alternative voices and closed the space for dialogue and debate.

Challenging Oppression

The pendulum also swings to the other extreme. WOZA, the women of Venezuela, and Iran are striving toward a fundamental grassroots-driven transformation of politics and power in their countries. Their efforts can be framed within conflict transformation theory, which has evolved significantly since the 1980s. Transformation offers a holistic approach to addressing conflict, and encompasses concepts of transition. Drawing on the works of Johan Galtung, Edward Azar, Reimo Vyrynen, and others, Hugh Miall offers five types of transformation that can take place, or transformers who can take action, to address conflict without resorting to violence.[46] First, there is context transformation, which refers to changes in the regional or international environment, which in turn impact the relations between a state and society. For example, the end of the Cold War catalyzed the political changes across eastern European countries. Second, there is structural transformation, which reflects changes in the basic relations and power structures that affect the conflict. It can be a rebalancing of relations to create more symmetry, change in control of power, or basic goals of different parties. The transition from apartheid to democracy in South Africa was partly due to this recalibration of power relations. Third, there can be an actor-driven transformation. This includes not only a change in or addition of actors or political parties, but also a shift in positions, goals, or the general approach of key players to the situation. Fourth, there can be an issues-based transformation, wherein major parties reframe, redefine, or shift their positions in relation to key issues so that compromise is possible. Fifth, a personal change of heart or mind among individual leaders or small groups creates a willingness to soften positions or make conciliatory gestures at key moments; this can be critical to transforming a situation. In practice, a combination of the above is needed to bring the necessary changes. Women's mobilization efforts often commence with a focus on issues, with a view to influencing changes within the political leadership.

In January 2006, for example, WOZA and its counterpart, Men of Zimbabwe Arise, mobilized support for a people's charter in demand for social justice. Their strategy was to listen to the concerns and desires of people across the country. The charter, drawn up following meetings with over 10,000 people countrywide in some 284 meetings, is a compilation of the issues most critical to the lives of Zimbabweans. Its goal is to influence the political direction of the country by demanding that leaders promise accountability and commitment to the issues.[47]

In May 2007, with regional talks on the horizon, WOZA articulated its vision of the country through a ten-point declaration. This vision included a condemnation of all forms of violence; an all-stakeholders' conference to initiate a constitution-drafting process; an audit of civil servants, the judiciary, and law enforcement officials to determine their nonpartisan status and provision of retraining offenders; a land audit; and engagement with the international community.[48]

In Iran in 2006, women from across the political and religious ideological divides launched a campaign to collect 1 million signatures in support of changing gender-based discriminatory laws. Framing this as a social issue that affects primarily women, regardless of class or religious leaning, the movement has gained significant support in cities and provinces. The impact is particularly notable in the context of the leadership's responses. For example, in May 2007, Ayatollah Ali Akbar Hashemi Rafsanjani, the former president and supreme-leader-hopeful, stated that given women's contributions to the economy, they deserve equal treatment to men. Days later, two other heavyweight ayatollahs, one a renowned conservative, echoed the statement. Ayatollah Gheravian said, "Some jurists reach their opinions through scientific and philosophical deliberation, while others rely more heavily on traditions and narratives. With the advancement of science and technology in the future, however, we are moving in a direction in which jurists must rely more heavily on logic and reason in forming their opinions." He continued, "Equality between men and women is the result of rational thought in Ijtihad (Islamic jurisprudence)," implying that clerics are now seeking to correct a narrative that has no roots in the Quran.[49] Such a discourse and its immense implications for legislative change in the near future would not have happened even five years earlier. It is a result of ongoing social transformation in the country and the campaign's successful strategy of outreach to constituencies that are critical to the ruling elite.

From a strategic standpoint, the Zimbabweans and Iranians are both challenging the existing power base and status quo, not through overt political dissent but through a lens of social justice. Their actions clearly heighten tensions and conflict. But their commitment to peaceful engagement and outreach to a mass public base, while subversive, is constructive, and it can thus create formidable challenges to the state. In

Iran, the state's sensitivities to the campaign are evident in three ways. First, there is a concern about the outreach to 1 million people and the possible consequences; second, the regime is intolerant of public demonstrations and protests, perhaps fearing that such gatherings could catalyze greater public dissent; and third, there is concern that the targeted laws are derived from Islam, and thus any changes are perceived by some conservatives as a direct challenge to the very essence of the Islamic state. In Zimbabwe, too, the state is intolerant of public demonstrations, and the crackdowns are harsh. At the time of this writing, Jenni Williams and others were again incarcerated.

Yet for the activists, the goal is not to challenge the existence of the state or to dismantle an entire political structure for their own benefit. Rather, it is to find an alternative paradigm through which issues that could lead to heightened tension and violence are addressed. The vision of such groups—increasingly found around the world, often led or supported heavily by women, is of a state that fosters greater social justice, transparency, freedom, and democracy. The goals are perhaps no different from those of many other disaffected and disenfranchised groups, but their strict adherence to Gandhian nonviolence is notable and a factor that taps into women's tendency to avoid the use of violence as a means of resolving disputes. A key question, however, is whether the women who take to the streets or collect signatures so courageously are willing to assume the mantle of political leadership as well. The insistence on staying in the realm of civil society, which is common to many women, can be detrimental to their own pursuits.

Many groups emerging since 1995 build on a rich history of women's activism throughout the Cold War years. The Argentine Mothers of the Plaza de Mayo, who first gathered on April 30, 1977, in the plaza outside the presidential palace in Buenos Aires to protest their missing sons and daughters, are still celebrated, long after the military junta they opposed collapsed in 1983.[50] The mothers first stood in a group, but because doing so was tantamount to a demonstration, they began to walk around the plaza. As the movement grew and became a regular Thursday event, the mothers remained silent. They did not hold up signs or protest government action. Instead they wore white head scarves embroidered with the names of their children.

At their core, such groups are typically pacifist and often feminist. By embracing and strategically using the motherhood identity, however, they are simultaneously reaching out widely to women and directly challenging the moral authority of states that typically define themselves through social conservatism heavily dosed with militarism and traditional family values that uphold motherhood as the ultimate virtue. The sudden emergence of mothers as the prime voices of dissent catches most dictatorial or militaristic regimes off guard. In the case of Argentina, for example, the junta, which had successfully eliminated political opponents by claiming they were subversives and traitors to the nation, and by "disappearing" them, at first could not apply the same tactics to a group of seemingly innocent and clearly unarmed housewives.

The impact of these seemingly innocuous and incongruous groups of activists—grandmas and moms for the most part—is also difficult to measure. Oftentimes, their success or potential impact is best measured by the ways in which the government reacts to them. Riot police, crackdowns, arrests, and beatings are not uncommon experiences. In Argentina, the military reacted violently within eight months of the first protests. In Zimbabwe, from the second demonstration, WOZA has been under police attack. In Venezuela, penal code reforms in 2005 even led to the criminalization of protesting with pots and pans.[51] In Iran, women protestors have been arrested and beaten. Those who speak out against the Islamic dress, let alone the regime itself, are branded as traitors to the nation. As of June 2007, at least five women's rights activists and members of the 1-million-signature campaign have been formally charged and sentenced to jail for acting against national security. Such events typically strengthen the resolve of the women involved to continue their efforts. In their view, facing opposition and attack is better than being ignored and deemed irrelevant. But their situation can also be precarious, as often fear and pressure from family can result in women's retreat from public space when the violence escalates.

At a minimum, women's activism does sensitize the public about injustice, and demands of accountability from their governments do raise awareness. At a maximum, their actions have catalyzed mass public support and been a key factor in the transformation of the political arena. In Lebanon in 2005, for example, a twenty-three-year-old female supporter of former prime minister Rafik Hariri inspired the outpouring of young people, many of them women, into the streets, which, within days, turned into a nationwide call for a change in government and the withdrawal of Syrian troops. In the United States, Code Pink may not have prevented the war, but it has been central to the US antiwar movement. Active on every front across the country, Code Pink influenced the 2006 US congressional elections, where the Democratic Party swept into victory on the antiwar agenda. In Argentina, the mothers' continued protest was a key pressure point and contributor to the weakening of the military junta. Certainly the prevalence of human

rights abuses and the issue of the disappeared in the 1983 elections campaign were in large part due to their activities.[52] But such impact is still
rare and related to the context in which the women are active. The
Argentinians protested for years and were *an important* factor (but not
the factor) in the eventual downfall of the junta. In Lebanon, the prime
minister's assassination triggered a national reaction. The protest tapped
into that moment of national unity.

Hoping for the Best, Not Planning for the Worst

It is rare, however, to find women's groups with an adherence to nonviolence and commitment to transformation of the state (be it for increased freedom of expression, democracy, human rights, legislation to
end discrimination, or the end of a military occupation) that explicitly
consider and plan against the use of violence by others (the state or
other nonstate actors). In other words, women activists, similar to ordinary people and peace activists more generally, are not effective at
strategizing for worst-case scenarios. Hope for change and a better future
is a powerful fuel and motivator, but it is not a strategy for dealing with
the reality of communal violence or warfare. Perhaps it goes against
human nature; perhaps change comes slowly and anything worse is too
difficult to imagine; or perhaps it is easier to think of the eruption and
escalation of violence—the chaos and random attacks; the assault and
rape of women; betrayal by a neighbor, school friends, or colleagues—
as something that happens to others, in faraway countries. Many a resi-
dent of Sarajevo thought so, even as Serbian troops were rampaging
across the countryside, just a hundred miles away. Many Iraqis who supported the ouster of Saddam could not fathom a worse situation or
believe that sectarianism and criminality would become the norm.

The consequences of this oversight can be dire. Where violence
emerges and escalates, it can sweep away the middle ground and the
initiatives of moderates, including women. For example, in 2000 as the
second intifada (uprising) erupted in Palestine, the women's movement
was thrown into disarray. The collapse of the peace process itself was
not a surprise to many people. Among Palestinians especially, the continued expansion of Israeli settlements and stagnation in the economy
were among other critical issues that heightened tensions and sowed
dissatisfaction throughout the Palestinian population. The chaos and
sudden militarization of the intifada were, however, a surprise and
shock to many. In the first intifada, which had been largely nonviolent,
women played a central role in public demonstrations and the political
arena; in the second, they were noticeably absent. Like others, their

knowledge and concern about the demise of the peace process had not automatically led to planning and preparedness to cope with the outburst and escalation of violence. For those who remained engaged, it has taken years to regroup and rebuild the trust and relationships that were badly frayed.

There are exceptions, particularly in instances where violence, albeit on a smaller scale, has come and is acknowledged as a real and present threat. In the oil-rich Niger Delta region of Nigeria, where tensions between local populations and international oil companies have escalated and flared into violence, in 2002, women led a nonviolent sit-in against Chevron/Texaco.[53] It was in sharp contrast to previous armed protests led by local men against the oil companies. The women, like others in their communities, demanded support, compensation for environmental damage, and increased oil revenue for their region. They were no more or less resentful than the men, but in their approach they opened a space for dialogue with the oil company. Chevron/Texaco took the opportunity to talk with the women and agreed to a series of community-based programs, including creating jobs for locals; starting a microcredit program for women; and funding schools, clinics, water, and electricity systems in the area. The initiatives alleviated tensions by transforming the interaction between the company and the community. "We now have a different philosophy," said one company executive to the BBC at the time, "and that is do more with communities."[54] Did they keep their word? Were they able to strengthen and expand the relationship to include others in the community? It is difficult to say. In the spring of 2006, tensions and disputes between local communities and oil companies ran high again. Women from the region wanted to take action, recognizing that armed groups posed a threat to their own communities. But the onus for taking action cannot be placed on a group of women lawyers or NGO leaders alone. The problem, as many say, goes back to poor development and education, lack of skills, and thus high unemployment among youth. Short-term preventive measures or catalytic programs to generate income and skills can be useful, but effective conflict transformation requires sustained support and involvement from multiple sectors in society, particularly the government.[55]

Minding the Gap: Short-Term Prevention, Long-Term Transformation

The situation in South Africa from 1991 to 1994, when the National Peace Accord (NPA) was signed and President Nelson Mandela was sworn into office, offers one of the best examples of linking the need for short-term violence prevention with the longer-term goal of nonviolent transformation and peacebuilding. Violence was escalating in South Africa in 1991, at a time when preliminary negotiations were under way between the apartheid regime and the opposition movement, led by Nelson Mandela and the African National Congress (ANC). According to Susan Collin Marks, the leadership on both sides acknowledged that it was in their interest to stop the violence and to work together as partners rather than enemies; otherwise, democracy would not take root.[56]

Through countless consultations and support from respected leaders across the business, religious, and other communities, they formulated the NPA. In September 1991, the government (including security forces), major political parties, business, trade unions, traditional leaders, and the churches signed it. They bound themselves to a code of conduct not only for police and security officers, but also for community development and, most significantly, local peace committees. The goal of the NPA and its network of local peace committees was to reduce violence and solve problems collaboratively within and across communities. As the peace committees went into action, their members mediated between the ANC and the government, improved relations among blacks in their own communities, brokered deals between warring factions, and generally were in place to mediate and prevent violent confrontations in communities. "[The] guiding spirit," Collin Marks writes, "was peacemaking in action."[57] It was, she writes, a means through which South Africans, black or white, factory worker or business mogul, could meet and work together to prevent the eruption of violence. That and the transformation of conflict through collaborative problem solving were inseparable to this notion of peacemaking. The long-term vision of a democratic state grounded in reconciliation and coexistence was directly linked to short-term mitigation of violence and tensions.

South African Women

South African women were important to the process. They were pivotal to the entire anti-apartheid movement and transition to peace. Though women were underrepresented on the local peace committees, South Africans and UN personnel noted the qualitative difference that women peace monitors made in enabling access to and fostering trust with communities. In one province, a committee decided that of every four monitors sent out, at least one had to be a woman, as they "bring down the temperature."[58] Women for Peace in the Alexandria township, a site known for violence between the ANC and the Inkatha Freedom Party (IFP), was among the most successful peace committees. Women for Peace's emergence in 1993 significantly improved the environment.[59] "Women were what made the committee effective," recounted one UN observer later; "with men it was war all the time . . . the women were keen to get peaceful resolution. . . . [It] helped get men to buy in. . . . Sometimes I would hear them [the men] talking among themselves . . . saying 'we need to show respect for our mothers.'"[60]

The South African experience is one of few models of integrated conflict prevention and nonviolent transformation work in practice. But much about the South African process is unique, including the nature of the opposition movement and the strategies it developed to generate and sustain mass public support, nationally and internationally. Even though it cannot be replicated overnight in another context, the lessons and experience should be effectively captured or integrated into international conflict prevention practice. Most pertinently, perhaps, the notion of community involvement and inclusiveness that gives the silent majority of peace supporters a voice needs to be more systematically and widely embraced.

A major flaw in existing efforts is the imbalanced attention that analysts give to sources and drivers of conflict, as opposed to sources and actors with the potential to mitigate conflict and "bring the temperature down." International development agencies tend to work with their traditional development partners. They are not always familiar with the emerging range of networks and organizations involved in conflict resolution and nonviolent efforts, nor do they always have the capacity to engage in conflict-sensitive analysis. This is detrimental for the women who dare to take a stand, because the international entities that could be their natural allies are often ignorant of their existence. In turn, this oversight is detrimental to the effectiveness of the international agencies that work on prevention. As one UN officer notes, "We keep focusing on bringing organized groups to the table, but women are organized in a different way so they do not appear in the picture. They are not invited to the table. Women play more subtle, constructive roles, so unless you change your criteria for selection about whom you invite at the table, they will never get in the picture. We have to change the paradigms."[61]

A focus on women typically leads to questions about men and broader cultural norms. An analysis of women's experiences can identify profound societal inequalities that not only affect women's and men's lives but also point to imbalances in economic and political power that require more systemic overhaul. A situation analysis that allows for the inclusion of women's voices and more in-depth, gendered analyses is not a simple tweaking of the way business is done. In and of itself it is a catalyst for transformation, a realignment of priorities, a widening of the circle of stakeholders and programming in every aspect of conflict prevention and development work. Yet a willingness to change the paradigm—the lens through which situations are viewed; the actors deemed to be important enough to engage; the fair balance among causes, consequences, and solutions to conflict—and, within this, giving attention to women, do not come easily to external actors, particularly if they answer to governments interested in preserving the status quo.

Where there have been attempts, it has been a slow process of relationship and trust building. In recent years, the UN has evolved its programming to encourage national and local capacity building with support from bilateral donors.[62] In Guyana, for example, starting in 2002 the UNDP tackled issues of social tension, primarily between Indo-Guyanese and Afro-Guyanese, and sought to correct deficiencies in electoral strategy to quell potential violence in the 2006 elections. A concerted partnership strategy was put in place, drawing together UN entities and other international actors with national counterparts under the umbrella of a Social Cohesion Program (SCP).[63] They worked with women's, youth, and media groups to mitigate politically driven tensions between the communities and promote peacebuilding in the run-up to parliamentary elections. The program, modeled on a "sprinkler" system, as described by one official, was designed to respond to potentially inflammatory remarks or events, before they escalated and spread.[64]

In West Africa, the UN Department of Political Affairs (DPA) worked directly with a regional women's peace network (the Mano River Women's Peace Network) to prevent the spread of conflict across Sierra Leone, Liberia, and Guinea. Even in Zimbabwe in 2006, efforts were under way to bring government, opposition groups, and civil society groups together as a step toward preventing the rise of conflict. It was also a means of encouraging interaction and highlighting interdependence and opportunities for mutual resolution of the conflict.

These are a few examples. Increasingly, the UN and national-level counterparts, including civil society, are attempting to work collaboratively with a conflict prevention agenda. These are tentative steps, nonetheless. Governments are still wary of interventions, so much so that international agencies use euphemisms such as social cohesion, political reform, or even peace and development to avoid the lightning rod effect of the term *conflict prevention*. Are they effective? "The short answer," writes the UN's Chetan Kumar, "is that we do not know yet;

time will tell." He points to the need to watch "'process indicators' . . . that critically monitor the nature of the conversation that takes place between key political and civic leaders . . . the media . . . and whether the conflict management culture is changed."[65]

As for women's peace and conflict prevention initiatives, it is still unclear whether they will be acknowledged and integrated fully into the new processes or whether their exclusion will be institutionalized. Guyana and West Africa set positive precedents. Will the agencies and individuals involved in this work draw and apply the lessons elsewhere? Time will tell.

Conclusion

Are women relevant to conflict prevention? Clearly they are. Information from and about them provides insight into a society. They are also important change agents. Women's actions to prevent the rise of violence and promote change through nonviolent means are important to recognize and support. But alone they cannot prevent the next violent conflict—prompted by the United States or resulting from state-induced oppression in the Middle East, Africa, or Latin America. If the timing is right, women can mobilize effectively. Supported by other sectors in their own society, they can tip the balance away from violence. But like others, particularly in the initial stages, they can be swayed by manipulation of identity politics and paralyzed with fear. The result is, too often, when they do enter the fray, the fighters are already recruited and the arms distributed. Their warnings against political manipulation, holding back their sons and daughters, street protests—silent or noisy— even coming together across the lines of conflict, are not enough to stop the tidal wave of war.

In Burundi, some 300,000 people died during the years of civil war. In comparison, the women's activities (or even the broader efforts of civil society) seem inconsequential. However small or late the steps, though, they made a difference in the lives of many people. The question is, with additional support, what else could they have achieved?

Although a neat, chronological typology of terms and actions would be helpful—with conflict prevention at one end of the spectrum and peacebuilding at the other—in reality, as South Africa shows, conflict prevention, peacemaking, and transformation fuse together. Recognition of that fact is easiest when violence is already present, when people have seen and felt it. They know that it can recur at any time in their own midst and will thus consciously and proactively seek to avert it.

In Nigeria too, the oil companies changed their approach when they acknowledged that the escalation of violence was possible. At that moment, they also realized and appreciated the opportunity provided by the women. It was before the tipping point and slide toward inevitable communal violence. But small-scale initiatives are not enough. The causes and catalysts for violence needed to be addressed. In 2006, the violence was again escalating: Will the lessons from the past be remembered? More women are engaged, but is anyone talking to them? But what is that tipping point to change the conflict dynamics? To many of the ethnically mixed sophisticated population of Sarajevo in 1991, war was not a possibility. For most Rwandans in 1994, genocide was impossible to fathom.

In 2007, is it too late to stop the slide in Zimbabwe, or can something be done, particularly given that opposition groups are still staging a nonviolent struggle? Efforts are under way to promote a dialogue of coexistence between the government and the opposition. But can it lead to substantive changes and a shift in control of power, or will it be derailed? According to media reports in June 2007, there were disagreements as to which groups should be at the talks hosted by Thabo Mbeki, the South African president. If limited to political parties only, says one analyst, "Many people . . . would challenge the legitimacy of a process they saw as hurried for political expediency, rather than a comprehensive process leading to complete political, economic and social transformation."[66] On the other hand, a more inclusive process, deemed "ideal" by some analysts, would take longer. With Mbeki's presidency coming to an end, the job may be left incomplete. While much is still uncertain, at least a process is being put in place, with the possibility of substantive changes.

What about Iran? The failure in Iraq is causing many US politicians and pundits to be cautious about military intervention against Iran, but the rhetorical heat is rising. The domestic situation in Iran is not improving either. Different political factions are struggling to get ahead with eyes on the 2008 parliamentary and 2009 presidential elections. The level of public dissent is on the rise, with protests by women, students, workers, and ethnic minorities. Yet the hard-line elements in the government seem unwilling to engage in any dialogue. In the words of Jenni Williams, "Can the love of power be won over by the power of love" for the country?[67] In the interest of ordinary citizens and the nation, can the state and its dissenters find a framework in which the political conflict and struggle for power are linked to a discourse of plurality, coexistence, and interdependence?

Peaceful conflict transformation is feasible, but where the state is still strong, it requires foresight and proactive efforts on the part of governments and civil society. Partnerships and the inclusion of all stakeholders are necessary ingredients, as in the case of South Africa. Leadership is essential to draw in extended constituencies toward a dialogue of coexistence and democracy. But questions about the nature of leadership and timing, as well as opportunities to tip the scales in one direction or the other, have not been adequately resolved. As Kumar says, "Internal capacity-building is imperative. If societies do not encourage and develop their own infrastructure for peace, peace is unlikely to be sustainable."[68]

There is still no coherent approach, however. Instead, we watch the deterioration and eventually assume that violence is inevitable, so the best that can be done is to prepare for the consequences. This permeates every level of thinking. The Darfur situation illustrates that way of thinking most graphically. The warnings of genocide, the campaigns, and public outrage have had limited effect on the lives and security of ordinary people in the region. The presence of African Union peacekeepers creates some limits but barely stems the flow of violence. Collectively we tolerate the rape and murder, as if they were inevitable and unstoppable. Knowing about the situation has not resulted in effective action by world leaders to prevent its escalation. The resistance and recalcitrance of the Sudanese government and its allies to outside intervention simply highlight the limitations of international will and action.

Many argue that too much talk of violence is also dangerous, sowing fear and division among communities and ultimately becoming a self-fulfilling prophecy and prompting preemptive violent action. By the same token, however, ignoring the possibility of violence can also lead to self-delusion. A balance is needed. In this quagmire of theory and uncertainty, clearly women peace activists or human rights activists are not a panacea. But they cannot be ignored either. They have the means and the skills, and above all the commitment and persistence, to push for change peacefully. They need support and capacity building to engage more effectively and strategically in conflict transformation. As stakeholders in society, their perspectives are important, and their participation is essential. Yet, when the international community steps in, too often it ignores their skills and contributions and does little to encourage or foster their involvement.

In the end, transforming a conflict from one that is expressed through violence to one expressed through peaceful means and structures is still easier said than done. We have come a long way, learned to read the signs, and see the writing on the wall. We understand the need to engage a cross section of stakeholders, but actions by major entities are still circumscribed. There needs to be a broadening of perspectives, an acknowledgment of the need to take a long-term approach and of the contributions that different actors can make. The linkages between prevention and transformation need to be stronger. There also needs to be a change in mindset: that violence can be prevented, and peaceful transformation of conflict is possible. Perhaps then, the inevitable will cease to be so.

Notes

1. David Rose, "Neo Culpa," *Vanity Fair,* November 2006, available at http://www.vanityfair.com/politics/features/2006/12/neocons200612.

2. "Zimbabwean Activist Vows to Fight On," Amnesty International, May 2005, available at http://web.amnesty.org/wire/May2005/WOZA.

3. Think tanks such as the US Institute of Peace, the Council on Foreign Relations, the Center for Strategic and International Studies, and others ran seminars and roundtable discussions and issued reports with recommendations on effective postconflict operations and "winning the peace."

4. Information available at http://www.codepink4peace.org/article.php?id =347, retrieved December 16, 2005.

5. Jenni Williams, presentation at the Woodrow Wilson Center for International Scholars and in discussion with the author, Washington, DC, September 2005.

6. Alexandra Balandia Ruizpineda, "Women in the Nonviolent Resistance Movement in Venezuela," in *Conflict Prevention and Transformation: Women's Vital Contributions* (Washington, DC: Hunt Alternatives Fund, 2005).

7. The Iraq War proves that even interstate wars are difficult to prevent.

8. Reports of the Carnegie Commission on Preventing Deadly Conflict are available at http://www.carnegie.org/sub/research.

9. Carnegie Commission on Deadly Conflict, *Preventing Deadly Conflict, Final Report,* Carnegie Commission of New York, 1999, available at http://wwics.si.edu/subsites/ccpdc/pubs/rept97/finfr.htm.

10. Examples of this debate include Carla Koppell and Anita Sharma, *Preventing the Next Wave of Conflict: Understanding Non-traditional Threats to Global Security* (Washington, DC: Woodrow Wilson Center for International Scholars, 2003).

11. The Human Security Center at the University of British Columbia, *Human Security Report 2005: War and Peace in the Twenty-First Century* (Oxford, UK: Oxford University Press, 2005), pp. 147–155.

12. Ibid.

13. Ibid.

14. World Bank, *Conflict Prevention and Reconstruction,* available at www.worldbank.org.

15. Martin Weiss, *World Bank Post-Conflict Aid: Oversight Issues for Congress,* RS21819 (Washington, DC: Congressional Research Service Report for Congress, April 19, 2004).

16. The Human Security Center at the University of British Columbia, *Human Security Report 2005,* pp. 147–155, available at http://www.humansecurityreport.info, retrieved July 18, 2006.

17. *An Agenda for Peace: Preventive Diplomacy, Peacemaking, and Peacekeeping* (New York: UN, 1992), available at http://www.un.org/docs/SG/agpeace.html.

18. For more on this discussion, see Francis Deng and Roberta Cohen, *Masses in Flight: The Global Crisis of Internal Displacement* (Washington, DC: Brookings Institution, 1998).

19. Msekiwa Makwanya, "Zimbabwe: Blair Legacy—Mugabe Ostracisation a Mistake," May 21, 2007, available at http://allafrica.com/stories/200705210229.html.

20. Robert Tait, "President's Future in Crisis as MPs Rebel and Economic Crisis Grows," *Guardian Unlimited,* January 16, 2007, available at http://www.guardian.co.uk/iran/story/0,,1991316,00.html.

21. For a selection of early conflict indicators developed by a cross section of research institutions, see *Conflict and Peace Analysis and Response Manual,* 2nd edition (London: FEWER, 1999), Annex 1, available at http://www.reliefweb.int/library/documents/studman2.pdf.

22. Eugenia Piza-Lopez and Susanne Schmeidl, *Gender and Conflict Early Warning: A Framework for Action* (London: International Alert, Swiss Peace Foundation, 2002).

23. In the nineteenth century, coal miners took a canary with them into the mine as an early warning sign of toxic fumes. Canaries are particularly sensitive to colorless, odorless fumes. If the canary showed signs of distress, it indicated that the air was not safe.

24. Jan Goodwin, "International Report," *Marie Claire,* November 1, 2005, available at http://www.accessmylibrary.com.

25. Discussions with the author, London, July 2006.

26. Ellen Johnson-Sirleaf and Elizabeth Rehn, *Women, War, and Peace* (New York: UNIFEM, 2002).

27. Women activists discussed their situation with the author, Fiji, June 2006.

28. These views were shared with the author by a former senior diplomat from the region, New York, January 2005.

29. International Labour Organization, *Situation of Workers in Occupied Arab Territories Continues to Deteriorate,* press release (Geneva: ILO, May 27, 2005), available at http://www.ilo.org, retrieved July 26, 2006.

30. Piza-Lopez and Schmeidl, *Gender and Conflict Early Warning.*

31. Elizabeth Powley, *Strengthening Governance: The Role of Women in Rwanda's Transition* (Washington, DC: Hunt Alternatives Fund, 2004).

32. Elizabeth Powley, quoting Heather B. Hamilton, "Rwanda's Women: The Key to Reconstruction," in "The Future of the African Great Lakes Region," *Journal of Humanitarian Assistance* 3, May 19, 2002, available at http://www.jha.ac/greatlakes/b001.htm.

33. Index Mundi, *Iran Total Fertility Rate,* 2006, available at http://www.indexmundi.com/iran/total_fertility_rate.html.

34. Comments made to the author by a range of people, Tehran, Iran, May 2004.

35. Interview with the author, Tehran, 2004.

36. Author's interview with leading reform politician, Tehran, Iran, 2004.

37. Food and Agricultural Organization, *Afghanistan's Women: The Hidden Strength of a War-Torn Land* (Geneva: FAO, 2002), available at http://www.fao.org.

38. Quoted in Sanam Naraghi Anderlini, *Women's Leadership, Gender, and Peace: Reflections on a Meeting at the Ford Foundation* (New York: Ford Foundation, 2000), pp. 16–17.

39. Ibid.

40. For more information, see Bernard Broughton and Sarah Maguire, *The Interagency Real-Time Evaluation of the Humanitarian Response to the Darfur Crisis* (New York: United Nations, January 2006), p. 33, available at documents.wfp.org/stellent/groups/public/documents/reports/wfp092382.pdf.

41. Ibid.

42. Discussions with Palestinian women activists, Ramallah, and noted in unpublished draft report on women's activism in Palestine and Israel, courtesy of Hunt Alternatives Fund, 2005.

43. Author's personal discussion with the former US diplomat to Burundi, 2005.

44. "The Business of Peacebuilding Continues," *Fem'Talk E-news: Blue Ribbon Peace Special,* Bulletin 15/2006, available at http://www.peacewomen.org.

45. Ibid.

46. Hugh Miall, "Conflict Transformation: A Multi-Dimensional Task," in *Berghof Handbook for Conflict Transformation,* David Bloomfield, Martina Fischer, Beatrix Schmelzle (eds.) (Wiesbaden, Germany: Berghof Research Center for Constructive Conflict Management, 2004), available at http://www.berghof-handbook.net.

47. For more information and updates, see www.wozazimbabwe.org.

48. WOZA/MOZA, "Ten Steps to a New Zimbabwe," May 27, 2007, www.wozazimbabwe.org.

49. Nader Karami, "Grand Ayatollah Endorses End to Gender Discrimination," *Roozonline,* June 5, 2007, available at http://www.roozonline.com.

50. Joshua Paulson, "Mothers of the Plaza de Mayo, Argentina 1977–1983," in *Waging Nonviolent Struggle,* Gene Sharp (ed.) (Boston: Extending Horizon, 2005), pp. 217–221.

51. Jolynn Shoemaker (ed.), *Conflict Prevention and Transformation: Women's Vital Contributions* (Washington, DC: Hunt Alternatives Fund, 2005).

52. Paulson, "Mothers of the Plaza de Mayo."

53. Felicity Hill, "Engendering Early Warning Mechanisms for Effective Conflict Prevention: The Elusive Role of Women in Early Warning," in *Conflict Trends,* no. 3 (Durban, ZA: African Centre for the Constructive Resolution of Disputes), October 2003.

54. "Deal Reached in Nigeria Oil Protest," *BBC News World Edition,* July 16, 2002, available at http://news.bbc.co.uk/2/hi/africa/2129281.stm, retrieved July 18, 2006.

55. Nigerian women's rights groups shared their views and concerns with the author, New York, March 2006.

56. Susan Collin Marks, *Watching the Wind: Conflict Resolution During South Africa's Transition to Democracy* (Washington, DC: United States Institute of Peace, 2000), pp. 9–17.

57. Ibid.

58. Genderlinks, *Mainstreaming a Gender Perspective in Multidimensional Peacekeeping Operations: South Africa Case Study* (Johannesburg, ZA: Genderlinks, n.d.).

59. Sanam Naraghi Anderlini, *Negotiating the Transition to Democracy and Reforming the Security Sector: The Vital Role of South African Women* (Washington, DC: Hunt Alternatives Fund, 2004).

60. Quoted in Genderlinks, *Mainstreaming a Gender Perspective.*

61. Informal discussion with the author, June 2005.

62. Chetan Kumar, "United Nations Catalytic Processes for Peace-building," in *What Really Works in Preventing and Rebuilding Failed States,* Occasional Paper Series, issue 2, December 2006 (Washington, DC: Woodrow Wilson Center for International Scholars).

63. "UNDP's Support for Peacebuilding, Democracy and Elections in Guyana," January 2007, available at http://content.undp.org.

64. In discussion with the author, New York, January 2006.

65. Ibid.

66. Norman Chitapi, "Too Many Cooks Could Spoil Mediation Process," *Africa Report,* June 6, 2007 (London: Institute of War and Peace Reporting).

67. "Jenni Williams Speaks About Women of Zimbabwe Arise," 2006, available at http://radio.oneworld.net/mediamanage/view/6267.

68. Kumar, "United Nations."

three

Getting to the Peace Table

> You need us because we women are willing to sit together on the same
> side of the table and together look at our complex joint history, with
> the commitment and intention of not getting up until—in respect and
> reciprocity—we can get up together and begin our new history and
> fulfill our joint destiny.
>
> —Terry Greenblatt, speaking before the
> UN Security Council, May 2002

In the peaks and troughs that mark Israeli-Palestinian relations, 2002
came close to the bottom. With the Oslo process in shreds, violence was
again the modus operandi. Israel responded to Palestinian suicide bomb-
ings in spring 2002 by cracking down on a massive scale. The army
rolled into the West Bank and Gaza, imposing twenty-four-hour lock-
down curfews on every Palestinian man, woman, and child for days,
weeks, and months on end. Yet in October, marking the second anniversary of Resolution 1325, Maha Abu Dayyeh Shamas, a Palestinian, and
Terry Greenblatt, an Israeli, appeared at the Security Council and spoke
of peace and cooperation. "Peace is made between peoples and not
between leaders. A process that should lead to a political solution that is
sustainable and consequently permanent . . . should not be left to the
confines of the generals, and should be transparent to the relevant societies," said Shamas, executive director of the Jerusalem-based Women's
Legal Aid and Counseling Service.

> The participation of women in any future peace process is essential to
> maintain connection to the realities of the relevant societies. . . .
> Women have proven themselves to be more dedicated to the process
> of reaching out. . . . We want to approach peace-building in a way that

53

will promote long-term stability. We want to explain to each other what it is like to live in Israel and Palestine, to develop transparent procedures so that any peace will be one between individuals and not politicians. . . . If we leave it only to men we get Israeli generals and Palestinians who will not be defeated and there is no room to negotiate.[1]

UN Security Council Resolution 1325 specifically calls on all actors to include women in peace processes. It is a recognition of women's potential contributions to peacemaking and their commitment, as demonstrated by Shamas's statement. Yet in 2006, there were no women in the multiparty Nepali peace negotiations. In Uganda at the time of writing, the opposition group, the Lord's Resistance Army (LRA), had a single woman on its team, but the government had none. Women remain absent as third-party mediators and even as representatives of the UN Secretary-General in most conflict-affected countries.[2]

Why? What hinders women's inclusion in formal peace processes? How have women overcome the challenges? Among those who have participated in negotiations, what difference did they make? In this chapter I draw attention to two dimensions of women's peacebuilding initiatives: (1) their efforts to gain public and political support for peace talks and (2) their contributions to peace negotiations. I explore the difficulties women encounter and the tactics and strategies they use to gain recognition and participation. Where women have been involved, I examine their contributions to the substance and process of negotiations. In doing so, I highlight the shortcomings of existing peace negotiation structures in addressing the complexity of civil wars.

Struggling for Normalcy in Times of War

The initial onslaught of violence and rise of militarization can push women out of the public sphere. But as warfare seeps into the home and the private sphere, women's activism takes new shape. Some, like the Women in Black of the Balkans, persist in their silent demonstrations. Others take on the task of providing food and shelter, medical care, education, and security for their families and community. When repression mounts, says Asian human rights activist Rita Manchanda, "The men retreat because they are too vulnerable. Instead the women come out in their traditional roles as nurturers and as protectors of the community."[3]

A recurring theme among many women's grassroots organizations is their resistance to militarization. In South Africa they fought conscription.

In Israel, women's organizations have drawn attention to the inhumane treatment of Palestinians by Israeli forces at security checkpoints. Their concern is twofold: the treatment of Palestinians and the effects of militarization on their own Israeli boys and girls. In the Philippines women initiated village peace zones to protect their children from recruitment by militias and the state army. In the Balkans, the Caucasus, Colombia, and Palestine, women have resisted the military recruitment of husbands and sons by hiding them, marrying them off, lying to the authorities, and even arriving at the front lines to take them home.[4]

Often the same women who initially take a stand to prevent war are the first to regroup and call for a negotiated peace and end to war. But they are joined by others who are catapulted into the unfamiliar terrain of politics due to the violence in their lives. For Visaka Dharmadasa of Sri Lanka, the moment came when her son, a soldier in the Sri Lankan army, disappeared in a battle against the Liberation Tamil Tigers of Eelam in 1998; for Ugandan Angelina Atyam it came when her fourteen-year-old daughter was among over 100 girls kidnapped by the LRA in northern Uganda overnight from a boarding school; for Cindy Sheehan, an American, it came when her son died in Iraq. The countries differ, the women vary, but their experiences and motivations to "do something" are strikingly similar.

The "something" can originate with profound sadness, perhaps anger, and a need to understand why her child is gone. The reactions that follow vary. Some demand an end to war; others seek information and explanation: Where is my son? What did the government know, and what measures are in place to protect others? Some seek compensation for their children and have needs as widows. These seemingly simple demands propel women not only into the political arena but also into the terrain of security and military experts. The questions they ask, the responses they get—many of which can be patronizing—push them further. They find themselves directly at odds with their own political and military leaders.

The step into the world of politics and national security also often leads women into dialogue and engagement with their erstwhile enemies, typically women from the "other side." What they find is a shared experience of violence and pain, of being women in societies dominated by men, of fear and mistrust of each other's communities, and of common hopes for future based on peace, justice, and normalcy. The similarity, in the words of one Bosnian woman on meeting her Serbian counterpart, "is like looking into the mirror."[5] "It doesn't matter which side you are on," echoes South African Thandi Modise, former guerrilla fighter and politician. "The fact is on both sides women will be raped, children will be maimed, and we won't know where the corpses are."[6]

This reaching across and search for a moderate space is never easy. The simple act of meeting each other at a time when fear, mistrust, and insecurity reign can be life-threatening. It is always a struggle to move beyond religious, ethnic, or familial affiliations to focus on peace and coexistence. Yet from Liberia to the Philippines, the Solomon Islands to Sri Lanka, women are stepping into the fray and finding common ground: slim and thin at times, but a starting point from which a common agenda emerges.

On the Streets

Often women's first foray into the political space and demand for peace comes in the form of mass public demonstrations. Northern Ireland in 1970 witnessed the mass mobilization of some 3,000 women, pushing prams with food to those who had none. The sight threw the British army into disarray. In 1976 Mairead Corrigan and Betty Williams again led the way, following the deaths of four children. They galvanized the public, signed petitions, and called for peace. For their efforts they were awarded the Nobel Peace Prize in 1977.

Nearly two decades later in Liberia, Mary Brownell, a school-teacher, took on a similar challenge. With warlordism devastating the nation and a dozen peace agreements in shreds, Brownell, together with a group of friends, decided to mobilize women "to bring pressure on the warlords to stop the fighting."[7] The group grew slowly. "Some of them weren't sure we'd make it, because," they said, "[the warlords] fight us with their guns, and we have nothing. So I said, 'let's go in faith.'" Eventually over the radio, they called for a mass meeting, inviting all women, "from all walks of life," to attend a public meeting at the civic hall. Over 400 women showed up. Like their Irish counterparts, the Liberians demonstrated and built public support and legitimacy. The Liberian Women's Initiative (LWI) was born. They raised funds through whatever means possible—from bake sales to donations—to attend peace talks held across the region.

In 1996, after the failure of some fourteen cease-fire agreements, the Liberians agreed to end fighting and hold elections. The LWI was critical to this progress. At every instance, they encouraged and lobbied the warring parties to accept compromises. They ran workshops in which members of opposing parties were forced to partner with each other to complete simple tasks. They held parties accountable at every point. They kept their public support through their demonstrations. They were the first sector of society to speak up to the fighters.

In 1996 in Colombia, women activists and organizations were leaders in the Mandate for Peace, Life, and Freedom campaign. Ten million people signed petitions in favor of a negotiated solution between the government and left-wing guerrillas (the Revolutionary Armed Forces of Colombia, or FARC, and the National Liberation Army, or ELN) in a nonbinding ballot in the elections of 1997.[8] The mass public demonstrations and peace marches led by a coalition of NGOs and networks do not fully explain then president Andrés Pastrana's decision to instigate a dialogue with the FARC, writes Catalina Rojas, but Colombians across the political spectrum agree that they were catalytic.[9]

Across the world, in Sri Lanka, Neela Marikkar, an advertising executive, was pivotal in getting the business community to use its clout to demand a negotiated settlement to a twenty-year war. The Sri Lankan conflict broke out in 1983. As a multiethnic, multireligious, multilingual society, its troubles were rooted in the country's colonial past. The British favored the English-speaking minority Tamil population, but with independence came a Sinhalese-dominated government. Citing the need to redress the imbalance caused by British rule, a nationalist Sinhalese government passed laws that favored the Sinhalese Buddhist population overtly. They included naming Sinhalese as the sole national language, thereby disenfranchising countless Tamils from government structures and educational opportunities. By 1983, tensions had reached a fever pitch. The LTTE, an armed rebel movement, emerged. They demanded an independent homeland in the north and east of the country. The war engulfed wider sectors of the population as the years progressed, with attacks and counterattacks on both sides.

In July 2001, the LTTE bombed Colombo airport, sending insurance premiums for imports and exports skyrocketing. The business community finally felt the impact of the twenty-year war. As founder of Sri Lanka First, a group of business leaders advocating for a negotiated end to the civil war, Marikkar initiated a mass public advertising campaign, encouraging Sri Lankans to step out of their homes and offices at midday on September 19, 2001, to hold hands and show the government they wanted peace. Of the country's population of 18 million, 1 million joined, standing in the midday sun for fifteen minutes, holding hands. It was an important moment.[10] The government was dissolved within weeks following a vote of no confidence. Elections in the autumn of 2001 brought a new government to power with the peace mandate. The LTTE and later the government declared a truce in 2002, and six rounds of direct talks took place before they hit an impasse in April 2003.[11]

In Nepal, where a Maoist insurgency and oppressive governmental responses have devastated the country over ten years, society organizations representing women, castes, and ethnic groups played a pivotal role in the people's movement in April 2006. The protests catalyzed multiparty peace talks and a comprehensive peace accord in November 2006.

This public mobilization is an effective prompt, a wake-up call to armed groups and government to initiate a cease-fire and dialogue without losing face. The effect can be long- or short-lived. It is rare, however, for those who mobilized in the civic sector, particularly women, to gain access or representation at the actual negotiations. The rosy language of international policies is not being implemented effectively by the very multilateral institutions and national governments that passed and are bound by the policies.

About Us, Without Us:
Why Women Are Absent from Formal Peace Talks

Some activists claim misogyny or sexism for women's exclusion from peace processes. For those, like the Northern Irish discussed below, who have faced the taunts and insults of men ("silly cow," and mooing noises in public forums), the claims are not always unsubstantiated. But the reality is more complex. The paucity of women in leadership positions in political parties, the state, or nonstate groups is perhaps the most pertinent reason for their absence from peace talks. Even where women hold leadership positions in opposition groups or the government, as in El Salvador, Uganda, or Sri Lanka, they remain largely excluded from high-level decisionmaking. Oftentimes their exclusion from peace talks is directly linked to their marginalization in major governmental positions. In Uganda for example, the explanation given to one female member of parliament was that the delegation was selected on the basis of posts: namely the defense minister, the chief of staff of the army, and so forth. Women do not hold such positions; thus they are absent from the talks.[12]

From the standpoint of women who mobilize in civil society, the lack of strategic planning and reluctance by some to engage in formal politics often compound the problem. Women's grassroots groups do not always perceive their actions as overtly political. Even those who challenge government actions and have taken on sensitive and highly political issues can regard themselves as predominantly apolitical and "just wanting peace."[13] In their early years, women's groups often have limited exposure to and experience with national politics, let alone international diplomacy. They can therefore be slow to devise comprehensive political strategies or to enter the national political arena as a formal entity. Although they may succeed in raising public awareness and support, they often remain in the informal sphere, a ready comfort zone, and do not focus their efforts on attaining representation at peace talks.

There are also instances in which women peace activists deliberately reject direct engagement and choose to withdraw from interactions with the formal sector (i.e., governments, rebel groups, or others). In Colombia and elsewhere, some groups take a firm stance against dialogue with armed groups or the government, based on their actions and the belief that the premise for talks is immoral. In effect they boycott formal processes deliberately, preferring to maintain a moral and ethical high ground. Is it an effective strategy? The reality in most instances is that the negotiations and compromises will be made regardless of whether women and civil society more broadly support them. Thus the challenge for many such groups is whether to forgo their moral high ground in exchange for the possibility of engaging in a process with the hope of having a positive impact. There is no clear-cut answer, and the conflict can result in civil society entities splintering (pro- and anti-negotiations) and weakening at times.

Ultimately, however, the exclusion of women, particularly those representing civil society organizations, results from systemic flaws in the structure and process of peace negotiations. Just as conflict prevention structures were designed in the era of international conflict, peace negotiations are also modeled on processes to end interstate wars. Herein lies the problem. International peace negotiations are largely focused on ending wars *between* countries. Cease-fire agreements, military retreats, and in principle a return of each side to its own mutually recognized territory are central features. Those who negotiate are political and military leaders on either side. Mistrust occurs on a national level, and relations (if not trust) are gradually restored through diplomatic and economic ties. Soldiers are demobilized and sent home to communities that may have changed with the war, but are not devastated. They are more likely to be welcomed than shunned. Each side has time to heal within its own safe space before reaching out to their enemies on their own terms, in their own time, if ever at all.

Ordinary Rwandans and Bosnians, Sudanese, Somalis, or even Palestinians and Israelis don't have that luxury. To be sure, the end of war means a return home for some. But when home is next door to the man who killed one's son or raped a daughter, it can be a harrowing place. The end of civil war does not bring retreat and a safe haven for surviving victims or perpetrators, because too often, there are no front lines from which to retreat. Refugees and the internally displaced have no place to return to. Homes, cities, villages, and communities were the battlefields. Generals, defense ministers, and political leaders may be well placed to agree to the cessation of hostilities and discuss power sharing, but they alone cannot bring peace within communities or trust between neighbors.

Peace Talks: Ending War, Bringing Peace

In the context of civil wars, peace negotiations have broader goals: to end war *and* bring peace. At a distance they may seem one and the same. In practice, they are profoundly different; intertwined and interdependent, but emphasizing different issues and relying on different sets of actors to ensure success. Clearly cease-fires must be set and complied with, and those who participated in the war making have to be present. In civil wars, however, peacebuilding is a far more complex endeavor. It involves providing basic security and services, building trust between opposing parties, recognizing the need for coexistence and interdependence, ensuring the rule of law, fostering justice and human rights, and establishing leadership that is legitimate in the eyes of the entire population. The consensus of armed groups to desist from violence is critical, but the rest is largely the domain of others. It requires the involvement and participation of those who have knowledge, understanding, and experience in the provision of these services, and those who have lived through the violence but maintained the norms of peace. The war makers rarely have the requisite experience and expertise in peacemaking or coexistence. Yet they are charged with the responsibility and power to bring peace.

Policymakers and international bureaucrats are often quick to defend the exclusionary nature of peace negotiations. War makers are the primary targets, and they need to reach a compromise, the bureaucrats argue. Getting agreement from them to come to the table is hard enough; reaching consensus on who else should be present on an equal footing is nearly impossible. The implicit message is, "We cannot rock the boat," regardless of whether the boat itself is leaking. When civil society organizations call for inclusive processes, often their legitimacy is questioned. Who are they? Whom do they represent? How can their objectivity be ensured? Although these are valid concerns, they are rarely, if ever, applied to the political and military leaders who claim to be representative of their societies but often appear to gain their legitimacy through the barrel of a gun.

Leaving Women Out: Reasons and Excuses

As for women's exclusion from formal processes, the reasons given are abundant. A common refrain among policymakers is that the peace table is not a venue for discussions of gender equality or women's issues. These are important issues, they say, but should come at a later stage. Implicit in such comments is the notion that women care only about issues of equality and that women's issues are their sole concern. There is still little understanding or acceptance that all issues are women's issues (and typical "women's issues" are very relevant to men as well). There is even less consciousness of and much skepticism about the capacities, knowledge, and experiences of women to engage and contribute effectively to negotiating and building peace and security.

Women's exclusion is embedded in local culture. Parties to the negotiations determine who represents them in negotiations, say international policymakers. The international community or third-party mediators cannot meddle in such issues. It is akin to social engineering, and certainly the peace table is not the place to address these "cultural norms." Yet mediators can often place conditions on talks. They can also provide advice and guidance. Most notably, as representatives of the international community they can call for adherence to international standards, including implementation of Resolution 1325. Often parties to peace talks (particularly nonstate groups) are willing to adhere to international norms to improve their own credibility as viable political entities, not just an armed group. Yet mediators seem to forgo such factors, and demand for compliance with standards (especially relating to the treatment of women) is rarely if ever made.

In addition, the credibility of women's civil society groups is often questioned. They do not represent the broad population. They are the elite. Their views and interests are no different than those of the men. Although in some cases those claims may be true, they also apply to men. In Burundi, for example, many of the seventeen parties to peace talks had no public support. In Nepal, for many in the public, the eight political parties to the talks were led by high-caste representatives and have not been effective in representing the concerns of the socially excluded ethnic and lower-caste population. A group's lack of representation or elitism is never used as a rationale for the exclusion of entrenched political actors. Even when there is recognition of the need for a more inclusive process, it is often cast aside in bargaining and comprises that bring parties to the table.

There is also a prevailing belief that peace accords are gender-neutral. International policymakers highlight references to human rights and justice broadly, suggesting that they encompass everyone, including women. No, says one former US ambassador to Africa. "Gender-neutral" translates into discrimination against women because the impact of decisions made at the table are rarely considered through the experiences of women who have to live with them. Reflecting on his involvement in Angola, Ambassador Don Steinberg notes that the weakness of the peace agreements on key issues such as reintegration of combatants became apparent when it was too late. The men, unskilled in anything other than warfare, returned to homes where women had learned to live without them. The result was an increase in domestic violence, alcoholism, and drug abuse.[14]

Women's presence for the sake of being women is also often questioned. After all, women are not immune to political or ethnic affiliation, and so the argument goes, they are adequately represented through their male leaders. Although that may be true in some instances, the systemic acceptance of women's absence from peace negotiations worldwide is notable. If Muslims or Hindus, Jews or any particular race of people were systematically absent, there would be an outcry and accusations of prejudice and oppression. Yet exclusion on the basis of sex is readily tolerated.

Other peculiar excuses include the idea that women should not be at the negotiations because they will make compromises, and besides, they had nothing to do with the war. On this, Swanee Hunt, a former US ambassador to Austria, notes how in Bosnia "women . . . disavowed the violence . . . but they leaned forward, rather than pulling back, to confront the challenges of postwar Bosnia." So she argues, "it is precisely because this was *not* their war, that they should shape the peace."[15]

The reasons and excuses given for excluding them hamper and frustrate many women but do not dissuade them. Once conscious and mobilized, they want to claim their space and express their opinions, concerns, and solutions in formal processes. They see peace negotiations as a moment in history and a critical window for change, a time when opposing sides tackle principles of democracy, freedom, self-determination, liberation from racial or ethnic oppression, and equality. The absence of these principles often motivates people to take up arms and go to war. For the women putting their lives on the line, freedom is not limited to freedom from sexual violence or even political oppression. It is also freedom from social and gender-based discrimination. Self-determination is not an abstract notion relating to national identity and statehood alone. It is about having the right to chart one's own course in society. Their implicit stance is that decisions about their future should not be made without their involvement.

Raising Their Voices, Demanding to Be Heard and Seen

In targeting the political arena and demanding negotiations, women have adopted different approaches. Some draw from or build on women's rights movements, with an explicit message of equality and demands for the right to participate in decisionmaking and the firm belief that peace processes should promote more equitable relations between men and women. Others build on their socially accepted identities as mothers or daughters, or along ethnic, religious, or tribal lines, and focus on critical peace and security issues. Both phenomena are often present in the conflict settings and interchange. There can be significant ideological clashes and disagreements on strategy. But when they can come together and share a common platform, they are a force to be reckoned with. As discussed below, the tactics they use vary across conflicts, cultures, time, and space, and they range from noisy street protests to quiet mediation, national political participation, and international lobbying to get their voices heard. The challenge is not only to open the political space, but also to create a strong public constituency that gives credibility to their demands.

Behind the Scenes

Women leaders who build credibility through public demonstrations and street protests sometimes move toward behind-the-scenes and track-two mediation. The Liberians perfected the art of "corridor lobbying," literally waiting in corridors talking to negotiators as they entered and exited the room during breaks in the 1994 Accra conference. They issued statements and formulated resolutions that they presented to mediators from the Economic Community of West African States (ECOWAS). Of the many activists, Ruth Ceaser says, they "would look at the documents and make sure that things [were] all right, that the resources were available, the meetings [were] held . . . [they were] like the engine that moves a car."[16]

Through contacts with regional media, particularly the Ghanaian press and international journalists covering the process, they also ensured that their exclusion was publicly acknowledged. At the same time, they spoke about the plight of women and children. They also took on the responsibility of documenting attacks against civilians and issuing a position statement on the conduct of the conflict, supported by "hundreds of women," says Theresa Leigh-Sherman. The persistence paid off at Accra, when Ghanaian president Jerry Rawlings invited the delegation to give a presentation to the negotiators. Of the recommendations they made, one, concerning the absence of women from negotiations, stunned observers. "Our lack of representation in the ongoing peace process is a denial of one of our fundamental rights; the right to be seen, be heard and be counted. This [denial] also deprives the country [of] access to the opinion of 51 percent of its human resources in solving problems, which affect our lives as people."[17] It was a simple statement of fact, at once obvious, shocking, and critical. With it, the Liberians set a precedent for full participation.

In the years that followed, as the war continued, the women's reputation grew. By 1996, a women's delegation was invited to another round of talks, but not as formal participants. Ruth Sando Perry, a member of another delegation but also an activist in the women's peace effort, was, however, nominated as the head of the council of state that would oversee elections in 1997. Even, then, Perry recalls being initially barred from the conference because she was not "accredited."[18]

In some instances individual women have become central to government-opposition mediation, often as a result of immense personal loss. Visaka Dharmadasa's son was a soldier when he disappeared in Sri Lanka in 1998. Desperate for news about him, she reached out to other families and formed the Association of Parents of Servicemen Missing in Action. The organization advocates on behalf of missing servicemen and offers counseling and advice to families. Dharmadasa has drawn on her personal loss to take a step beyond, reaching out to Tamil mothers on "the other side." Over the years, she has led a public rally of Sinhalese and Tamil mothers, 12,000 of them, as a reminder to the government and public of the plight of the missing. She has also run workshops on rehabilitation of soldiers and reconciliation between the warring sides; educated soldiers, youth, and community leaders about international standards of conduct in war; proposed guidelines to the army for identifying soldiers' bodies; and is suing the government to force DNA testing of soldiers' remains.[19]

In 1999, writes journalist Beena Sarwar, Dharmadasa led a group of five mothers, members of her association, into Tamil territory, ostensibly to visit a Christian shrine, but in reality to meet with the LTTE. The women met with young LTTE soldiers, no different from their own sons. They sat on the floor opposite them and offered food. They "broke the ice by asking a young soldier about his children, pretending to be surprised that he didn't have claws, or horns on his head."[20] They offered cakes and books. "We found that they did not have hatred towards us, and nor did we towards them," Dharmadasa recalls. She never asked them about her own son and is quick to acknowledge that her pain (and his, if he is alive) is matched and perhaps more acute among the Tamil population. Later, when the LTTE risked their own lives to get Dharmadasa and her group across the divide, the relationship deepened.[21] The trust that exists has sustained their contact, even when formal peace talks stalled.

She has been tireless in her efforts to bring about peace talks and at the forefront of demanding women's participation in the peace process. She successfully lobbied the Norwegians, who were mediating talks. When talks about formal negotiations began in 2002, a Gender Subcommittee was formed comprising only women, representatives nominated by the government and the LTTE. Even the Norwegian facilitator was a woman. It is perhaps the first time that women made up 100 percent of the official delegations and mediation team within a formal peace process.

In 2003, when the talks stalled, the LTTE shunned other mediators, including the Norwegians. Instead they called on her to convey their messages to the government, explaining their temporary withdrawal. Dharmadasa is widely recognized and trusted for her commitment to ending the violence through negotiations.

In Sri Lanka's landscape of peace and civil society activism, there are many people who seek recognition. Dharmadasa is not one of them. "I live in Candy," she says, "that is where the LTTE finds me." She poses no threat, has no hidden agenda, and above all recognizes the precarious situation in which she finds herself. In no way does she want to be perceived as a threat. A move to Colombo, an offer she has received many times, and attention would be detrimental to her work and her cause. The LTTE know and trust her not as a politician or diplomat, she says; with them, "I'm just a simple mother."[22]

North across the Bay of Bengal, beyond Bangladesh in India's northeastern corner among the forty tribes of the Naga Hills, other "simple" mothers—other women—are mediating in the midst of another conflict. The Nagas number about 3 million people, speaking some sixty different dialects. The tribes straddle internal Indian provinces and international borders. They are an indigenous people, secluded and self-sufficient, with a tradition of intervillage warfare that dates back centuries. Throughout their history, writes Rita Manchanda, women have been the sanctioned arbiters and peacemakers, known as the Demi or Pukrelia, though their involvement in public affairs was considered an "ill omen."[23] The current struggle, like so many others, dates back to the last days of the Raj, when India won its independence. The Nagas, believing themselves to be a distinct people with a history and culture separate from those of mainland India, have fought for independence for over half a century. The struggle is ongoing, and the parties to the conflict come and go: armed groups and subgroups; the government of India; the Indian state of Nagaland, formed in 1963 and comprising Naga and non-Naga peoples; a variety of tribes; and border states. Cease-fires are signed, but violence continues, and negotiations are sporadic. In the midst of such confusion, a broad-based peace constituency is emerging in which women's organizations play a prominent role. In 1997 a cease-fire agreement was signed, but it was precarious. Many of the factions were reluctant to adhere to the provisions. Eight years later in 2005, largely due to the sustained efforts of civil society and a popular base, abandoning the peace process, bumpy as it seemed, was not a viable option for the various parties.[24]

The women involved come from distinct ideological backgrounds. On the one hand, the Naga Mothers Association (NMA), formed in 1984, draws on traditional identities of women as peacemakers, to assert their role as arbiters and mediators, expanding the middle ground for peace. On the other hand, the Naga Women's Union of Manipur (NWUM), formed in 1994 in preparation for the Fourth World Conference in Beijing, asserts women's rights more broadly. Although its founding principles include promoting traditional values, it is active in safeguarding women's legal rights, including marriage and divorce, inheritance and property ownership rights, and above all, participation in village and tribal authorities.

On the question of peace, the two work symbiotically, advocating the message of peace, diffusing tensions, reconciling warring parties, and drawing on their distinct identities and constituencies to maximize effect. Informally, says Manchanda, Naga women have mediated within their own communities and with state and other nonstate entities. They have formed human barriers to protect their villages from Indian security forces and demanded the release of their relatives in face-to-face meetings with military commanders. They have lobbied for the removal of army posts in areas where they have provoked violence near villages.

The NMA has reinforced its role as the traditional peacemaker and is respected and trusted for the neutral stance it takes when mediating between factions. In urban areas, tribal leaders request the presence of women at talks with underground leaders as a means of keeping discussions peaceful. Though maintaining dialogue is difficult at times, particularly in the aftermath of attacks, the women work through their social and informal networks to sustain lines of communication and defuse tensions.

A continent away, in northern Uganda, Angelina Atyam's journey from midwife and mother to peace activist and trusted mediator parallels Dharmadasa's experience. The conflict began in 1986 with the LRA, a part-cult, part-rebel movement led by Joseph Kony. In its earlier years, the movement sought to appeal to the Acholi people of northern Uganda by reacting to President Yoweri Museveni's ouster of the country's former leader, who was an Acholi. But the LRA has no popular support, and in its twenty years of fighting it derived strength from the abduction and subjugation of some 30,000 children, boys and girls of all ages, who were forced to fight. Those who try to escape are beaten to death, those who survived and escaped tell a similar tale. Many were sent back to their own villages to kill their parents and others they knew. The girls have been raped and forced into "marriage" with rebel commanders. They have lived in the bush, in ill health and with little food. Violence has permeated their lives.

In 1996, the LRA abducted Angelina's fourteen-year-old daughter along with over 100 other girls, during a night raid on her boarding school. "When they were taken at first, we just cried and wailed, but then we decided we must do something," she explained in 2004.[25] With others, she founded the Concerned Parents Association (CPA), an NGO dedicated to advocating for the unconditional release of children; providing trainings in rehabilitation and reintegration of combatants, with an emphasis on education and health; and asking for a peaceful resolution of the conflict, with reconciliation and forgiveness.

Atyam launched her crusade from village to village, country to country, talking to politicians and the powerful about the plight of Ugandan children. The war that displaced 1.5 million people went unnoticed for years, but Atyam's crusade shone a national and international light on the region and the escalation of violence. Wary of the attention, Kony summoned her to a meeting, offering her daughter, Charlotte, back in return for her silence. Angelina refused. "If I had asked for Charlotte and she came back—what about the rest? What about the other parents? What about this very many children? What about their mothers? The pain I feel, is what also they feel," she said in a 2006 interview with MSNBC.[26] In 2004, Charlotte escaped with her two young sons. But Atyam continues her work on behalf of the other children. Over the years, she has become a recognized and trusted figure. "We as parents are saying that we don't believe in putting out a fire with petrol. We think it's high time somebody talks," she said to Dutch radio in 2004.[27] In 2005, when the prospect of peace talks was looming, Atyam was a member of the six-person delegation that met with world leaders to support the process.

Political Parties

The trajectory of public protest, humanitarian assistance, and informal mediation does lead to formalized representation at peace talks for some. Not because as women they are invited, but because they subvert existing norms and structures and create their own place.

In Northern Ireland, the peace marches and attempts at resolving the conflict in the 1970s failed, and the women's peace movement waned. By the 1980s, however, women were again working with each other across religious communities on issues of common concern— child care, equal pay, social welfare. As they dealt with these bread-and-butter issues, their points of commonality, especially their daily fears and hopes for the future, began to overwhelm any differences in religion. The relations they established and the trust they built through working together on nonsensitive issues laid the foundation for their involvement in political and conflict-related issues.

In 1996, US senator George Mitchell took up the task of mediating peace talks. Arriving in Northern Ireland, the senator noted the disparity of views and plethora of political parties, not only across sides but also on each side. As a way of ensuring inclusiveness and fair representation of the people, Mitchell proposed that admission to the all-party talks would be via elections, with the top ten parties gaining seats at the negotiations. That alarmed leaders of the women's movement, who recognized the risk of being marginalized. At first they approached various political parties with a view to bringing their agenda and constituency to them, but the parties showed little interest in supporting their views or, indeed, women's participation. Desperate and with six weeks to go, they called an open meeting. From across the religious, geographical, and social sectors the women came, from some 200 organizations, with their roots in nationalist and republican traditions, unionist and loyalist communities. They transformed their network into a political party, one that provided a space for people who were uncomfortable with defining and limiting themselves in terms of the agenda, identities, and values espoused by the mainstream culture.

Although supported by both men and women, the Northern Ireland Women's Coalition (NIWC) was the first explicitly women's political party to emerge. It had no money for campaigning, no headquarters except people's homes, and no name recognition. In the run-up to the elections, kitchen table politics took on new meaning, as the women used household goods, old supermarket boxes, and whatever means available to produce campaign materials; support their seventy candidates; and spread their message of inclusion, equality, and human rights. Their constituency was strong enough. When the election results were tallied, NWIC came in ninth overall, giving it a legitimate seat at the peace table.[28]

A few years later and a world away, Somali peace talks began in Djibouti. Only the country's five clans were recognized as legitimate entities for participation. All were led by men, and none considered women sufficiently important to include them on the negotiating teams. For Asha Hagi Elmi Amin, founder of the Save Somali Women and Children (SSWC), an organization that provided assistance and care to war-torn communities, the exclusion was untenable. Like other Somali women from the outset of war in 1990, Asha was torn between the clans. "My father was from one clan, my husband from another."[29] Literally and metaphorically, she was caught in no-man's-land, belonging to both clans but not fully trusted by either. "I realized the only identity no one could take away from me, was being a woman. My clan is womanhood."[30] When the peace talks began in 2000, the UN invited Amin as an observer. Ignored by representatives of the five clans and thus not considered to be a formal participant, Amin decided to both play by and subvert the rules. Together with other women, she formed a sixth clan, the women's clan. It did not come easily: for six months they struggled among themselves and battled with the other clans and the international community to gain formal recognition. "People were suspicious of us . . . because we wanted to use women as bridges of peace . . . we wanted to unite Somali women as one. . . . Some war lords tried to destroy us," said Amin in 2005. But they were unsuccessful. "They are the same ones that realize that only God can stop us . . . so now they shake our hand."[31]

In January 2004, as leader of the sixth clan, Amin was the only woman to cochair the final phase of the Somali National Reconciliation Conference and the first woman to sign the peace accord.[32] Together with twenty-two other women, they went on to join the Somali Parliament of the Transitional Federal Government (TFG). By 2005, when the Islamic Courts threatened the fragile state, the parliamentary women led a women's peace rally in support of the state.[33] Amin also reached out to the Islamic Courts in 2006 in an effort to sustain peace and, despite the personal risks involved, was a vocal critic of the Ethiopian interventions and escalating violence in early 2007. Her antiviolence stance is clear: the regional situation will improve through trade, development, and dialogue on rights and security. For Amin, intimidation, revenge, and occupation are detrimental to any peace process.[34]

Working with Internationals

Outreach to the international community is another of the tactics and strategies that women adopt. They have worked from two ends of the spectrum: from the local to the global and from the global back to the local.

At the local level. Reaching out to the diplomatic and UN community is an effective means of elevating women's voice and legitimacy in situations in which their own national leaders ignore them. The Liberians went from embassy to embassy, faxing and disseminating their material at every turn. They also leveraged their international contacts to push for formal recognition and representation. In the Somali case, the UN's simple act of inviting SSWC to observe the Djibouti talks was enough to motivate and enable Amin to push for the creation of the sixth clan. In Sri Lanka the Norwegians, as sponsors of the talks, supported the idea of a gender subcommittee. In most instances, the impetus came from the women themselves; the international community's efforts were limited but catalytic.

The Liberians and Sierra Leoneans who led mass demonstrations for peace watched their countries spiral back into war throughout the late 1990s. They regrouped. In 2000, with support from Femme Afrique Solidarité (FAS), a Geneva-based NGO, they established the Mano River Women's Peace Network (MARWOPNET), a regional movement with links across Guinea, Liberia, and Sierra Leone, networking through the elite and the grassroots and lobbying the international community. MARWOPNET, whose Liberian members were relegated to the corridors in the 1996 peace process, was an official signatory to the Liberian peace accords in 2004. It remains an influential presence in the region.

In the Democratic Republic of Congo (DRC), the Inter-Congolese Dialogue started in 2001 as a push to bring a devastating war to an end. The war began in 1998 and has been described by some as Africa's first world war, involving seven regional nations. The brutality of fighting, coupled with a humanitarian crisis that led to disease and starvation, resulted in an estimated 3.3 million deaths among women, children, and the elderly by the war's end in 2003. When the dialogue started, Congolese women drew on Security Council Resolution 1325 to demand participation. The UN Development Fund for Women (UNIFEM), in partnership with FAS and Women as Partners for Peace in Africa (WOPPA), worked with the women to ensure that their concerns were reflected in the official agenda. As talks faltered, FAS and WOPPA, with funding from the Canadian government, brought women together from across ethnic and political divisions to build a common peace platform. When the process resumed in 2003, there were thirty-six women among the 300 delegates.[35]

The Afghan peace talks in Bonn 2001 were a watershed for women's inclusion. Not because of the numbers—there were only five women—but because it was the first time that major international players, notably the United States, had made an explicit call for women's inclusion at the start of a process. The push did not come in a vacuum. It was the result of years of concerted lobbying on the part of US-based organizations such as the Feminist Majority Foundation. The precedent set made it easier for Iraqi women to seek and attain participation in the decision-making that goes on about the future of their country, but still it did not come easily.

In 2003, with the Iraq War starting, Hunt Alternatives Fund, a US-based private foundation, funded the first of a series of gatherings for Iraqi women in Washington, D.C.[36] For many of the participants, Shias and Sunnis, Assyrians and Kurds, it was the first time they were speaking collectively as Iraqi women about their experiences of life under the Ba'athist regime of Saddam Hussein. Their interactions with the US government, World Bank, and UN raised women's profile and catapulted them into the political arena. They formed organizations to bring the Iraqi diaspora closer to those active inside the country. They forged links with the policy community and, despite the violence, are struggling to maintain a presence and voice at the heart of Iraqi politics. Building on its experiences with Iraqi women, Hunt Alternatives Fund's program, the Initiative for Inclusive Security (formerly known as Women Waging Peace), has continued to support Sudanese, Colombian, and other women. Similarly, the University of San Diego's Kroc Institute provides an annual venue at which women peacebuilders and policymakers can reflect and draw on experiences.

Taking a stand at the global level. The global campaign that led to Security Council Resolution 1325 is perhaps the most significant political success that women peace activists have had. It was and is a challenge to the status quo. In aiming for a Security Council resolution, they sought to bridge the chasm between their grassroots communities in war-torn countries and the New York skyline. Among those who joined the campaign for a Security Council resolution, many knew too well that the compromises and decisions made at the peace table had life-and-death significance for them and their families. So the strategic targeting of the Security Council and push for a resolution that endorsed women's inclusion in peacemaking was not only a deliberate attempt at shifting the paradigm and the norms governing peace processes, but also a means of ensuring that they had a chance to determine the future—theirs and their society's—at the point in time when foundations were being laid.

On paper, the effort was very successful. Resolution 1325 calls on governments to ensure the wider participation of women in all phases of conflict prevention, resolution, and peacebuilding. It also "calls on all actors involved, when negotiating and implementing peace agreements, to adopt a gender perspective, including, inter alia . . . measures that support local women's peace initiatives and indigenous processes for conflict resolution, and that involve women in all of the implementation mechanisms of the peace agreements."[37] The reference to all actors and the call to support women's peace initiatives are particularly significant. It is the first time that international law has acknowledged that nonstate actors have a right to be included in peace negotiations.

In practice, the realization of the spirit and word of the resolution remains patchy. Not surprisingly, however, women activists globally have seized on the resolution and been its most ardent supporters and users. Israeli and Palestinian women who have been at the frontiers of peacemaking since the 1980s have taken the vision to a new level. Guided by the spirit and language of Resolution 1325 and dismayed by the continual failure of the formal processes, a group of twenty Israelis and twenty Palestinian women leaders, together with their counterparts from the UN and the European Union, launched the International Women's Commission (IWC) in 2006. Speaking with one voice and a common vision, they advocate for a return to negotiations to work toward "a just and sustainable peace based on the two-state solution."[38]

Resolution 1325 emerged as the result of a tripartite partnership of civil society, the UN, and governments. The IWC is replicating that notion. Its members are women with proven leadership records. Some are well-known politicians, whereas others are longtime civil society actors and international policymakers. In their work, they are proving that such a partnership is possible and necessary for the resolution of the Israeli-Palestinian conflict. "We call upon the Quartet [the UN, the

EU, Russia, and the United States] and other members of the international community to fulfill their obligations in ensuring the end of the occupation, guaranteeing legal protection, and initiating negotiations between the parties," their formal statement reads. "We urge civil society institutions and women in our societies, in Europe, the United States and throughout the world to demand that their governments be proactive third parties in ending our protracted conflict. The International Women's Commission is ready to engage fully in this process, and make the promise of Security Council Resolution 1325 a reality."[39]

Has Resolution 1325 brought women to the peace table? Certainly since it was passed, women's demands for inclusion have been heard more often in formal channels. The Security Council is bound by its own mandate to address the issues at least once a year. The question remains: almost a decade after its adoption, has the resolution been effectively implemented? Not exactly. There is still plenty of inertia and foot dragging among politicians and diplomats. But with pressure from civil society, reference to its provisions arises more regularly in the context of discussions about specific conflicts. In Colombia, Israel, and Palestine, governments have integrated the mandate to include women in peace processes in national policies and even legislation. In 2006, the United Kingdom issued its national action plan for the implementation of the resolution. Others are following suit.

Under pressure from member states, various departments and agencies within the UN have produced action plans for a systemic implementation of the resolution. The Women, Peace, and Security Working Group, comprising a range of international NGOs, has been at the forefront of monitoring the Security Council's own actions. As a result of their advocacy, women from conflict areas have had the opportunity to speak to the council.

At the time of this writing, the UN Population Fund (UNFPA), together with international donors, was attempting to integrate the provisions of the resolution into aspects of the peace process in Nepal, including issues relating to governance, reintegration, and transitional justice. Internationally, activists have translated the resolution into over seventy languages. It has been distributed and explained in workshops and conferences worldwide. In the Balkans and across Africa, women's groups have joined to produce documentary films, mimes, and cartoon versions of the resolution for training among illiterate populations. Resolution 1325 is proving to be a useful hook, a legal framework, and a blueprint for more inclusive peacemaking, but implementing it remains an uphill battle against business as usual.

At the Table: Making a Difference

For the women who have won the battle to get to the peace table, the struggle takes a new turn as negotiations begin. On the one hand, they face the challenge of maintaining their presence and not being subject to the whims or pressures of political or military factions to marginalize them. On the other, they have to demonstrate their ability to influence and make a difference. As gender specialist Pamela Fishman writes, "Power is not just having the ability to impose one's will. It is having the ability to impose one's definition of what is possible, what is right, what is real and what is rational."[40] For women in peace negotiations, the challenge is therefore not only to tackle the key agenda items but also to raise other issues. Those who come with experiences from the ground and express civilians' views struggle to provide alternative perspectives on what is "important," "right," and "rational." Those who succeed alter the substance of the talks by introducing new issues to the agenda and providing new insights. They affect the process, dynamics, relations, and ways in which negotiations are conducted. But perhaps most importantly, they come to the table with a more holistic understanding about the actual purpose of the talks and the centrality of interdependence.

Peace processes, reflects Howard Wolpe, former US congressman, diplomat, and US special envoy to the Burundi negotiations, "require in the first instance, abandonment of the zero-sum, win-lose paradigm induced by war."[41] Parties must reach the point of recognizing their common interests and inextricable interdependence. Yet again and again, peace talks are conducted in a win-lose atmosphere, in which the individuals at the table, often men, are fighting for their own gain. Reflecting on the Burundian process throughout the 1990s, Imelda Nzirora summed up this attitude. "Our Burundian brothers who are members of political parties put the division of the 'national' pie first . . . they are thinking, 'at the end of the negotiations, what position and post will we get?' But that isn't what interests us women. We are interested in returning to peace, so that our sisters and the women in the country side can cultivate their land, move about without fear of being killed today or tomorrow."[42]

Overwhelmingly, women activists, those who make it to the negotiations and those who do not, consider peace talks as the time to acknowledge the concrete and tangible consequences of war and the opportunity to build a more positive and equitable society From southern Sudan to Northern Ireland, from the Middle East to Central America, the Balkans, or the Philippines, women articulate a holistic vision of peace. They link personal peace—peace of mind—to their need for a peaceful society predicted on principles of social justice, equality, rights and responsibilities, and the most basic universal human needs: health, education, security, freedom of movement, and legal and political rights. It is at once complex and so simple, ambitious and yet so basic and profoundly normal.

As Vjosa Dubruna, a Kosovar pediatrician and human rights activist, says, "my understanding of peace is really based on my experience of it. Peace isn't just the absence of war, but a stable life. Freedom. And something that comes with freedom: true respect for diversity."[43] Liberian Mary Brownell echoes this desire for normalcy. "We wanted peace. You want to walk down the street. You don't want to look behind for stray bullets to come from nowhere and strike you. We wanted to be free and satisfied, have the peace of mind. We wanted our children to go to school, to be educated. Because many of us were not in a position to send our children to school so they never had the chance to go into the schoolhouse. Let our children go back to school. Let us move about freely, attend our business, make our market, live a normal life."[44]

This purpose and vision inform women's contributions to the substance and process of peace talks. As discussed below, there are common trends evident across conflict areas where women have become involved in talks. They influence and expand the agenda and issues up for discussion. They bring the voices and experiences of victims. They tend to maintain closer ties to the grassroots and a popular base, communicating their concerns at the negotiations and relaying decisions made back to them. Finally, they bring distinctive approaches and skills that affect the tone and dynamics of the process.

Expanding the Agenda

For many women, there are no lines between private and public spaces. The perspectives they bring to the peace table stem largely from their circles of concern, the voices and experiences they are closest to, from within the home and the community. As mothers, wives, daughters, sisters, teachers, social workers, doctors, human rights activists, lawyers, and local politicians, they are at the front line of coping with the direct and indirect consequences of violence on a daily basis. They document, heal, protect, and resist. The consequences of war are not just those who die in battle or the politics of power, but the destruction of livelihoods, the spread of disease, the absence of education and schooling, the devastation of farmlands and communities, the end of normalcy, the onset of profound trauma.

The peace table, therefore, is their chance to address the underlying structural causes of conflict and to pursue a goal of social justice for all. It is also the moment to ensure that issues of discrimination as they affect any sector of society, including women, are addressed. The recognition of mutual pain and interdependence that they gain through their collaborative efforts at the community level comes to the peace table. It is also an opportunity to address key challenges from new and alternative perspectives. As discussed in Chapter 5, in South Africa, for example, women's involvement in discussions of security sector reform was central to reformulating the national security paradigm and enhancing the credibility of and public trust in the security sector.

For Hanan Mikhail Ashrawi, a key participant in the pre-Oslo talks between Israel and Palestine, women's approach to the talks was fundamentally and qualitatively different from the men's. "We looked at peacemaking not as a personal agenda, for power, but as a set of issues dealing with life and death." While the men avoided and postponed difficult issues, as was evident in the Oslo years, the women, who included political figures such as Naomi Chazan, unloaded "historical, existential, human luggage" from the outset and addressed the process comprehensively.[45]

In the Naga peace process too, women were key to shaping the agenda. In 2001, they, along with other civil society activists, successfully broadened the cease-fire to include protecting civilians from abuse and attack by armed groups. The change reflected a growing recognition that any negotiations had to place civilian security and the concerns of ordinary people high on the agenda. In Sri Lanka, Astrid Heiberg, the Norwegian mediator of talks between women selected by the LTTE and government, recalled their focus on people's basic needs—clean water, fuel, food—compared to prestige projects such as road building that were more popular with men.[46]

Even in El Salvador, where the women "commandantes" who sat at the table were there by virtue of their military rank, not gender or civil society experience, they displayed a keener sense of responsibility toward their constituents than their male counterparts. It was particularly notable when time came for the allocation of land to male and female supporters of the Farabundo Martì Liberation National Front (FMLN) guerrillas. The women were being marginalized, and it was the intervention and insistence of the women commandantes that ensured their equal inclusion as beneficiaries in the disarmament, demobilization, and reintegration programs.[47] In Northern Ireland, NIWC representative Monica McWilliams focused on the underlying economic factors that fueled conflict. In addition to addressing issues of human rights, she raised the question of skills building and reintegration challenges for former fighters.

Elsewhere, as women and leaders with constituencies, these negotiators are often the first to introduce issues of discrimination and exclusion, not just on the basis of gender, but of race, religion, ethnicity, and class. They demand equality in the eyes and practice of the law. Introducing a gendered lens—that is, examining the issues through the experiences of women and men—helps in tackling fundamental structural inequalities. On the one hand, these women wish to reduce the victimization of women in general, to give them more freedom and rights under the law. It is also a means of highlighting the humanity of the boys and men caught up in fighting and acknowledging their fears, concerns, and aspirations. On the other hand, addressing the developmental needs of women is, as South African Cheryl Carolus suggests, essential if the goal is to achieve sustainable development and stability for society as a whole. "When you exclude 53 percent of your population from actually playing a meaningful role in the transformation of our society, you are doing society a huge disservice."[48]

In Guatemala, the example of Luz Mendez, the lone woman in the formal delegation of the Guatemalan National Revolutionary Unity (URNG), indicates that women in the civil society forum widened the space and discourse to address the needs of indigenous people, the handicapped, and other marginalized groups. Spanning three decades, Guatemala's civil war was a typical Cold War phenomenon. It began in 1960, when leftist rebels and guerilla forces launched a struggle against the US-backed military. The conflict escalated through the 1970s, engulfing the countryside and the large poverty-stricken indigenous population. In 1982, opposition groups formed the URNG, and the army intensified its attacks. A year later, as the URNG weakened, with prompting by the United States, the army returned the country to civilian rule. Presidential and legislative elections were held in 1985, and peace negotiations began in 1987. Civil society groups were active and vocal about human rights abuses throughout the conflict and, as peace talks started, the church pushed for the formation of an assembly through which civil society could engage in the negotiations. The Assembly for Civil Society (ACS) included human rights organizations, trade unions, indigenous associations, and representatives of the women's movement. Throughout the nearly decade-long negotiations, the ACS offered proposals, identified issues of concern, and made recommendations to the formal parties.

The women's movement, in particular, brought up such issues as access to land, credits, and other productive resources; health programs;

equal opportunities for training and education; the right to a paid job; elimination of legal discrimination; penalties for sexual harassment; the creation of spaces and institutions for the defense of the rights of indigenous people; and mechanisms to promote the political participation of women. They also ensured that the peace agreements recognized women's contributions to the country's economic, social, and political development.[49] In doing so, they were pointing to the profound root causes of conflict in Guatemalan society that affected a vast cross section of the population, not just themselves. The demand for equal opportunities for everyone was also a means of ensuring that all Guatemalans had a chance for a better and more peaceful future.

Ensuring Victims' Voices Are Heard

Women also bring the voices of the victims to the peace table, says Baroness May Blood, one of two representatives from the NIWC at the Northern Ireland peace talks. As a down-to-earth, sleeves-rolled-up, no-nonsense type, Blood was a community worker for years, dealing firsthand with the direct and indirect trauma that came with the violence. Helen Jackson, then a UK member of parliament and present at the negotiations, confirms that the women's movement had a specific focus. "They . . . gave a human face to the conflict, and highlighted the personal consequences of war."[50]

In Liberia too, the first chance they had to speak to political leaders, the women spoke of the war's invisible victims. "We talked about the killing and how these men were opening these women's stomachs and betting on [the sex of] the babies. We talked about everything, because the women were tired," recalls Leigh-Sherman. "We made recommendations. . . . The nine presidents that were there and . . . CNN, BBC, everybody was in tears, because these were the facts that these people didn't know about."[51]

Giving voice to victims, humanizing the conflict, and drawing on women were tactics that Malian women also used in the 1990s. Mariam Maiga, who was trained as a pharmacist and later became a peace activist, says, "Wives of combatants were taken to hospitals so that they could see first hand the effects of their husbands' work. We sent missions to opinion leaders in order to alert them to the destructive capacity of military action."[52]

Women are committed to bringing what Hanan Ashrawi calls the underbelly of war to the peace table. Cambodian Mu Sochua, NGO leader and former minister, sums up much of what women around the world say. "We negotiate differently because we are confronted with an issue in a situation that we no longer can live with. . . . Women from the grassroots, women who have experienced violence or have helped people in situations of violence . . . won't let go. . . . they cry out . . . because it is not acceptable [to let go]."[53]

Building Consensus: Strengthening the Foundation

If women are conduits for bringing the voices and concerns of victims and civilians to the table, they are also conduits for taking the negotiations back to the grassroots and their constituencies. From Burundi to Bougainville, women are known for ensuring that the essence of the discussions, particularly the compromise being made, is conveyed to ordinary people. In Northern Ireland, they led demands for the creation of a civic forum where representatives of civil society organizations—trade unions, NGOs, and others—could provide input into the negotiations and keep updated on the process. As in Guatemala, where the civil society forum maintained its links to the formal process, the involvement of nonstate actors with significant constituencies in the process is an effective means of taking society along at the pace of the talks. It deepens understanding of the difficulties that negotiations entail and broadens the sense of ownership and, most importantly, commitment to the actual process.

The sustained link to the grassroots or a constituency strengthens women at the negotiating table, giving them both the legitimacy and the mandate to take positions and to be clear where compromise is acceptable and where it is not. In South Africa, for example, the ANC's Women's League mobilized its popular base and reached out to women across the political and civil society spectrum. In 1992, women held the first public cross-party meeting of South Africans and formed the Women's National Coalition. As the negotiations progressed, they fanned out across the country, consulting some 3 million women about economic, social, political, legislative, and security issues. In the end, they emerged with a twelve-point agenda known as the Women's Charter. They drew on this vast constituency to assert their right to participate on an equal footing and in equal numbers (50 percent) in the negotiations process. They also used the charter to legitimize the demands they made in the name of South African women. During the multiparty negotiations process (MPNP), they formed a women's caucus, where they came together across political parties to discuss strategies and ensure that the needs of their grassroots constituencies—women and others—were being addressed in every area under discussion, from governance to security.[54]

Building Trust

"Building trust is perhaps the most difficult but also most essential job of the peacemaker," said Nobel Laureate Oscar Arias in 2001. "For all parties to a conflict to be willing and able to compromise, it will be necessary to trust [each other]." For this trust to emerge, modes of political discourse and communication need to change, writes Wolpe, from the abrasive to one of mutual respect and willingness to listen to the other.[55] The late Mo Mowlam, UK secretary of state for Northern Ireland during the most critical years of peace talks, said, "You have to ask why do they need to shout?" The blame culture, she argued, does not work when the goal is to move forward. "You have to see in what ways you can build trust and confidence . . . you can only do this if you give people a sense of hope. Then the fear and distrust begin to decline. The aggression declines too."[56]

There is no definitive proof of women's trustworthiness or of their ability to build trust more effectively than men. The paucity of women involved in peace processes does not allow for the testing of any hypothesis one way or the other. Yet the anecdotal evidence suggests that women are, at the very least, perceived to be more trustworthy, sometimes because women are less often implicated in war. Other times, it is a result of the tactics women themselves use. They come forward as representatives of the people, with no agenda of personal gain.

If nothing else, women regard trust building as a priority and take advantage of opportunities to foster trust and strengthen communication between warring parties. In India, the Naga women, knowing that motherhood confers status, make strategic use of it. "Our advantage [with the underground troops] is that we approach them as mothers," says NMA president Neidunuo Angami, "therefore we are trusted by all sides."[57]

The trust comes through a combination of neutrality, the willingness to engage with all sides, and honesty. The NIWC's willingness to speak to all sides, extremists among Catholics and Protestants, won them deep trust. Throughout the talks, they were respected for their commitment to getting to peace, and taking every step necessary to get there, regardless of their personal status.

For many women, trust is also based on truth telling. "To build trust, you must speak the truth from the beginning, said Nani Chanishvili, a Georgian academic, politician, and peace activist, in 1999. "It's painful, but it's important."[58] As Ashrawi reflected in 1999, although honesty is not always the easiest approach, it is the key to ensuring more effective dialogue. "When we understood that we were being honest with each other, it meant we respected each other enough to articulate the issues. That I think created a qualitatively different type of . . . approach."[59]

Women are also often more personal in their interactions, Heiberg notes. In Sri Lanka, although there were only two rounds of talks, the women were involved in exchanging books and going on excursions to war-devastated areas. Such rituals as serving tea and acting as hostesses, drawing on social patterns of behavior, created a congenial atmosphere in which people talked together and generated trust.[60]

The trust emerges not just between the negotiators but also between them and their respective constituencies. For Mary Brownell, women's sincerity and honesty earned them the support of a wide cross section of Liberian society and the respect of the international community and faction leaders. "We were sincere. We were not after financial gain," said Brownell in 1999. "They couldn't say that they could buy us off by offering us a few thousand dollars to close our mouths. Even those who attempted it, we rejected it. So they saw that we were sincere. What we had to say we said it, whether they liked it or not. This is why they respected us."[61]

Communication and Empathy

Honesty and directness do not imply being adversarial or aggressive. From observers at the Burundi talks to participants in Northern Ireland, South Africa, and elsewhere, the experience and the message are the same: women deal with conflict differently. Where there is confrontation, they tend to first seek out areas of commonality, as opposed to focusing on differences.

Psychologist Simon Baron-Cohen makes a similar assertion based on years of empirical work. His work builds on that of Deborah Tannen and others whose research shows the different communication styles of males and females.[62] Pointing to differences in expressing disagreement, he says girls "are more likely to soften the blow by expressing their opinion in the form of a question, rather than an assertion."[63] They also "express anger less directly and propose compromises more often." This manner of communication relates to concerns about the other. The result can be that the exchange is "less dominating, less confrontational and less humiliating for the other person."[64]

In peace talks, the attention to practical issues affecting daily life and security, where the opposite sides' experiences and concerns are more similar, often provide a solid platform from which to address more contentious issues. In the Sri Lankan process, Heiberg observed the women's ready willingness to view a problem collectively and seek solutions together, with less concern about their stated positions. In contrast, she noted, drawing on years of experience as a politician in Norway, men tend to be concerned about and rooted in their formal positions, ready to shift only when they observe concessions from the other side. "Female interactions are transcultural," says Heiberg. "What I saw in Sri Lanka is what I saw in Norway twenty years ago. There is a female code of behavior."[65]

Heiberg's observations concur with Baron-Cohen's views about key differences between men's and women's social behavior. He attributes them in part to differences in brain type. The female brain, he writes, "is predominantly hard-wired for empathy. The male brain is predominantly hard-wired for understanding and building systems."[66] His studies reveal how girls show higher levels of emotional sensitivity toward each other and to newcomers. The "female agenda," he writes, "is more centered on another person's emotional state," whereas "the male social agenda is more self-centered."[67] These statements are not absolute and cannot be applied to every individual. But the difference in degree is worth considering.

In the context of peace negotiations, there are no quantitative data to confirm the anecdotes, but the experiences are strikingly similar. Many observers claim that women are better at listening and empathizing. Heiberg contends that, in her experience, women are not better at listening per se but at sharing: sharing the space for talking, for presenting and respecting ideas, and for ensuring that "everyone gets something."[68] In South Africa, Carolus credits women for their ability to listen, empathize, and foster an environment conducive to talks. The skills women gain through their domestic sphere and responsibilities—as mothers, or caregivers to the elderly and ill—become positive attributes in the negotiations. In effect, women's socialization strengthens their communication, empathy, trust building, and conflict resolution capacities, all of which are key ingredients for peacemaking. It is not an essentialist or biological notion; rather, it is an acknowledgment of the value of women's gendered skills and social experiences.

Similarly, among the Naga, it is commonly accepted that women and mothers are more effective at mediation and negotiation. Quoting local activists, Rita Manchanda writes, "In a situation of anger when men can not talk to men without violence, it is the mothers who . . . can deal with anger and pacify them . . . it is to do what the men cannot do. . . . In fact, it is expected that women are needed to reach the warring factions, defuse intercommunity tension, open channels of communication and build a dialogue of understanding and trust."[69]

In Northern Ireland too, Mo Mowlam was widely admired and adored for her capacity to listen and empathize with people. Ironically, Mowlam herself, while admitting to being a good listener, was wary of attributing that to her sex, preferring to link it to her working-class roots. But those who worked with her and experienced her presence have fewer qualms about attributing many of her qualities to her identity as a woman. "Mo Mowlam related very quickly and naturally with the sort of issues that the women in the community wanted to raise with her . . . the immediate empathy with the community, [and] home-based family issues," said one of her colleagues in 1999.[70]

As much as women themselves display less aggression, their presence also affects the behavior of their male colleagues. In Georgia, said Chanishvili, the presence of women altered the men's stance. "Because when there are women present, men speak in another way. . . . They try not to be so aggressive. They speak as members of society, not just as men, hunters, warriors."[71] Again, this points to the notion that women can temper the level of hostility that may exist and contribute to a more conducive environment for dialogue.

Listening, empathy, and respect for the other's humanity and pain seem nebulous and "fuzzy" in the midst of violence and warfare. Yet these soft, intangible issues are often the hardest issues to resolve. They can make or break trust and with it the entire process of peace negotiations. Where women have participated, they are credited for making a notable difference in creating such an environment and making the process not only more humane but more healing.

Challenges and Opportunities

Neither the journey nor the actual process of negotiations is ever easy for women. Those who make it don't have an easy time. In Northern Ireland's civic forum, the men "mooed" as the women entered, ridiculing the ladies' coalition and at times bursting into the song "Stand by Your Man." In Burundi, women were accused of betraying their own. Women have been locked out of negotiations, misinformed, and had their proposals ignored. In Colombia, women activists, like others who are outspoken, are killed. But the discrimination and mistreatment rarely deter them. In Northern Ireland, NIWC members took to naming and shaming. Each day, they would write up the names of the men who had "mooed and booed" them. It was effective, and in time the NIWC representatives were the trusted mediators between groups on either side. But there is no doubt that the obstacles women activists face can be daunting.

One negative consequence is that often women spend much of their energy on fighting to get a seat at the table, rather than conveying their message or engaging in the negotiations. This distills their message into one of demanding a right to participate, rather than bringing attention to the issues they raise or the contributions they can make. The persistent inertia or implicit refusal of other actors to enable women's inclusion can fuel the perception that women are only in it for themselves.

In part, the problem results from the tensions among women peace activists. Those who come from a background in feminism and women's rights tend to focus more on rights—the "what can peace do for women" perspective. Those from the peace movement or who come to activism as a result of experiences of conflict-induced violence tend to focus more on ending the war—the "how can we as women contribute to peacemaking" perspective. In other words, their demand and desire for inclusion in decisionmaking are not primarily motivated by the idea of using the peacemaking process to promote gender equality. Of course, the two dimensions are not mutually exclusive. One often leads to the next, and they are inevitably intertwined. For example, the Liberian women entered the fray to end the war, but quickly realized that their exclusion was bound up with patriarchal attitudes toward women and deep-seated discrimination. Similarly, the South African women who fought for liberation from apartheid in the ANC recognized that to attain equality and self-determination they had to address the gender dynamics in their own political structures.

Nonetheless, it is a fine balance. Too often, international actors intervening on behalf of women raise the issue of women's needs and rights, which can overshadow those who use their identities and roles as women in their society to resolve conflicts and address issues that endanger peacemaking. The explicit focus on women's needs and rights can also create a public and political backlash, as women are branded "extreme feminists" and unrepresentative of the majority. To avoid being discredited and labeled negatively, women's groups have to devise alternative tactics. The struggle between building a popular base and retaining strong feminist credentials, however, can be a challenge for some.

Women's concerns about the needs of victims and other issues can also distract their attention from the key agenda issues—the deal makers and breakers—over which compromises are often difficult for all concerned. It is a delicate balance. Ideally, other actors should be taking up the plight of victims or express concern about the effects of discrimination or the negative implications of their decisions on excluded groups. But they tend not to do so. Thus women are forced to continue their advocacy and lobbying, thereby diminishing their opportunities to engage and tackle more prominent issues relating to security, power sharing, and so on.

In part, women peace activists need to move beyond the issues of common concern and experience to those where there is significant disagreement within and among their respective communities. The trust building, empathy, and humanizing that come from finding common experiences as women are powerful fuel for enabling women to tackle the core causes of conflict. Israeli and Palestinian women are leading examples in this regard. Together they sought to tackle many of the core issues (the question of returning refugees, the status of Jerusalem, and so forth) through a gender lens, unpacking and redefining the issues of rights, peace, and justice in ways that embraced the diversity of the population in their communities. For example, Palestinian and Israeli women, through Jerusalem Link, were among the first groups to jointly and publicly agree to a two-state solution in 1993.[72] At the time it was daring. Over a decade later, it has become the norm.

Similarly, in May 2006, when the world was shunning the Hamas-led government in Palestine, the International Women's Commission—composed of leading Israeli and Palestinian women and women leaders on the global stage (including the UN and the EU)—was urging the international community to engage with and not isolate the Palestinian Authority. The commission warned of the detrimental humanitarian impact that economic and political boycotts would have on ordinary citizens. Months later, as its predictions came true, the commission called on the UN's Human Rights Council to investigate the killings in the Gaza Strip. In March 2007, again at a time when many countries were shunning the unity government, the IWC issued another statement calling on the international community to normalize its relations: "Now is the time for courageous leaders to transcend fear and get down to work towards resolving all the difficult issues. Women of the IWC are showing the way."[73] Invariably, the commission maintains its call for a more inclusive peacemaking effort, as noted in its May 2007 statement: "The IWC appeals to the international community and to Israeli and Palestinian authorities, as well as to civil society in both communities, to join together in an inclusive and transparent effort to extricate us from the shackles of the past and help us create a just and peaceful future based on the principles of justice, equality, tolerance and mutual respect."[74]

Arguably, asking women to tackle and resolve the big issues may be setting the bar too high, but it is not. Rather it should be seen as an opportunity to prove that the addition of alternative perspectives can help to bridge the bigger divides. International actors and mediators should credit and draw on the stage-setting and relationship-building efforts of women as entry points into negotiations on the most contentious issues.

Planning for inevitable reversals of peace processes is also essential. As bridge builders and voices from the middle ground, women gain support when a process is going well. But if the process fails once the compromises are on paper and the hard work of implementation comes into play, the situation can unravel. Opponents can return to extreme positions if they believe that promises are not being kept, and extremists can come to the fore, discrediting the moderates for being too soft. In Northern Ireland, the NIWC, though extremely effective as mediators and critical to mobilizing the public to vote in favor of the 1998 Good Friday Agreement and continuation of the peace talks, lost support in the intervening years. As implementation stalled, positions hardened, and the middle ground was lost. The attacks on key candidates resumed, and the party lost all its parliamentary seats in 2004.

To sustain their links and strengthen the middle ground, women and the larger peace constituency need to plan through potential worst-case scenarios to counter the attacks and accusations of selling out. But external actors also need to acknowledge and give credit to these voices of reconciliation and moderation in the midst of militarization and confrontation. Too often they do too little.

Finally, claiming a space and voice in negotiations is clearly difficult, but staying the course as it evolves into governance is equally important. To avoid the evaporation of the issues they raised in peace negotiations, women need to step in, stay, and influence the political process. A woman interested in promoting peace, says longtime peace and women's rights activist Naomi Chazan, "[has] to go into politics even if it is hard."[75] On the one hand, women's own reluctance and apprehension about entering politics creates a dilemma. Many civil society activists are unwilling to make the transition from one sphere to the next. But it needs to be done, at least by some. The networks between civil society and political structures need to be strengthened. To stay in, however, also means facing the entrenched political system and those who have no interest in transformation. This battle with the momentum of business as usual can lead to the demise of individual women or new voices in politics. It is often compounded by the international community's ignorance of the changes that have taken place, together with their focus on state building that can inadvertently result in support for the old status quo and reversal of any gains made toward a more inclusive society.

Conclusion

Not every woman who has a say in peace negotiations carries a holistic vision or a commitment to the needs of surviving victims. Often those who make it to the talks are part and parcel of existing political parties or tokens. Not every woman considers the increased presence of women in peace talks a necessity. There is many a queen bee in the world of politics, willing to ignore or sever ties to women's constituencies to further their own positions. By no means can all women bridge the divide and join together. Sudden events—a bombing, the breaking of a ceasefire, an attack on civilians—can overwhelm them. But there are countless women who remain committed to making peace and representing the voices of their communities. The individuals and organizations discussed here and throughout this book epitomize this creed. The relationship is two-way: whether in formal politics or in civil society, they represent their constituencies, and in turn they garner the support of this often-silent majority.

Many a detractor argues that too many parties and too much depth and breadth are overwhelming and beyond the scope of peace negotiations, that the focus should be on ending the war, with the rest coming later. Among Guatemalans who lived through six arduous years of talks, many take a different view. As in other places, the implementation of the peace accords has been slow and at times a downright failure. The absence of the elite from the process had negative repercussions. But Guatemala did not return to all-out warfare. That is in part a testament to the extended and inclusive process, which gave civil society representatives and their constituencies a sense of ownership. They, like the formal negotiating teams, lived through the six years of back and forth. They gave input and saw their issues being taken up, addressed, and recorded. They also understood the compromises being made. Frustrating as it is to see many of the goals and benchmarks still exist only on paper, the peace accords themselves are not simply a reminder of where they were but a road map of where they want to be, a joint vision and blueprint for the society that came from a cross section of Guatemalan society. As a negotiations process, it sets an important example.

But the paradigm of shifting negotiations from simply ending war to that of building peace is slow to change. Zero-sum-ism is still too prevalent. Inclusivity in the substance of the agenda or among the participants at the table remains more the exception than the rule. The international foot dragging about changing this paradigm also goes on. Certainly there are constraints: governments and armed opposition groups typically prefer limited intervention. But as mediators, observers, and funders of peace processes, the international community could be setting a different tone, pointing out the pitfalls of exclusionary processes, and encouraging a more comprehensive approach. Of course, it is easier to aim low. That approach is shortsighted, however, because it fails to recognize the willingness and commitment of ordinary people to make peace work. It is also unwise, as it ignores the skills, abilities, experiences, and commitment of those who have made peace and those who have to live with the consequences of failed talks.

As for the question of women, perhaps there are still too few real examples to make a strong case. But the discussion above highlights commonality not just in women's perceptions but also in the contributions of those who have been involved in negotiations. If nothing else, the demands by women have helped broaden the discourse and debate around the purpose and substance of peace talks. Within the UN system, the need for gender sensitivity in the language of peace agreements is more readily understood and accepted. References to the needs of women and children and the plight of victims are becoming standard. Although many a national or international bureaucrat might still raise an eyebrow or implicitly belittle the notion that women have a right to participate in decisionmaking related to peacebuilding, they are increasingly faced with disapproval and opposition—within and without their own institutions. The women themselves are no longer derided. Mindsets and practices are slowly shifting.

The discussions are also compelling some academics and practitioners to consider more critically the actual and potential differences in men's and women's approaches to negotiations. Ironically, often women themselves are not fully aware of their comparative strengths (as communicators and trust builders, as symbols and representatives of the silent majority, as leaders, etc.) and how to maximize and draw attention to them as important ingredients in the very difficult business of peacebuilding. Advocates of women's inclusion, experts in peacemaking, researchers, policymakers, and others should also pay more attention to identifying and understanding these strengths—whether they are due to biological, social, educational, professional, or other factors—and draw them into the peacemaking process. If, for example, as psychologist and longtime culture of peace advocate David Adams says, a "peace identity" is drawn from a sense of community and belonging, and women are effective in finding the common ground and drawing on informal social networks, then we should be learning from them.[76]

Similarly, if empathy, relationship building, and communication are important to the process, then how can the approaches taken by women be drawn on to complement those of men? At present, women seem to face a no-win situation. If they are cooperative or less direct in their style of communication, they are accused of lacking confidence or professionalism, but those who are more assertive can be accused of being too aggressive. Men who are more inclusive are credited for being progressive, however, whereas those who are assertive are heralded as strong leaders.[77] If negotiations are genuinely about bringing peace, then the comparative strengths of both men and women should be acknowledged and drawn up.

On trust, how did the women of Northern Ireland, Somalia, and elsewhere succeed in turning the initial skepticism, disrespect, and distrust they encountered into a deep trust? What can they teach us about their successes and pitfalls? How can we help them and other women grow stronger? Perhaps most importantly, in what ways could and should the international community support and amplify their voices when the rhetoric of extremist and hate revs up again?

Women do not have all the answers. Among those who have been negotiators and mediators, their achievements have ebbed and flowed with the conflicts themselves. But as Terry Greenblatt, former director of the Israeli women's peace organization Bat Shalom, said to the UN Security Council in 2002: "Even when we are women whose very existence and narrative contradicts each other, we will talk—we will not shoot."[78] There are lessons to draw from these experiences, and those in the business of peacemaking cannot afford to judge them prematurely, dismiss, or ignore them. At the very least, as Greenblatt said, "You need us because we women are willing to sit together on the same side of the table and together look at our complex joint history, with the commitment and intention of not getting up until—in respect and reciprocity—we can get up together and begin our new history and fulfill our joint destiny."[79]

Notes

1. Speech delivered to the UN Security Council, May 7, 2002, available at http://www.peacewomen.org/un/sc/is_pal_arria/UNSCStatement-Maha.pdf, retrieved January 22, 2007.

2. For more on women as mediators, see Antonia Potter, "We the Women: Why Conflict Mediation Is Not Just a Job for Men," *Opinion,* October 2005 (Geneva: Center for Humanitarian Dialogue).

3. Rita Manchanda, "Trapped by Extremism: Women in the Kashmiri Conflict," in *Women and Violent Conflict: Global Perspectives Conference Report,* Sanam Anderlini, Rita Manchanda, and Shireen Kermali (eds.) (London: International Alert, 1999), pp. 30–31.

4. As mentioned in Dyan Mazurana and Susan McKay, *Women and Peacebuilding: Essays on Human Rights and Democratic Development 8* (Montreal: International Center for Human Rights and Democratic Development, 1999), pp. 18–19.

5. Author's personal discussions with Bosnian peace activist, Geneva, Switzerland, January 2000.

6. Thandi Modise, "Conference Presentation," in *Women and Violent Conflict: Global Perspectives Conference Report,* Sanam Anderlini, Rita Manchanda, and Shireen Kermali (eds.) (London: International Alert, 1999), pp. 23–24.

7. Quoted in Sanam Naraghi Anderlini, *Women at the Peace Table: Making a Difference* (New York: UNIFEM, 2000).

8. Both organizations are known by their Spanish acronyms.

9. Catalina Rojas, *In the Midst of War: Colombian Women's Contributions to Peace* (Washington, DC: Hunt Alternatives Fund, 2004).

10. Neela Marikkar, *Empowering the Silent Majority,* available at http://www.womenwagingpeace.net, retrieved January 9, 2006.

11. Violence increased through 2006, and at the time of writing, media sources indicated that a return to direct negotiations was highly unlikely. See "Sri Lanka Peace Talks Now a Mirage, India Feels," *Malaysia Sun,* January 11, 2007, available at http://story.malaysiasun.com.

12. Ugandan MPs speaking on a panel, "Women Leaders Reflect on the Prospects for Peace in Northern Uganda," Washington, DC, Woodrow Wilson Center for International Scholars, January 17, 2007.

13. Carmel Roulston, "Conference Presentation," in *Women and Violent Conflict: Global Perspectives Conference Report,* Sanam Anderlini, Rita Manchanda, and Shireen Kermali (eds.) (London: International Alert, 1999).

14. Speech by Don Steinberg, Initiative for Inclusive Security, Policy Forum, January 16, 2007, Washington, DC.

15. Swanee Hunt, *This Was Not Our War* (Durham, NC: Duke University Press, 2004), p. xxiv.

16. African Women and Peace Support Group, *Liberian Women Peacemakers* (Asmara, Eritrea: Africa World Press, 2004), pp. 26–31.

17. Ibid.

18. Ibid.

19. Visaka Dharmadasa, *About Us,* Initiative for Inclusive Security Network Members, available at http://www.womenwagingpeace.net, retrieved July 26, 2006.

20. Beena Sarwar, *Some Mother's Son,* available at http://www.counter currents.org/hr-sarwar210604.html.

21. Ibid.

22. Discussions with the author, New York, March 2003.

23. Rita Manchanda, *Naga Women Making a Difference: Peacebuilding in Northeastern India* (Washington, DC: Hunt Alternatives Fund, 2005), p. 4.

24. Ibid.

25. Christian Aid, *Interview with Angelina Atyam from Northern Uganda,* 11.04, available at http://www.christianaid.org.uk, retrieved July 25, 2006.

26. Angelina Atyam, interviewed for "Children of War in Uganda," *Dateline,* MSNBC, September 26, 2006, available at http://www.msnbc.msn.com.

27. Eric Beauchemin, *Talking with the Devil,* Radio Netherlands, 2004, available at http://www.radionetherlands.nl/features/humanrights/devil.html.

28. More information available in Kate Fearon, *Women's Work: The Story of the Northern Ireland Women's Coalition* (Belfast: Blackstaff, 1999).

29. Personal discussion with the author, New York, December 2005.

30. Shelley Anderson, "My Only Clan Is Womanhood: Building Women's Peace Identities," International Fellowship on Reconciliation, May 2005, available at http://www.ifor.org/WPP/article_May_05.pdf.

31. Ibid.

32. Rosemary Okello, *The Sixth Clan at the Somalia Negotiating Table,* available at http://www.awcfs.org, retrieved January 9, 2006.

33. Salad Duhul, "Somali Women Demonstrate to Support State," *Somaliland Times,* November 2006, available at http://www.somalilandtimes.net.

34. Correspondence with the author, January 2007.

35. UNIFEM, *Securing the Peace: Guiding the International Community Towards Women's Effective Participation Throughout Peace Processes* (New York: UNIFEM, October 2005), p. 6.

36. Hunt Alternatives Fund runs the Initiative for Inclusive Security, formerly known as Women Waging Peace.

37. Security Council Resolution 1325, New York, United Nations, 2000.

38. *Israeli and Palestinian Women Leaders Call for a Return to Peace Negotiations,* press release, UNIFEM, New York, May 3, 2006, available at http://domino.un.org/UNISPAL.NSF, retrieved July 25, 2006.

39. Ibid.

40. Pamela Fishman, "Interaction: The Work Women Do," in *Language, Gender, and Society,* B. Thorne, C. Kramarae, and N. Henley (eds.) (Rowley, MA: Newbury House, 1983), pp. 89–101.

41. Howard Wolpe et al., "Rebuilding Peace and State Capacity in War-Torn Burundi," *Round Table* 93, no. 375 (July 2004): 457–467.

42. Anderlini, *Women at the Peace Table,* p. 33.

43. Vjosa Dubruna, quoted from interview, "Building a New Kosovo," available at http://www.womenwagingpeace.net/content/articles/0310a.html.

44. Ibid.

45. Ibid.

46. Discussion with the author, November 2006.

47. Pampell Conaway and Salome Martinez, *Adding Value: Women's Contributions to Reintegration and Reconstruction in El Salvador* (Washington, DC: Hunt Alternatives Fund, 2004).

48. Ibid.

49. Discussions with the author, Washington, DC, 2003.

50. Anderlini, *Women at the Peace Table,* pp. 32–33.

51. Quoted in "African Women and Peace Support Group," *Liberian Women Peacemakers,* Africa World Press, 2004, pp. 26–31.

52. Mariam Djibrilla Maiga, in *Women, Violent Conflict, and Peacebuilding: Global Perspectives,* Sanam Naraghi Anderlini, Rita Manchanda, and Shireen Karmali (eds.) (London: International Alert, 1999), pp. 44–45.

53. Anderlini, *Women at the Peace Table*.

54. Sanam Anderlini, *Negotiating the Transition to Democracy and Reforming the Security Sector: The Vital Contributions of South African Women* (Washington, DC: Hunt Alternatives Fund, 2004), http://www.huntalternatives.org.

55. Wolpe et al., "Rebuilding Peace."

56. Quoted in Anderlini, *Women at the Peace Table,* p. 38.

57. Manchanda, *Naga Women Making a Difference,* p. 17.

58. Interview with the author, 1999.

59. Anderlini, *Women at the Peace Table,* p. 32.

60. Personal conversation with the author, 2006.

61. Anderlini, *Women at the Peace Table,* p. 31.

62. Deborah Tannen's book, *You Just Don't Understand: Women and Men in Conversation,* first published in 1990, is among the best-known texts on gender differences in communication.

63. Simon Baron-Cohen, *The Essential Difference* (New York: Basic, 2003), p. 47.

64. Ibid.

65. Interview with the author, November 2006.

66. Baron-Cohen, *The Essential Difference,* p. 1.

67. Ibid., p. 45.

68. Author interview, November 2006.

69. Manchanda, *Naga Women Making a Difference,* p. 14.

70. Anderlini, *Women at the Peace Table*.

71. Ibid.

72. For more information, see Jewish Alliance for Justice and Peace, http://ga3.org/btvshalom/notice-description.tcl?newsletter_id=3535885.

73. International Women's Commission, "IWC Call to Normalize Relations with the New Palestinian Government," March 22, 2007, available at www.iw-peace.org.

74. Ibid.

75. Sonia Rao, "Chazan Discusses Women, Peace," *The Observer Online,* October 13, 2006, available at http://media.www.ndsmcobserver.com.

76. Quoted in Shelley Anderson, "My Only Clan Is Womanhood: Building Women's Peace Identities," International Fellowship on Reconciliation, May 2005, available at http://www.ifor.org/WPP/article_May_05.pdf.

77. Many women peacemakers speak of these perceptions based on personal experience. Deborah Tannen raises and analyzes this in the context of the workplace in *Talking from 9 to 5: Women and Men at Work* (New York: HarperCollins, 1995).

78. Terry Greenblatt, speech to the UN Security Council, 2002, available at http://www.fire.or.cr/mayo02/batshalomeng.htm, retrieved January 22, 2007.

79. Ibid.

four

Disarming, Demobilizing, and Reintegrating Fighters

Disarmament and demobilization are quite easy in the DDR process. However, reintegration is the difficult and complex part of the process.
—Sudanese woman ex-fighter

I have seen women being able to disarm a drunk or rowdy man or group of men, whereas a police or outsider would have enflamed the situation.

—UN personnel

Picture two meetings nearly two years apart: the same theme, but a universe of difference. The first was in Washington, D.C., in 2004. A representative of the World Bank speaks to a crowded room. Disarmament, demobilization, and reintegration (DDR) programs are, by definition, short-term interventions, he said. The bank's national partner is the government, in this case the government of Sierra Leone. The government determines who does and does not qualify for DDR programming and benefits. That the government was implicated in the war is brushed aside for the moment. The figures for the Sierra Leone DDR programming are impressive: 72,500 combatants, $48 million. A success, then? That answer lies in the eyes or the experiences of the beholder, and the second meeting.

In Addis Ababa in late 2005,[1] a workshop was in progress: Anna,[2] a Sierra Leonean woman, introduces herself to another packed room. She tells her story. She was a mother of five when the Revolutionary United Front of Sierra Leone (RUF/SL) attacked her village. The men forced her to watch and laugh as they slaughtered her father and other family members. One child died. They abducted her and her four remaining children and took them into the bush. Another child disappeared in the intervening months. She was forced to "marry" the man, an RUF commander, who killed her father. "I was lucky," she says. "He did not rape me." As a commander's wife, she had influence in the camps, and she used her position to protect younger women and children, boys and plenty of girls. She also fought. Later she escaped and now lives in a remote rural area, running a community-based organization caring for people like herself: over 100 women and children forced into rebel fighting, trying to reintegrate into society. She gets no benefits from the government or the DDR program. She receives no support for her current efforts.

Emily stands; she speaks of her family being slaughtered as she lay under a dead body, hiding.[3] Like Anna, she was abducted and forced to fight. She became a commander in the RUF. When the war stopped, she returned home to care for her children. Later she returned to the capital to discover that the DDR program registration was closed. She received no benefits, no support, and no acknowledgment of her existence. Emily is responsible for the livelihood of ten people but has nothing.

Among the countless UN declarations and policies regarding women's rights, Security Council Resolution 1325 was the first to explicitly mention that those involved in the planning and implementation of DDR programs should "consider the different needs of female and male ex-combatants and . . . take into account the needs of their dependents."[4] This statement opened the door for broader discussions about DDR and the role of women. In 2002, a UN experts meeting issued its findings, noting that "women have an essential role in helping to create the conditions for the cessation of violent conflict, in such activities as monitoring peace, dealing with trauma . . . [and] collecting and destroying weapons."[5]

The underlying premise was that women have a role as civilians. There was little mention of women in armed groups. In the ensuing years, scholars, notably Vanessa Farr and Dyan Mazurana, have shone greater light on women and girls' experiences in armed groups, particularly their marginalization from DDR processes. Farr suggests that field programs overlook the needs of women combatants, in part because they do not fit the stereotype of women as caregivers.[6]

UNIFEM supported work in this area, publishing *Getting It Right, Doing It Right: Gender and DDR* in 2004 as preliminary guidance on addressing women in DDR programming. The report recommends that the gendered dimensions of armed forces should be analyzed at the earliest possible time to ensure that the issues facing women and men (and boys and girls) are integrated into program planning. It calls for sex-dis-aggregated data and, along with other reports, for a broadening of criteria for eligibility in DDR programs. Given the multiple roles that women and girls play as fighters, supporters, and dependents, they must not be excluded from the benefits of DDR programming. The report also refers to the design of cantonment sites, stating the need for separate and secure facilities for women and men. It notes the difficulties, rejection, and trauma that women and girls in particular face during reintegration.[7]

In 2006, the UN launched the comprehensive Integrated Disarmament, Demobilization, and Reintegration Standards (IDDRS).[8] They echo and elaborate on the practical points raised in *Getting It Right, Doing It Right,* offering practitioners a host of ready tools and checklists to ensure the equitable treatment of males and females in DDR programming.

Much of this emerging discourse centers on women's experiences of marginalization, their right to be included in DDR programs, and recommendations to the policy community to address this gap. Less is said about whether and how the inclusion of women in DDR, those in armed groups and those outside—as mandated by Resolution 1325—could produce better results overall. In this chapter I focus on that dimension of the debate. I take the fact that women have the right to equal opportunities and treatment in DDR programming as a given, regardless of whether they make a difference to the overall outcome of the process. Nonetheless, it is important to examine whether and how attention to women in these situations can improve the scope of such interventions. This is particularly important, given the skepticism that continues to prevail internationally regarding the disarmament, demobilization, and reintegration of armed groups. Reflecting on women's involvement and contributions to DDR processes through parallel and contrasting examples from El Salvador, Sierra Leone, and elsewhere, I highlight how paying attention to women in three distinct roles—as combatants, as auxiliary or essential support staff within fighting forces, and as civilians in communities—can contribute to the substance and process of DDR.[9]

What Is DDR?

The disarmament, demobilization, and reintegration of fighters—state armies, guerrillas, or militias—are among the most sensitive and critical issues addressed in peace negotiations.[10] For good reason: fighters need to be disarmed, their units disbanded, and their affiliations and loyalties to commanders severed. Otherwise, the potential for a return to fighting is too high. Successful DDR is, as the World Bank says, "the key to an effective transition from war to peace."[11] Farr takes the point one step further. "DDR is also a process that is symbolic as well as practical, to offer fighters a new identity that is compatible with peaceful development and sustainable growth."[12]

The principal elements and premise are seemingly logical. The first phase in the process—disarmament—is defined by the UN as "the collection of small arms and light and heavy weapons within a conflict zone."[13] Assembly is the first step. As former fighters gather into camps, or "cantonment" areas, they are given food aid, shelter, clothing, medical attention, basic education, and orientation programs.[14] In general, physical disarmament occurs at this point: weapons are confiscated, stored, and eventually destroyed.

Step two, demobilization, "is the formal disbanding of military formations and, at the individual level, . . . the process of releasing combatants from a mobilized state."[15] Ex-combatants are typically discharged over a period of time; transported to their home districts, or granted small initial reinsertion packages. Sometimes former fighters are eager to go home; at other times, depending on their actions, they may be fearful of returning to communities where they might face rejection and hostility.

Nicole Ball considers the last step, reintegration, as a two-part process involving initial reinsertion and long-term reintegration. Reinsertion refers to the period when an ex-combatant re-enters his or her former home or enters a new community. Reinsertion assistance is generally provided to former fighters in the form of cash during the demobilization phase—either in a lump sum distribution or in installments over time. In addition, basic materials may be provided, such as household goods, agricultural supplies, or stipends for education.

Reintegration refers to the long-term process of reentry into the community, the building of livelihoods, and the process of returning to a peacetime lifestyle. In general, ex-combatants with demobilization papers receive modest packages of benefits. Former fighters may enter job placement services or participate in short-term skills training, credit schemes, scholarships, or rehabilitation programs. International actors work with NGOs to establish workshops and other forms of skills training. They range from carpentry to tailoring and hairdressing but rarely match the economic needs of the country, take account of the market's capacity to absorb the newly trained, or address the expectations and aspirations of the fighters themselves. Banks and local authorities may channel credit programs, and scholarships may be provided to a handful of designated leaders. In instances in which land distribution is included in the reintegration process, it is done in conjunction with government offices and as part of an overall national reconstruction plan.

The integration of fighters from all sides of a conflict into the new national security forces is often a specific goal of peace agreements and, by extension, DDR processes. More often than not, however, applicants for the newly reformed police, military, or other security forces far outnumber available posts. Although much is said about "downsizing" existing national forces to enable the integration of opposition groups, political and economic realities rarely allow it. Army salaries feed many mouths, and as the Iraq situation proved, firing existing military personnel in the immediate aftermath of a conflict is not prudent from a security standpoint. Therefore, in the transition period, security forces often remain far larger than is necessary (South Africa is a case in point).

Sustained social and economic reintegration is another explicit goal, but often the understated and underfunded assumption underlying DDR processes. In some cases, the international community may include a second "R" in DDR: rehabilitation. It encompasses difficult issues, such as the need to address the psychological and emotional aspects of returning home, as well as problems that arise in relation to the wider community. It is a long-term process. Nearly all DDR programs address rehabilitation in some form, but DDR (as opposed to DDRR) is still the more commonly used refrain. The IDDRS is clear about the need for reintegration: "If reintegration fails, the achievements of the disarmament and demobilization phase are undermined, instability increases, and sustainable reconstruction and development are put at risk."[16]

Yet just as conflict prevention and peace negotiations processes are outdated, DDR programs are also stuck in the paradigm of wars past. The field experience and policy doctrines clearly point to the need for sustained reintegration programming, but the political forces that determine resources and funding provisions lag behind. The focus is still on the "DD," with an assumption that the "R" will happen one way or another: soldiers will go back to barracks or return home and be absorbed into a community. The assumption carries with it immense cynicism, for as the World Bank itself estimates, countries emerging from conflict have a 44 percent chance of sliding back into violence within five years.[17] And even if war does not break out, crime levels spike and violence becomes a more permanent fact of life. In the words of Johan Galtung, a state of "negative peace" becomes the accepted norm.[18]

In effect, the clear definitions, logical steps, and formulations belie a messy reality. DDR is an "emergency process," writes Farr. The international community is faced with a catch-22. On the one hand, DDR is essential to strengthening the fragile peace. On the other hand, the insecurity and the atmosphere of tension and lagging mistrust in the immediate aftermath of a peace accord make many an army, militia, or armed movement reluctant to hand over the majority of their weapons and demobilize every fighter.

Disarmament is often ad hoc, with many weapons remaining in circulation. The pervasiveness of small arms and light weapons, portable and easy to hide, often dismantled and assembled in a matter of minutes, makes disarmament even more difficult to implement. Typically, many of the weapons used in wartime remain in society and become instruments of violence and instability for years to come.

Demobilization is not easy either. DDR planners typically rely on the leaders of fighting forces to provide accurate data on the makeup of their forces. In traditional armies it is a matter of course. Even in wars of liberation and conflicts based on ideology or self-determination—such as in Central America and South Africa—the leadership typically has an interest in ensuring that "their people" benefit from the process. Where the state has collapsed or warlordism and thuggery have taken hold, however, the leadership may not know who is in its ranks or may have no interest in revealing its full hand. Where underage fighters are prominent, as in Nepal in 2006 or Liberia in 2003, rebel and government leaders may deny their existence to avoid international condemnation. In Nepal, the Maoist leadership, when pushed, implied that the underage members of their movement were predominantly orphans of the war. In the process of negotiating the peace accord, they agreed that if some underage fighters were found, they would send them home. The reality of whether "home" exists, or whether families and communities would accept the fighters, particularly the women and girls who broke all social taboos, is left unanswered. This lack of transparency about who is in the ranks and what happens to the underaged is at times an insurance plan to remobilize in case negotiations fail.

The amorphous nature of "fighting forces" that have emerged from the new forms of war is a major complication. Men and boys come and go, as in Afghanistan, shifting alliances, joining up, and returning home, depending on the season, the intensity of violence, and the pay. In Sierra Leone, the term *sobel* was coined for those who were national soldiers by day but rebels and looters by night. Finally, regardless of the country or the conflict, women and children are involved, including as frontline fighters, far more often than is usually predicted or admitted.

The lack of accurate information can wreak havoc on planning and particularly on resource allocation. In Sierra Leone, for example, the initial estimate of the number of fighters was 45,000. Ultimately, 72,500 had passed through the DDR program, yet estimates suggest that the actual number of fighters was 137,865.[19] By the time the disarmament and demobilization were done, much of the money earmarked for the entire process had already dried up.

As Farr says, the need to restore a semblance of security often forces DDR planners to "provide quick and dirty interventions" to minimize any potential for spoiling the process.[20] The implicit assumption is that "spoilers" are most likely to be combatants, who are stereotypically expected to be young men. That has significant implications for the design of DDR processes. First, typically only combatants qualify for DDR benefits. Second, the underlying assumption guiding the design of facilities, the benefits packages, and other aspects of the process is that these combatants are men. Third, whatever the initial intent may be, the operating principle in most instances is disarmament and demobilization as soon as possible, resulting in significantly less attention and fewer resources dedicated to the medium- and longer-term reintegration needs of either the combatants or the communities that they reenter. Such an inadequate process not only harms the likes of Anna and Emily and all the children who are increasingly a part of military movements but also works against the ultimate goal of such processes: sustained peace.

Missing the Point About Women

It is easy for armchair activists to criticize existing practices and point to gaps and weaknesses. For the internationals, there is a sense that outsiders never fully take account of the constraints that exist, particularly in their dealings with often reticent national governments. Although they acknowledge the purpose of, and value in, the reams of guidelines regarding good practices in DDR and the supplemental policies and resolutions that highlight questions of gender and community, there is also palpable frustration. Gender equality and women's rights are all well and good, but negotiators have other priorities. The usually unstated opinion is that although the equal treatment of women and support for victims are honorable ideals to pursue, the reality of a war-torn society does not allow for such luxuries. Sometimes, international actors are quick to reject responsibility for the inclusion and equal treatment of women. The commanders determine who qualifies for DDR, and they, as external actors, cannot intervene. This may well be true, but it is difficult to imagine that the international community would collectively shrug its shoulders if, for example, the most hardened fighters of the RUF or LURD had not come forth to register for the DDR process. In effect, the international system has its double standards and contributes to the perpetual exclusion of women. It is an attitude that permeates every level of bureaucracy at international, regional, and national levels and is profoundly insulting to women and girls in war zones. More to the point, however, it is reflective of ignorance about the roles of women and girls (under eighteen) in armed groups and their relevance to the very process and goals of "DD" in the short term and "R" in the long term, as discussed below.

Thwarting the Spoilers: Women Combatants and DDR

The potential spoilers may typically be younger men or disaffected middle-rank leaders, but there are other factors to consider. First, the tenacity of women who join up voluntarily cannot be underestimated. In Sri Lanka, Nepal, the DRC, and elsewhere, women who joined opposition movements as a means of exiting traditional life are often more reluctant to lay down their weapons than the male fighters. Coming from societies in which women are often heavily discriminated against or have personal experiences of violence, they view the weapons they wield as a direct source of respect, empowerment, and protection. In the words of one Congolese former female combatant, "We used to protect ourselves by weapons. Now there is no one to protect us."[21]

In Sri Lanka women fighters garner immense respect and are renowned for their fighting prowess. If this respect is at risk in any DDR negotiations or processes, they could be resistant to participating. In Nepal, women, particularly the younger ones, are unlikely candidates for reinsertion into lives of near-servitude. Will they try to retain or take up arms if they are treated poorly? Too soon to say, but if the peace process that began in 2006 fails, the women combatants should not be underestimated. But the words and experience of women fighters from the DRC should be instructive. "After DDR was started in DRC we chose to be civilians and surrendered our weapons, but we still regret being civilians," said one fighter at a workshop in 2005.

> We have been forgotten in trying to make a living and survive. Being women, we have nothing to live on. We thought we would be given something to live on in return for becoming civilians. We cannot find husbands; no one wants to marry us. We don't have enough food to eat. Women ex-combatants in our country develop negative attitudes. We have bad reputations. We are unable to express ourselves. We are now thinking to return to the bush because of lack of help.[22]

Second, the efficiency and effectiveness of armed groups, particularly armed opposition movements, depend heavily on either the communities in which they have support or the communities that they themselves create and move with. Women feature strongly in this regard. In Sierra Leone, an estimated 44 percent of women and girls were given basic military training by their captor "husbands" or commanders, and nearly all performed other duties as cooks, spies, messengers, food producers, communications technicians, and medical personnel. In Uganda, the LRA also has used young girls for multiple functions: fighters, sex slaves, cooks, spies, and medics. A decade earlier and a continent away in El Salvador, 30 percent of fighters in the FMLN were women, as were 40 percent of the *tenederos,* who provided support to base camps.[23] Even in the South Pacific island of Bougainville (province of Papua New Guinea), women were critical to the sustainability of the armed groups throughout the 1989–1998 war, providing food and fuel.[24]

In other words, women and girls play a fundamental role in the maintenance of armed movements. It is not a new phenomenon. In wars throughout time and space, women and girls have fought and supported armed causes. They can do things and go places that men cannot. They arouse less suspicion, precisely because they are perceived to be less violent. They have always been instrumental in maintaining camps, providing food, shelter, care, and moral support. In Sierra Leone, less than 10 percent regarded being a wife as their primary role. But the international community continues to resist this reality, instead relegating women and girls to roles such as sex slaves, passive wives, and camp followers, ignoring any influence or role they may have in sustaining the war or potential they may have to mitigate the effort of the spoilers.

In northern Uganda, southern Sudan, and the DRC, where the LRA has operated, boys and girls are involved in fighting. Mazurana, a longtime researcher in the region, notes that the movement has tended to release boys more readily than girls.[25] Her hypothesis is that these young women and girls are critical to the maintenance of rebel camps, producing and making food and caring for the injured. Although hard data are still lacking, preliminary investigations indicate that the women and girls are often in camp areas instead of conducting patrols or fighting, and therefore are more carefully guarded.[26] Without the women and girls, the camps and by extension the fighters cease to function effectively. If DDR programs deliberately targeted the female population of military forces—sought to inform them of the peace agreements reached and provisions for their demobilization and reintegration through local radio announcements, informal social networks, and NGOs active in conflict zones—they could in principle pull the proverbial rug from under the feet of the very men that are currently characterized as potential spoilers. Without effective infrastructure or base camp and no provisions, the armed groups would be far less threatening.

Instead, there is limited effort at reaching out to the women and girls. In Sierra Leone, for example, possession and knowledge of assembly and dismantling of an AK-47 were initially a prerequisite for qualification and entry into the DDR program. The leadership of armed groups did not convey the information through its ranks, particularly to the women and girls. Quite the opposite: countless women and girls reported that their commanders had ordered them to hand in their weapons, only to see them redistributed among the men and family members of the leaders. Other women and girls noted that they often shared weapons, as they undertook a variety of different roles and were excluded on the basis of not being "combatants."

Later the conditions changed to allow for groups to come forward with one weapon, but again, the information was not adequately conveyed to those in the bush. At the close of the program, women represented 6.5 percent of the total number of fighters registered, even though the initial governmental estimate for women at the outset of the process was 12 percent.[27]

The disparity between the number of girls (under the age of eighteen) within the forces and those entering the DDR process is most staggering. Of the estimated 12,056 girls in the Sierra Leonean fighting forces, only 506 (0.4 percent) participated in official DDR programs.[28] Many of the girls bore children and by traditional local mores were no longer considered to be girls, despite being under eighteen. The international and national staff conducting the DDR did not accept them as women fighters, and yet the girls themselves and the society around them no longer considered themselves children. The vast majority were, thus, excluded from the programs for child soldiers. There was also an erroneous belief that many of the traditional hunting groups turned Civilian Defense Forces (CDF) forbade the inclusion of females in their ranks. Eyewitness evidence and countless personal statements suggested otherwise. Still no provisions were made to reach out, inform, or support women emerging from those groups.

Pushing for Peace from the Inside

Discussions with over forty female ex-combatants across Africa in 2005 revealed that women within armed groups can also exert influence on the men with whom they have to live, are forced to marry, or consider as cohorts in armed groups. Anna, from Sierra Leone, reflected on her efforts to persuade her commander to treat the children and women better and to insist on this with his male counterparts. Dina, from Sudan, one of the few women to be involved in the peace process, was emphatic about the need to sustain and nurture the new and extremely fragile peace emerging between the government and her own movement, the Sudanese People's Liberation Army (SPLA).[29] The women are pressing the men to stay the course, she says: "We are more committed than some of the men." The Liberian women, some affiliated with Charles Taylor and others fighting for the rebel movement Liberians United for Reconciliation and Democracy (LURD), all high-ranking commanders, were also keen on maintaining the peace. They acknowledged the access and influence they could bring to bear on the men. As trusted insiders, they have great potential in influencing, mediating, and "turning down the heat." Yet, time and again, the international community barely acknowledges their existence and thus makes little effort to work with them to shore up support for the process.

In El Salvador, one of the few instances in which women combatants and supporters were included as beneficiaries of DDR programs, the immediate postwar transition was a difficult environment for women who had dedicated their lives to the FMLN. As they returned to civilian life, many faced social stigmas for breaking taboos and becoming fighters. The pressure to return to traditional life, coupled with war fatigue and their own desire to return to domesticity and families—aspects of life they had put on hold—contributed to the withdrawal of many women from the official programs. In many instances, however, the simple lack of child-care support to enable their involvement in trainings or work programs meant they had no real means of participating. Ultimately, many of the women, including senior figures, felt pressed to sacrifice their own ambitions and step back into traditional roles.[30]

Reflecting on their experiences a decade later, female ex-combatants in El Salvador at first felt they had made no contribution to the reintegration effort. With more reflection, however, they acknowledged that their sacrifices and willingness to step back into domesticity were critical contributions to the reintegration of their male ex-combatants and in many instance, husbands or partners. In effect, they were not just influencing them verbally to support the peace, but stepping back and giving them the space to have a prominent role in the public sphere, responsibilities, and much needed self-esteem, which were critical to their sustainable reintegration and thus the success of the peace process. It took five years before the nightmares faded and a semblance of normalcy entered their lives, say many of the former male FMLN fighters. They acknowledge that the women's sacrifices contributed to their recovery and reintegration.[31]

But the pressures to conform to traditional norms did not entirely negate the women's experiences, sense of empowerment, and confidence they gained during the war. For many, the skills they had acquired—from basic literacy to nursing, communications, organization, leadership—came to the fore over time and enabled them to contribute to the development of their communities. For example, in the low-lying, flood-prone Bajo Lempe region, where some child care and assistance were given to women, they emerged as leaders in emergency response efforts, maintaining and mending levees, monitoring local industry practices, and lobbying government for resources. "They are undertaking work in the church, schools . . . supporting economic development," says Arnoldo Garcia Cruz, president of the local development organization.[32]

Through personal relations forged during the conflict, women ex-combatants had a ready platform on which to build networks of community-based organizations. Working in remote rural areas, they were often a key source of education, training, and health care. A 1998 USAID study notes the importance of such NGOs to the success of reinsertion and reintegration. "NGOs as executing institutions greatly facilitated the implementation of the [national reconstruction plan] . . . [they were] essential for providing access to program services by the target population, a large percentage of which is located in remote, war-torn areas."[33]

In Africa too, women and girl combatants have displayed remarkable commitment to reintegrating into communities and working for peace. The skills they gained during their time as fighters range from map reading to negotiations, management of personnel and resources to planning, coordination, mobilizing groups and focusing on results-oriented activities. In other words, they have critical skills and social capital for peacebuilding and recovery.[34] Many have used their own initiative. In northern Uganda, teenage girls, former LRA fighters (themselves abducted and abused), run community projects supporting other "girl mothers," providing counseling for the young abductees and care for their children, and seeking reconciliation with communities they were often forced to terrorize. Twenty-one-year-old Daphne A., for example, abducted at the age of fifteen, who escaped by age nineteen with her child, was finishing high school in 2005.[35] Her ability to navigate the complex legalese of the international criminal court indictments of the LRA leaders, and the implications it has for peace, suggest a mature and intelligent young woman. She dreamed of being a lawyer "to bring justice" to Uganda.

Like their El Salvadoran counterparts, the young women from northern Uganda receive minimal recognition or support from the national government. The support they do get is largely sporadic and comes predominantly from international NGOs. Effective reintegration and outreach to rural areas in the aftermath of war are difficult for international actors. However, as these cases indicate, recognition of and support for female ex-combatants who are pushing for peace from within their movements and across their military affiliations would be an efficient use of social and financial resources. Yet their actual and potential contributions are barely recognized and thus not fulfilled.

The Role of Women in Community-Based Reintegration and Disarmament

Beyond women fighters and those associated with armed groups, there are countless other civilians in villages and communities across war-affected countries taking on the task of supporting reintegration and the rehabilitation of former combatants: men, women, and, where children are used, child soldiers. They take on the task because no one else does. In Sierra Leone, researcher Shellac Davies says, "The women argued that if those children were left uncared for now that peace has been achieved they would easily revert to their old ways . . . that left abandoned these child ex-combatants would have nothing positive to do and/ or think, and will prove a threat to the fragile peace now in existence."[36]

The work that women do makes a difference in the lives of ex-combatants. Esther works as a reintegration and HIV/AIDS officer for a community-based NGO that cares for child ex-combatants in Sierra Leone. Like Anna, she was abducted. Like Emily, she watched her relatives—three siblings, all university graduates—being killed. "After all that has happened to me, I still want to work with these children," she says. Her colleague Ramatu not only works with the children at the center by day but also has fostered five girl mothers and their children and two others, all former fighters, giving them a home and place to recover. In the survey conducted by Dyan Mazurana and Kristopher Carlson throughout 2003, 55 percent of respondents—young women and girls associated with fighting forces—"indicated that women in the community had played a significant role in their reintegration."[37]

In Uganda, Angelina Atyam's organization offers counseling to former child soldiers and their parents as part of their reintegration and rehabilitation support. Says Atyam, "We put a large emphasis on education and health."[38]

In addition to providing physical assistance to former fighters, these civil society groups gain a different perspective on the very business of

DDR. In Sri Lanka, Visaka Dharmadasa's work on missing soldiers has led her into the world of the military and a deeper understanding of the motivations and fears driving fighters. She reflects on how the very concept of DDR can be jarring for nonstate fighters. To them, she says, the terms "*dis*armament and *de*mobilization" denote disempowerment. They feel stripped of their means of protection, their livelihood, and their identity. It would be more effective to first demobilize and support their reintegration and, once they have a sense of security about life and their livelihood as civilians, address the question of disarmament.

Women in conflict zones have also been effective conduits for promoting disarmament and sustaining cease-fires. In Bougainville, as leading figures in their communities, particularly mothers of combatants, they were critical to the disarmament process, even when their own lives were at risk. In *Getting It Right,* UNIFEM quotes one UN worker's experience in the region: "I have seen women being able to disarm a drunk or rowdy man or group of men, whereas a police or outsider would have enflamed the situation."[39]

In Mali in 1997, representatives from the National Women's Movement for Peace and Unity acted as mediators between political and military figures and as liaisons with the international community. They held "sensitizing missions" in conflict areas, aiming to humanize the effects of war and bringing victims into focus. At a regional summit, they successfully advocated for a moratorium on arms that led to a national movement to destroy arms. The "Flames for Peace" ceremony was a major force in destroying small arms.[40]

In 2003 in Liberia, with a freshly signed peace agreement in place, women took their activism into fighters' camps. Initially, the UN Mission in Liberia (UNMIL) ignored them for their lack of expertise, but women peace activists were not dissuaded. They entered cantonments, engaged with fighters, and collected and destroyed AK-47s. When the formal process broke down, women contacted the leading generals to tackle the problem. UNMIL eventually revised its position and invited them as partners to the DDR process. Leymah Gbowee, a representative of the Liberian Women in Peacebuilding (WIPNET) program in 2003, worked with the UN system to disseminate information in communities to raise awareness and support.[41]

In Somalia, women took their activism from the corridors of power to the streets of Mogadishu. A 2005 UN report mentions the role of women: "Women's groups, along with other civil society and business groups, have played a prominent role in initiating and supporting pre-disarmament encampments in Mogadishu. They have also been successful

in convincing militia leaders in both Mogadishu and Kismayo to dismantle a large number of checkpoints and improve the security environment in those cities to some degree."[42] Before the December 2006 Ethiopian attacks, female members of parliament were among the first to reach
out to the Islamic Courts for a dialogue on security and the protection of
rights.[43]

Albania, following the conflict in neighboring Kosovo, was awash
with arms. As part of a pilot project run by UNIFEM from 2000 to
2002, women's organizations became involved in advocating for disarmament and weapons collection in several towns. They sensitized the
public through campaigns and the slogan "Life is better without guns."[44]
In the towns where the project was implemented, over 7,000 weapons
and 300 tons of ammunition were collected. The Albanian police also
acknowledged the importance of their support. Most significantly, in a
follow-up survey to the campaign, 62 percent of respondents said women
had influenced their family decision to hand in the weapons.[45]

Similar results occurred in Cambodia. In 2004, the Working Group
on Weapons Reduction conducted a survey on women's roles in weapons
reduction and peacebuilding. The survey concludes:

> in most cases involving weapons, women managed to do a better job
> than men because of their natural characteristics of being gentle. More
> significantly, some women were so brave that they dared confront
> people even when threatened with weapons. The braveness even shocked
> armed men as they had usually considered women as the weaker sex.
> And as a result, those armed men turned [ended] their disputes in a
> compromising way.[46]

The survey highlights women's roles at home, in their communities
through NGOs, and at the national level in terms of the tactics and
approaches they adopt to first build trust and then convince their counterparts—typically men—to hand in weapons. "I saw that most armed
people dared not hand over their weapon directly to the authority
because they are afraid of being accused of hiding illegal weapon. So,
they give it to their reliable community of NGOs," says one local commune chief.

Much of their success is also due to being explicitly nonthreaten-
ing in their approach. "Women's voice is so soft that we feel like listening," says one community member. Another recalls how "a woman
in our community who once came to educate us about weapon is in-
formative. Her explanation is clear, understandable, but sometime
funny." In contrasting these experiences to those of older men, one vil-

lager captures the essence of changing gender roles in postwar Cambodia and the increasing respect for women's approaches. "When uncle Sun, my neighbor, educate about something, no one listen to him because he speaks so loudly and he is aggressive too. If anyone protests against his ideas, he will get angry quickly. Sometimes he almost hit that person, too." What emerges from the survey is that Cambodian women, like their counterparts across the world, while still heavily discriminated against and struggling to improve their lot in life, are also using their perceived weakness or stereotypical roles as nurturers and the "gentler sex" to tackle the hardest security issues with great effect.

Yet these community-based women, working informally or within small organizations, receive little support and rarely a penny of the millions pledged by donor governments and spent on DD—and supposedly R—by national governments, the World Bank, and UN agencies.

The pilot project in Albania was not replicated or adapted to other contexts. Regardless of their commitment and success, local NGOs and newly minted community groups formed by female ex-combatants have little chance of accessing international funds. No matter what they do or how effective they are, they still have to prove their "impact and sustainability" to the faceless institutions that manage donor funds.

Conclusion

In the disarmament and demobilization phase, women and girls are again caught in no-man's-land. First, as fighters they are often excluded from DDR programs, for a variety of reasons: (1) they do not pose a major threat, nor possess sufficient leverage in their movements to demand equal treatment; (2) they do not fit stereotypical notions of fighting forces; (3) they are in a paradoxical situation—on the one hand, they are patronized, exploited, or ignored, on the other hand, as "fighters" they do not garner the sympathy, support, or attention of their communities, peace groups, or human rights groups; and (4) acknowledging that 30 percent of fighters in many nonstate or guerrilla movements are women would require a significant change in every aspect of DDR programming, and planners are hard-pressed to make such changes. In other words, they are not important enough to worry about.

Second, there is significant resistance to acknowledging that many women and girls, either those who were abducted and coerced or those who joined by choice, perform essential roles as auxiliary staff. Just as in any national army, they are critical to the functioning and war-making capacities of the movements. Yet unlike the auxiliary personnel in state armies who do receive benefits, those in nonstate movements are excluded from benefits because they fall outside the strict definition of *combatant.*

This invisibility and exclusion is not just bad for the women and girls; it is counterproductive to the short- and long-term goals of DDR. It shows disregard for the ways in which women and girls in armed forces can and do support the process and promote peace. It also reveals a shortsightedness that can have significant long-term consequences. Treating them as passive victims or "dependents" strips them of control of their lives and their sense of self-dignity. Moreover, by not acknowledging the skills and resources that they have attained, DDR processes risk losing tremendous social capital that could be utilized for postconflict reconstruction.

Without support, many of the women and girls who are demobilized have few choices for their own and their children's survival. Some turn to prostitution and by extension become victims and conduits of HIV/AIDS. Others drift into crime or back into the bush, rejoining remnants of the armed group. But by and large, the women and girl-mothers have a commitment to securing peace for themselves and their children. Excluding them means excluding their children, who might emerge as the next generation of disaffected youth.

Third, implementation of the R in DDR continues to be haphazard and poorly thought out. The reasons vary. Reintegration and rehabilitation are costly, complex, and long-term. The international community does not have the means or attention span to focus on each country for years on end. There is always another crisis, another DDR process to initiate in an emergency situation. Even when it does recognize the challenges, the UN system or other multilateral entities may be hampered by the parameters set by donors and member states. National governments are also reluctant to endure such deep interventions for so long. Yet without effective R, the DD can be irrelevant. Too often the men, having wielded power and authority through their guns, rampaging through the land and over people, return to the work they know best: fighting in gangs, for organized crime groups, or back as rebels. The women might resist, but they too are affected and as Haiti in 2005–2006 shows, the cycle of violence and conflict begins again. But DDR processes could be broadened to address combatants and their communities through a more integrated and systemic approach. Benefits could be distributed not only to the fighters but also to the communities. For example, the UN International Children's Fund (UNICEF) altered its approach in Sierra Leone by providing resources to schools that accepted former child combatants, rather than just providing funds to the fighters themselves. In this way, the community (including noncombatant children) benefited equally. The community-based approach is also a means of reducing tensions between combatants and civilians, particularly victims, who see fighters being rewarded for their actions, while victims receive nothing.

These approaches have gained momentum in recent years. DDR programming in Liberia in 2004 drew on some of the Sierra Leonean experience. Yet in the words of one Liberian activist, if it were not for the "constructive interference" of women's groups, the results would have been different.[47] In the African Great Lakes Region, efforts were under way at the time of this writing to ensure that women are included in the Multi-Country Demobilization and Reintegration Program that is targeting some 450,000 fighters across seven countries. Similarly, the North-South Sudanese peace process and related DDR programming are taking place, and the international community is paying special heed to women ex-combatants. In Colombia, an ambitious, nationally driven DDR program is under way with strong emphasis on reintegration and an accounting of not only the fighters but also their families and communities. Here, there is an appreciation of the integral role that women can play in sustaining reintegration efforts. But the policy talk in New York, Washington, or Geneva has yet to make a dent in field programs across the world. Even where there is progress on the question of women in and associated with armed forces, there is a disregard for the work of *noncombatant* women in communities, who take on many of the burdens of reintegrating and rehabilitating fighters because "no one else does."

Above and beyond international actors or fighters themselves, for these women, successful DDR is a matter of basic survival. They have neither an exit strategy nor weapons to wield if the peace fails and violence breaks out on their doorsteps. They work in insecure environments on the toughest of issues. From Bougainville to Sierra Leone or Sri Lanka, those working on any aspect of peacemaking, particularly in relation to disarmament issues, tread a fine line. To be effective, armed groups have to trust that they are neutral and independent. There is always the risk of being perceived as traitors, "sent in to disarm." Yet despite the pressures, they are committed to the work and continue with the most meager resources available. Their work is rarely acknowledged publicly. Even in instances in which the international community has supported women's efforts toward rehabilitation—for example, in Albania and El Salvador—the positive experiences are not documented effectively or conveyed within and across institutions in such a way as to systemize and upscale the practice, beyond the pilot efforts or discrete interventions.

Why not? The reasons vary and most likely extend beyond the scope of women and DDR issues. Lack of coordination, ineffective means of learning from experience, and no systematic prioritization of the issues are all factors. Advocates have highlighted the flaws in the processes: who to include, what benefits to provide to whom, how to broaden the programming to address rehabilitation. They have also taken a rights-based approach; regardless of whether women contribute or not to DDR processes, they have a right to be included and have equal opportunities to education, skills, and jobs. Some have also emphasized efficiency, as in this discussion.

Still, the cogs in the international wheel are slow to move, reluctant to alter practices, perhaps overwhelmed by what real change would entail. Doubtless, detractors argue that supporting women and girls in this context is not a priority or that their efforts lack impact. Whatever the reasons, there is a distinct disregard for international laws and ideals by the institutions that are meant to uphold them. This also indicates a profound disrespect for women like Anna, whose lives have been destroyed, and yet they are able to pick up the pieces, move on, and even support others.

Ultimately, this reluctance to review and revamp DDR programming to address the existing weaknesses points to a shortsightedness that is potentially dangerous. In a 2004 assessment of the Sierra Leone DDR program, scholars Macartan Humphreys and Jeremy Weinstein conclude that "ex-combatants [regard] the international community as the key disciplinary agent capable of making the government accountable to the demands of its constituents."[48] Yet they argue, as international attention shifts away from the country, the potential for violence can increase, and thus "the primary means of holding politicians accountable must come through internal mechanisms of influence and control, rather than from the intervention of outsiders." Women fighters or civilians time and again are proving their commitment to making the peace work and rehabilitating fighters. As NGOs and activists, they could form a key part of the internal mechanisms not only to hold politicians accountable, but also to influence and calm potentially disillusioned and impatient ex-fighters. Supporting them is not only practical and cost-effective, but it seems like a concrete means of bringing the R back into DDR, and making it not just a short-term intervention but also a long-term success.

Notes

1. Dyan Mazurana, *Women in Armed Opposition Groups in Africa and the Promotion of International Humanitarian Law and Human Rights* (Geneva: Geneva Call, 2006).
2. For security and confidentiality reasons, her real name is not used.
3. For security and confidentiality reasons, her real name is not used.
4. Security Council Resolution 1325, paragraph 8c (2000).
5. Secretary-General's Report to the General Assembly, *United Nations Study on Disarmament and Non-proliferation Education* (New York: United Nations, 2002), A/57/124, paragraph 36.
6. Vanessa Farr, "The Importance of a Gender Perspective to Successful Disarmament, Demobilization and Reintegration Processes," *Disarmament Forum* 4 (2003).
7. For more information, see UNIFEM, *Getting It Right, Doing It Right: Gender and Disarmament, Demobilization and Reintegration,* New York, 2004, available at http://www.womenwarpeace.org.
8. *IDDRS, Level 5: Women, Gender, and DDR,* available at http://www.unddr.org/iddrs/05.
9. References to El Salvador and Sierra Leone are drawn from case studies led by the Women Waging Peace Policy Commission, which the author directed from 2002 to 2005.
10. Parts of this section and further sections are drawn from Sanam Naraghi Anderlini and Camille Conaway, "From Combat to Community: The Role of Women in Disarmament, Demobilization, and Reintegration (DDR)," paper presented at McGill University conference on Gender and Security 2003, available at www.womenwagingpeace.net, retrieved July 18, 2006.
11. Nat Colletta, Marcus Kostner, and Ingo Wiederhofer, "Case Studies in War-to-Peace Transition: The Demobilization and Reintegration of Ex-Combatants in Ethiopia, Namibia, and Uganda," World Bank Discussion Paper 331, Washington, DC, 1996, p. xv.
12. Farr, "The Importance of a Gender Perspective."
13. Kofi Annan, *Report of the Secretary-General on the Role of the United Nations Peacekeeping in Disarmament, Demobilization and Reintegration* (New York: United Nations, 2000), p. 2.
14. United Nations Department for Disarmament Affairs, *Disarmament Issues,* New York, 2003.
15. Mats Berdal, "Disarmament and Demobilization After Civil Wars," *Adelphi Paper 303* (London: International Institute for Strategic Studies, 1996), p. 39.
16. *IDDRS, Level 5: Women, Gender, and DDR,* available at http://www.unddr.org/iddrs/05.
17. World Bank, Conflict Prevention and Reconstruction Unit, http://web.worldbank.org.
18. Johan Galtung, *Peace by Peaceful Means: Peace and Conflict, Development and Civilisation* (Oslo: International Peace Research Institute, 1996).
19. Dyan Mazurana and Kristopher Carlson, *From Combat to Community* (Washington, DC: Hunt Alternatives Fund, 2004).
20. Farr, "The Importance of a Gender Perspective."
21. Quoted in Dyan Mazurana, *Women in Armed Opposition Groups in Africa and the Promotion of International Humanitarian Law and Human Rights, Reports of a Workshop* (Geneva: Geneva Call, 2006), p. 33, available at http://

www.genevacall.org.

22. Ibid., p. 38.

23. Camille Pampell Conaway and Salomé Martinez, *Adding Value: Women's Contributions to Reintegration and Reconstruction in El Salvador* (Washington, DC: Hunt Alternatives Fund, 2004).

24. UNIFEM, *Case Study Bougainville, Papua New Guinea,* 2004, available at http://www.womenwarpeace.org.

25. Personal discussions with the author, 2004.

26. For more information, see *Survey of War Affected Youth, Phase 2: Girls and the LRA,* available at http://www.sway-uganda.org/sway2.htm.

27. Mazurana and Carlson, *From Combat to Community,* p. 18.

28. Ibid. Additional information was drawn from "Statistical Data from the National Committee on Disarmament, Demobilization and Reintegration," data provided to the author (Freetown, Sierra Leone: Government of Sierra Leone, 2002); *Statistical Data from the United Nations Children's Fund,* data provided to the author (Freetown, Sierra Leone: UNICEF, 2002).

29. For security and confidentiality reasons, her real name is not used.

30. Pampell Conaway and Martinez, *Adding Value,* p. 18.

31. Ibid.

32. Ibid., p. 22.

33. Lynn Stephen, Serena Cosgrove, and Kelly Ready, "Aftermath: Women's Organizations in Post-Conflict El Salvador," working paper no. 309 (Washington, DC: United States Agency for International Development, 2000), quoted in Pampell Conaway and Martinez, *Adding Value.*

34. Mazurana, *Women in Armed Opposition Groups.*

35. For security and confidentiality reasons, her real name is not used.

36. Shellac Davies, quoted in Mazurana and Carlson, *From Combat to Community.*

37. Ibid.

38. Interview with Angelina Atyam, northern Uganda, 2004, available at http://www.christianaid.org.uk, retrieved January 20, 2006.

39. UNIFEM, *Getting It Right, Doing It Right,* p. 24.

40. Miriam Maiga, "Joining Hands in Collecting Small Arms: The Mali Experience," in *Women, Violent Conflict, and Peacebuilding: Global Perspectives,* Sanam Naraghi Anderlini and R. Manchanda (eds.) (London: International Alert, 1999).

41. UNIFEM, "Women Building Peace Through Disarmament, Demobilization, and Reintegration," Beijing +10 Conference Review, available at http://www.peacewomen.org.

42. *UN Secretary-General's Report to the Security Council on the Situation in Somalia* (New York: United Nations, December 2005), S/2005/642, paragraphs 35–41.

43. At the time of this writing, legislators who had opposed the Ethiopian intervention were at risk of detention and some were in exile, including one prominent woman.

44. For more information, see http://www.bicc.de/weapons/events/unconf/workshop_texts/workshop_kushti.html.

45. United Nations Development Programme, "Women: The Untapped Resource," *Essentials 11* (2003).

46. Unpublished survey conducted by the Weapons Group on Arms Reduction with support from Hunt Alternatives Fund, 2004. The author is grateful to Hunt Alternatives for its kind permission to draw on this material.

47. The term was used by Liberian women peace activists who were describing their interventions at a panel titled "Priorities for Liberia's Reconstruction," Woodrow Wilson Center for International Scholars, Washington, DC, February 2007.

48. Macartan Humphreys and Jeremy Weinstein, *What the Fighters Say: A Survey of Ex-combatants in Sierra Leone* (New York: Columbia University, 2004), available at http://www.columbia.edu, retrieved July 18, 2006.

five

Postconflict Governance and Leadership

Women do not change institutions simply by assimilating into them, only by consciously deciding to fight for change. We need a feminism that teaches a woman to say no—not just to the date rapist or overly insistent boyfriend but, when necessary, to the military or corporate hierarchy within which she finds herself.

—Barbara Eichenreich

Women cannot afford to stay out of politics because that is where decisions are made. . . . Women need to develop self-confidence to fight for their rights. Women should respect tradition and culture but never let it be used as a weapon against them. All issues are women's issues.

—South African woman, ex-combatant, and politician

If media coverage is any indicator, 2006 was the year of women leaders. The success of Ellen Johnson-Sirleaf in Liberia, the first elected female African head of state, followed just months later by Michelle Bachelet's sweeping victory in Chile, brought the issue of women's leadership into sharp focus. If they were not enough, then news that Hamas had fielded women candidates, six of whom won seats, in its landslide victory against the ruling Fatah Party in Palestine certainly captured the headlines.

The attention alone is indicative of how far things have come and how far they still need to go. Bachelet and Johnson-Sirleaf join four other elected female presidents worldwide. In May 2007, together with constitutional monarchs, appointed and acting heads of state, and prime ministers, women led only nineteen of 192 member states (and two non-member states) of the United Nations.[1] The Hamas representatives are among a steady flow of women benefiting from the imposition of quota

systems to draw more women into political decisionmaking and legislatures. Globally the numbers are still low: women average 16.5 percent
of legislators worldwide, with the Nordic countries (including Finland)
and Rwanda leading with over 40 percent women and the Arab states on
the lower rungs at 6.8 percent (with the exception of Iraq, which has 25
percent).[2]

But the interest in Johnson-Sirleaf and Bachelet, more perhaps than
in Angela Merkel of Germany, who was elected as chancellor in 2005,
comes from their style and approach to politics. Unlike the handbag-
wielding "Iron Lady" Margaret Thatcher, and others who took pride in
being manlier than the men, Bachelet's feminine and feminist attributes
are emphasized. Bachelet certainly takes pride in representing women's
voices and paying tribute to her female constituents, setting her apart
from many a predecessor. Johnson-Sirleaf, too, although known as the
African "Iron Lady," is heralded not only for her qualifications, education, and competence but also for her connection to the wider populace,
particularly women, and for her promises of social inclusion. Across
West Africa, women are proud of Johnson-Sirleaf, believing that she
will represent them.

The Hamas women are similar and yet very different. They too rode
the wave of community service and grassroots connectivity. For the first
time, perhaps, they highlighted Hamas's community work to the wider
world. For many Palestinians the movement had been the key service
provider. "If the men's most visible role has been fighting Israel,
Hamas's social programs have attracted the loyalty of women," wrote
New York Times reporter Ian Fisher in 2006. "Hamas offers assistance
programs for widows of suicide bombers and for poor people, health
clinics, day care, kindergartens and preschools, in addition to beauty
parlors and women-only gyms."[3] Hamas drew on these links to mobilize
women as grassroots campaigners.

For those who assumed that women would tilt toward the more secular Fatah movement, the results were shocking. The contradictions, say
Palestinian pollster Khalil Shikaki, arise from the nature of the conflict
and occupation itself. On the one hand Palestinian women, like their
counterparts in other conflict-affected countries, have been part of the
political and increasingly military struggle. Unlike their counterparts in
other Arab countries, and despite pressures from a patriarchal society,
they have been a strong presence in the public and political arena for
decades. On the other hand, the harsh realities of occupation force
increased dependence on traditional social networks, including the family and mosques. Without a government to offer basic protection, says
Shikaki, "you need more conservative social values."[4]

These women exemplify the divergent trends among women leaders. Bachelet is the feminist ideal; Johnson-Sirleaf is the more traditional realist but a significant break from the African strongman stereotype and the epitome of trustworthiness and competence in a region plagued by corruption and ineptitude; and the Hamas members represent the crop of more conservative women who are entering politics either on the quota wave or based on their political affiliations and the societal trends that Shikaki notes. They are not easily categorized. Among the Palestinian women elected, one had three sons who were suicide bombers; another, Jamila Shanti, a philosophy professor at the Islamic University, speaks of the legitimacy of suicide bombers in the name of the Palestinian struggle. Yet she also talks of the need for legislative reform and an end to corruption and particularly discrimination against women. "Discrimination is not from Islam; it is from tradition," says Shanti. "[Change] may not be easy. Men may not agree," but the Hamas women are committed to bringing change.[5]

Despite their differences, to the electorates in Chile, Liberia, and Palestine these women leaders are a counterpoint to traditional political actors. Citizens of those countries voted for change from business as usual, in support of those who prioritized social services and were seen to be more honest. These women were also seen as a breath of fresh air in terms of their approach. In Chile, especially, said Mori Institute polling group director Marta Lagos in 2006, "It's important that she [Bachelet] is a woman, because she represents feminine leadership, neither authoritarian nor hierarchical."[6] Perhaps most significantly, these women symbolize change by virtue of being elected leaders in regions where women have traditionally taken a backseat in politics and public discourse.

Many people talk the talk of women's leadership in peace and security, particularly following the US invasion of Afghanistan in 2001. In recent years there has been an easy willingness among donors and multilateral agencies and NGOs to churn out statistics about women in legislatures, demand quotas for women on party lists and in parliament, and make assertions and repeat platitudes about the self-evidentiary nature of the positive attributes of women's leadership and inclusion in governance. Yet do women in decisionmaking positions bring about change? Can they make a difference?

In this chapter I explore women's contributions to postconflict governance, particularly in the transition or immediate postwar period. I touch on women's entry into the political arena in the aftermath of conflict, particularly from the standpoint of international support, and reflect on their transformative or added value—why they matter, what they bring, and what impact they have—through the existing prism and accepted wisdom of the international community and its criteria for good governance. In doing so, I also question aspects of conventional wisdom, drawing attention to key issues that remain largely neglected, and debate what leadership traits are valued, how priorities are identified, and how resources are allocated. I further suggest that although the rhetoric and actions of the international community vis-à-vis women are commendable, greater resources and commitment to transformation of the political arena are needed to enable women's effective and sustained participation. The danger otherwise is that the expectations placed on women in the most difficult of situations put them in a precarious position. They are, in other words, set up to fail. That situation may ultimately make support for women's participation in the political arena short-lived.

Women and the Political Pie After Conflict

It is striking but not altogether surprising that women leaders are emerging at local, provincial, and national levels in countries affected by violence, oppression, and division. Whether war pushes women into the public domain as breadwinners and single parents, propels them into activism to cope with personal tragedy, or mobilizes them for a cause, it quickly politicizes them too. Often in the aftermath of war and particularly during peace negotiations, there is bitter resentment and disappointment at not attaining the equality and rights they strived toward. In Central America, where women made up some 30 percent of guerrilla forces, the immediate postwar years witnessed a considerable push-back of women into traditional spheres. As discussed in Chapter 3, in El Salvador, they had few choices. Many wanted to return to normalcy and lives they had put on hold, but they also wanted to participate in community and public life. Yet the opportunities were few and far between, at times simply because child-care provisions were not available.

After liberation wars across Africa, many women came face-to-face with exclusion from decisionmaking and leadership in the postwar period. Similarly, in the Middle East, women were key actors in the first intifada (1987–1991) and initial negotiations that led to the 1993 Oslo process and subsequent creation of the Palestinian Authority, but they were soon marginalized from the peace process. Speaking in 1999, Hanan Ashrawi, former spokesperson for the Palestinian Authority and longtime peace and human rights activist, reflected,

There was a very patronising, patriarchal attitude [toward the women] of "good for you, you've done your national duty, now go back." You cannot take decisions on our behalf, so you want to reassert the traditional norms and patterns. Our women were resistant to this. . . . We questioned, we refused. Unfortunately, in our case, the system of the revolution reimposed itself on women. The system of tokenism took over.[7]

For many the situation described above is a wake-up call: if they do not take a stand for themselves and the values they represent, no one else will. "We became angry," recalled Bosnian Samra Filipovic-Hadziabdic, director of the Gender Equality Agency of Bosnia and Herzegovina (BiH) in 2006, "but we turned our anger into action."[8]

Despite the reams of international declarations and conventions, most notably the Convention on the Elimination of All Forms of Discrimination Against Women, ratified in 1979, or UN Resolution 1325, passed in 2000, international support for women's participation in post-conflict governance structures has not been systematic. That is not to say that efforts have not been made, but rather that international and national actors undertake small-scale and often disjointed, ad hoc projects. Too much depends on the will and interest of individuals.

In the case of BiH, for example, the UNDP, the Swedish International Development Agency (SIDA), and others sponsored onetime projects in support of women's rights and empowerment, but there was little coordination. In 1997, the Organization for Security and Cooperation in Europe mission in Sarajevo developed its "Women in Politics program to promote the sustained involvement of women in politics. It combined legislative approaches with capacity building and training initiatives. The program was integrated into the broader range of political initiatives run by the OSCE, but it was dependent on volunteer contributions for 50 percent of its funding.[9]

It was in part thanks to the efforts of the privately owned Hunt Alternatives Fund that women's political participation gained visibility. As foundation chair Swanee Hunt recalls, her program funded a visit by six women leaders from three nationalist political parties, a women's party, and two multiethnic coalitions from BiH to Washington, D.C., in 1998. The visit not only raised the women's profile but also provided them with the opportunity to find common ground. On their return, the group reached out to a wider cross section of women, and in partnership with the OSCE, held a cross-party women's conference, titled "Women: A New Political Future," in Sarajevo. "Two hundred women came from over two dozen political parties," writes Hunt in *This Was Not Our War.*

"This conference . . . helped create a momentum. One result was a rule requiring that women be one in three candidates distributed evenly throughout all party lists."[10] Although the ensuing rules did not guarantee a 33 percent quota for women in the BiH House of Representatives or at regional and cantonal levels, it did result in significant jumps in the percentage of women legislators.

East Timor in 2000 was another feat. The women's movement gained momentum in June 2000, at the first meeting of the Congress of Timorese Women, when some 400 women from the thirteen districts adopted the Platform for Action for the Advancement of Timorese Women. The organizations involved, ranging from grassroots groups to national entities working in diverse sectors, also created the East Timorese Women's Network (REDE) with fourteen founding members. The creation of the UN Transitional Administration in East Timor (UNTAET), and with it the arrival of Sherrill Whittington as gender adviser, boosted the women's profile. Working closely with local women's groups, Whittington succeeded in bringing gender equality issues out of the wilderness within the UN mission and into her interactions with the mission head, the late Sergio Viero de Mello. UNTAET addressed demands for equality within the mission, instituted affirmative action policies throughout its own structure, and provided incentives such as TV airtime to parties with a strong showing of women candidates, among other actions. It also introduced special measures in other sectors, notably police reform, where 40 percent of the initial wave of recruits were women. Although it never introduced baseline quotas for women in decisionmaking structures and the national legislature, together with UNIFEM, it did provide training, support, and mentoring to women interested in political work. Yet as this arm of the international community struggled to support the Timorese women, another arm, representing members of the donor community (themselves UN member states and signatories to CEDAW), was pointedly ambivalent. In 2004, reflecting on the discord, activist and member of the Constituent Assembly Milena Pires noted how some donors perceived the promotion of gender equality as a "luxury and inappropriate for East Timor at that time."[11]

Regardless of the gains or losses, the experiences of East Timor and BiH were local in character, dependent on the activities of the local women first and foremost, international NGOs, and even individual personnel within various international agencies who had a keen awareness of and determination to address women's political participation. There is insufficient will or effort put into integrating them into major governance interventions and institutionalizing practices globally. Consequently, such efforts do not yield substantial and sustained results.

Within the UN system, UNIFEM supports women's political participation but lacks the resources to be a strong driving force or voice among
the mainstream agencies. Elsewhere, such as in South Africa or Uganda
in the 1990s, external involvement was limited, not well understood by
the international community, and thus never effectively drawn upon or
adapted. For example, in South Africa, the Women's League of the ANC
worked closely with women from other political parties and government
to raise the profile of women. Collectively they fought and succeeded in
getting a quota for women. In Rwanda, the transitional government
devised an innovative system of triple balloting for local elections,
allowing women and youth to stand on separate ballots from mainstream candidates. The lessons in each case have not been effectively
captured, adapted, or adopted by the major entities supporting governance programming.

The consequence over the years has been that the experience, frus-
trations, successes, and failures of women's political participation in the
postconflict period, as related to governance and other issues, have not
resonated strongly at the highest levels in New York, Washington, Brussels, or London. Instead of building on experience, opportunities are
missed, and the lessons are rarely drawn or applied effectively.

Lifting the Veil: The Afghan Watershed

Afghanistan, or more specifically, the US administration's attention to
Afghan women in late 2001, brought a new prominence to women's
roles in postconflict governance. Newspaper articles, television footage,
and the documentary film *Beneath the Veil,* broadcast by CNN, brought
the brutality of the Taliban regime and its explicit misogyny into American living rooms. Women's rights organizations, such as the National
Organization for Women (NOW), the Feminist Majority Foundation,
and the Revolutionary Association of Afghan Women (RAWA), that had
kept the plight of Afghan women alive in policy circles and among their
own constituents became newsworthy. Yet the international system was
reluctant to engage. On November 1, 2001, writes journalist Sally Armstrong, Sir Kieran Prendergast, the former head of the UN Department
of Political Affairs, made a statement countering the provisions of UN
Resolution 1325. "Women cannot be included in peace negotiations," he
said, "because the situation is too complex."[12] But the NGO community
persisted, until three weeks later, the political tides finally turned. "First
Lady Laura Bush used the President's weekly radio address to speak out
for Afghan women," writes researcher and women's rights activist Masuda

Sultan.[13] The fight against terrorism, said Laura Bush, "is also a fight for the rights and dignity of women."

Afghan women, virtually enslaved and covered in billowing blue burkhas, were suddenly catapulted to the forefront of the US and, by extension, the international community's policy agenda. Overnight, UN agencies, the World Bank, and others jumped on the gender bandwagon, with representatives speaking eloquently of the role of women in the future of Afghanistan. The well-worn excuses of culture and political sensitivity used to push women's rights aside elsewhere were forgotten. Instead, it was assumed that not only did women have a right to be included, but also that their participation in politics would be a moderating force. Support for women's political participation in postconflict and Islamic states became a key element of the Bush agenda. "Across the world, the increasing participation of women in civic and political life has strengthened democracies," said President George W. Bush in March 2006. "A democracy is strong when women participate in the society."[14] Stated or unstated, the inclusion of women became a strategy not only to promote democracy but also to counter extremism and, by extension, terrorism.

As with so much else in Afghanistan, in the months and years that followed, the rhetoric was never matched by reality. For example, outsiders placed too much emphasis on lifting the burkha, without respecting the concerns and advice of Afghan women who warned against this blatant and cosmetic approach to women's rights. They rightly feared that the focus on the burkha would create a backlash and jeopardize their ability to meet their more basic needs. Issues of health, education, income generation, and security, which were foremost in the minds of Afghan women, did not receive the requisite attention or resources. The creation of women's centers and girls' schools in the midst of the rubble of war-torn towns and villages also became a source of tension. Many of the centers have been destroyed or left abandoned. Yet if they had been formed as community centers, with their use by all (including women) negotiated within the communities themselves, their chance of survival would have been greater. Certainly more consultation and engagement with a wide cross section of women themselves could have helped avoid many of the pitfalls. But for all the flaws in policymaking and programmatic challenges in that country, Afghanistan did set a precedent. The issue of women's political participation in the aftermath of war could no longer be blatantly ignored.

In 2002, as the Iraq War loomed on the horizon, and in 2004, as the North-South Sudan peace talks entered their final rounds, civil society organizations and UNIFEM again brought women's participation in peacemaking and governance to the attention of policymakers. Once highlighted, those issues were acknowledged and supported by major agencies and donors. The bureaucracies are now better equipped to respond, particularly in the context of elections. Publicly, no one dares suggest that support for women's political participation, either as voters or as candidates and decisionmakers, is untimely or a luxury in any context. The remaining challenge, though, is to ensure that external interventions do not harm or result in a backlash against women. At the very least, this requires both a thorough knowledge of the sociopolitical context and in-depth interactions (often by women) with women so that the approaches taken are not seen as a direct affront to local values. This is not giving in to cultural relativism; rather, it is drawing on the cultural context to determine the best course of action needed to secure women's participation and protection.

Good Governance

In the clamor to build peace in the aftermath of civil war, the thirst for workable formulae and successes that can be replicated is never-ending. Not surprisingly, the promotion and establishment of "good governance" is widely acknowledged as a key pillar of postconflict reconstruction. It cannot be addressed or judged in isolation from other elements (economic, social, or security conditions, for example), but in and of itself, good governance is of primary importance. The US Agency for International Development (USAID) defines good governance as "a government's ability to maintain social peace, guarantee law and order, promote or create conditions necessary for economic growth, and ensure a minimum level of social security." Key elements include "democracy (e.g., elections, human rights, and representation), [as well as] public accountability, responsiveness, transparency, and efficiency."[15] The World Bank identifies six indicators of good governance: voice and accountability, political stability and lack of violence, government effectiveness, regulatory quality, rule of law, and control of corruption.[16] Likewise, the UNDP emphasizes legislatures, electoral systems and processes, justice and human rights, access to information, decentralization and local governance, public administration, and civil service reform as elements of good governance.[17]

Focusing specifically on the transition from violent conflict to peace and normalization, the widely respected and influential Post-Conflict

Reconstruction project (PCR)[18] at the Center for Strategic and International Studies in Washington, D.C., identifies the following as key components to be addressed by international and national actors: the development of a national constitution; the establishment of a transitional government in the short term and executive authority in the long term; the strengthening of the legislature; the promotion of local governance and transparency; the development of measures to combat corruption; and participation in the form of elections, political parties, civil society, and media. Largely mirroring Western-style democratic ideals, these frameworks offer guidance and a vision of where a society ought to be, but they are technocratic in approach and at times a reflection of the working practices of institutions engaged in such issues, rather than the complexity of the society where they seek to practice. In the context of conflict-affected states particularly, the checklists and guidelines on good governance are too limited.

Scholar Roland Paris, for example, critiques the push toward democracy and market liberalization that has become the stock-in-trade of international agencies.[19] In his review of international peacekeeping and reconstruction efforts, Paris does not dispute the end goal. Rather, he argues for more emphasis on the strengthening of institutions and the development of strong and effective government, with key elements such as a vibrant civil society capable of holding the state accountable, before moving toward elections and open markets. In effect, he calls for greater attention to the foundations of the institutions that uphold the practice of good governance, instead of the typical push toward elections (which can exacerbate existing divisions) and open markets (which can generate significant uncertainty and insecurity for ordinary people).

Former US congressman and diplomat Howard Wolpe unravels the concept to an even greater degree, arguing that too often international efforts in the postconflict period neglect the state of mind of the presumed leaders and decisionmakers. The institutions can be formed, he says, but if the mindsets, fears, and deep-seated issues of mistrust and insecurity are not acknowledged and addressed, there is little chance of strengthening institutions or generating sustainability. He further contends that overlooking the basics—most notably the principles of cooperation and interdependence—that underlie democratic processes can be detrimental to the overall effort of promoting good governance. "The strength and stability of Western democratic societies rests as much upon cooperation as it does upon competition," he writes.[20] Drawing on Roger Fisher's work on interest-based conflict resolution, he points to several baseline features: the recognition of mutual interdependence; a strong dose of trust that all sides will play by the rules, particularly in dealing with conflict; and the use of communication styles that are not abrasive or threatening on a personal level but rather promote interaction and "better listening."[21]

By definition, says Wolpe, war-torn (even highly conflicted and dictatorial) societies do not share the "perceptual and attitudinal common ground that is a 'given' in Western democratic societies." Without these "four often neglected political imperatives," it is unlikely that political transformation and democratization processes and therefore the negotiated peace can be sustainable.[22]

How does that relate to and affect women? Despite the diversity of culture, the nature of war, or other factors across countries, several characteristics are common to women's governance-related activities. Often their approaches and interests are an extension of their work during and around the negotiations. Although they are typically circumscribed by limited resources and access to international technical and financial support, as discussed below, women not only are effective along the standard indicators mentioned above but also are seemingly natural proponents of the neglected issues raised by Paris and Wolpe.

Why Women Matter

A key dilemma facing the international community and societies emerging from war is to balance the need for new voices and perspectives against existing and often entrenched ones that may have given rise to the conflict. As Afghanistan, Somalia, and elsewhere show, it is a difficult task. Conflicts give rise to new perspectives, and previously excluded sectors of society expect and demand a role in decisionmaking. They may be among sectors that agitated for conflict or those who emerged as voices of moderation. But where compromises are reached, new players are pitted against old ones whose willingness to negotiate a settlement is matched by their expectations of power and influence in the aftermath of war. In other words, for many a warlord, Maoist rebel, or armed faction of a political party, the negotiations and postwar period are, effectively, payback time.

Prior to the 2001 US invasion of Afghanistan, the international community viewed this question of participation largely through the prism of identity or affiliation (ethnicity, religion, or political or military group), which might have been the basis for inclusion or exclusion in the past, and hence a rallying call for war. But this approach can backfire. In BiH for example, presidential elections reinforce ethnic divisions. Bosnians can only vote for Bosnian candidates, Croats for Croats, Serbs for Serbs. Even though the presidency passes from one to the other, there is little chance of promoting leadership that crosses these boundaries. Similarly in Iraq, although the objective has been full inclusion, the approach of highlighting ethnic and religious identities has generated greater division.

Gender as an alternative variable for participation and inclusion is of particular relevance. As at least 50 percent of the population—regardless of ethnicity, religion, political affiliation, and class—women are the most politically marginalized cross section of society. Thus, how they fare can be a significant indicator of the change taking place. This is especially true in deeply patriarchal societies—which include many conflict-affected countries. Increases in tolerance, coexistence, and plurality are reflected in the treatment of women; the access they enjoy; the changes in legislation regarding their social, economic, and political standing in society; and the positions they hold. Simultaneously, where political or identity issues are at the root of conflict, women can use their gendered identities and social experiences to bridge these chasms and set an example for others in their own identity groups. But it is neither easy nor automatic. Oftentimes, as in Latin America or South Asia, women's class and caste identities outweigh their ability to unite across gendered experiences. But as the examples of Northern Ireland, South Africa, and Rwanda show, women can lead the way by reconciling past injustices and creating alliances in formerly staid political structures.

A Force for Moderation?

The virtual slavery of Afghan women and US exploitation of their situation helped to bring gender inequality into mainstream foreign policy agendas and international discourse. The inclusion of women came with the assumption and expectation—in many cases rightly so—that they would be a moderating force. That assumption is not entirely new. The Rwandan transitional government was perhaps the first national government to view women as new voices and conduits for moderation and peace. The government viewed women's full participation as a political imperative that would draw in a previously excluded sector of society and shift away from the culture of political extremism. Given the demographics, the reasons were obvious: some 70 percent of the postgenocide population of Rwanda was female. As Elizabeth Powley writes, "[They] immediately assumed multiple roles as heads of household, community leaders, and financial providers. . . . Quite simply they are the majority constituency and the most productive segment of the population."[23]

In the transition years from 1995 to 2004, the Rwandan Government of National Unity (GNU), led by the Tutsi-dominated Rwandan Patriotic Front (RPF), pursued twin policies of decentralization and democratization, as well as explicitly addressing the participation of previously excluded sectors, notably women and youth. Several factors drove the policy on women: (1) their sheer majority and activism in the reconstruction of Rwanda; (2) the experiences of Uganda and South Africa, where women had gained significant presence in political circles, provided women in the RPF with role models; (3) women were significantly less implicated in the genocide than men but heavily victimized. There was an understanding that the public at large trusted them more than men in positions of leadership and that they had proven to be more effective at reconciliation, a priority for the RPF and the transitional government.[24]

Elsewhere, from Colombia to Cambodia, Iran, and Afghanistan, through turbulent times, when the opportunity was presented, women have been at the front lines, supporting candidates who stood for moderation, reform, and peace.[25] In Cambodia, political violence and economic difficulties persist, and cultural discrimination of women is entrenched. Yet since the cease-fire and negotiated settlement of 1991, communities are acknowledging that women entering local and national politics bring a different approach and perspective. "We want more Khmer women to be candidates," says one local politician, "because women don't solve problems by force and gunpoint."[26]

In Iran women were a key constituency of reform-minded president Mohammad Khatami in 1997 and 2000. In the 1997–2004 reform-era sixth majlis (parliament), women were at the forefront of key issues, including issues relating to gender equality that challenged key interpretations of Islamic law and, by extension, the nation's constitution. Among the first wave of Iranian women revolutionaries, the transformation is particularly notable. For example, feminist ideology was frowned upon and considered illegal for years in the aftermath of the revolution. Yet, speaking in 2004, a senior official in the Ministry of the Interior openly used the term "we feminists" and spoke of the rights of women to engage in decisionmaking. She, like others, reconciled her religious and political beliefs by widening the Islamic framework and finding legitimacy within it. To counter opposition, she further used the Islamic revolution's late leader, Ayatollah Ruhollah Khomeini, to legitimate the claim. "Iman Khomeini himself said that women must interfere in serious matters—this means not just the family," she said. "The Imam also said that when power and government were not in the hands of the people, women were *haram* [forbidden] in the majlis—but now [after the 1979 revolution], it does belong to the people—so we make no distinctions between men and women."[27] This framing of women's rights within Islamic discourse, as opposed to a secular standpoint, can be an effective shield for women against a traditional religious and patriarchal backlash.

In Afghanistan, despite endemic gender discrimination, including lack of education and access to resources, women have spoken out against extremism. Malalai Joya, the young delegate to the constitutional Loya Jirga (Great Council) of 2003, electrified the meeting with her denunciation of warlords and local commanders. Others, both those in civil society and their counterparts in the policy arena, walk a fine line between their struggle for rights and the potential for violent backlash. Nonetheless they have, writes Sultan, "helped ignite the national debate within government and civil society over a variety of issues relating to democracy, religion and freedom of expression."[28]

And in Iraq, amid the chaos and political horse trading that kept the country in limbo for months after the 2005 parliamentary elections, observers noted that the women parliamentarians, even those who emerged from more conservative religious parties, were more "forward leaning," willing to engage and seek common solutions. Most tellingly, they continued to participate in problem-solving efforts and meetings initiated by the international community, despite actual and potential threats to their lives.[29] Recommendations from an October 2006 gathering of women representing governmental entities and NGOs reflect the direct linkages between women's struggle for rights, broader adherence to human rights, and the ever-present threat of increased sectarianism and religious extremism. The participants point to the underrepresentation of women on the Constitution Reform Committee and the struggle to maintain their perspectives. They further note "reservation and worry over article 91/2 of the constitution which is suggesting [the inclusion] of seats for experts and clergymen within the Higher Federal Court . . . that will decrease and tamper with the role of the judiciary system."[30] They also call on the constitution to recognize that, as a member of the international community, Iraq is signatory to "several . . . human rights conventions [e.g., the Geneva Conventions and CEDAW], [and that] these international treatises [should] be considered as other sources of Iraqi legislation, to guarantee against law breaking by tribal norms and social traditions that dedicates [sic] violence and discrimination against women in particular."[31] Their calling card may be women's rights, but they are front and center in the struggle for human rights, tolerance, and democracy. Given the levels of violence and insecurity in Iraq, the willingness of women to work across the sectarian boundaries and partner with civil society is extraordinary.

Perhaps it is too soon to tell whether women's amenity to widening political discourse, seeking the middle ground, or tackling entrenched interests can make a noticeable and sustained difference in the politics of any country, be it one facing the threat of war, one emerging from war, or an industrial nation. In many instances it is perhaps too much to ask. As noted in Chapter 3, in Northern Ireland during the peace talks, political parties on all sides were willing to draw on the abilities and willingness of the NIWC to mediate and maintain the flow of talks. Yet in the aftermath, as the tough business of implementation came into play, issues such as decommissioning of fighters, the withdrawal of the British Army, the handover of weapons, and so forth became contentious. The rhetoric of extremists on both sides gained traction, and the middle ground disappeared. NIWC representatives found themselves lampooned, attacked, and accused of treachery in the 2003 Assembly elections.

In Afghanistan, as in Sierra Leone, the magnitude of nation building is overwhelming for all concerned. The ongoing power struggles between armed factions, including remnants of the Taliban, and the violence they wreak can destroy any effort at moderation. Just as in Northern Ireland, as the implementation of agreed compromises turns shaky, the extremes reemerge to wield power over weak governments. Against this backdrop, many of the Afghan women legislators may be severely constrained, targeted for stepping outside accepted social boundaries, and accused of incompetence. That said, their male counterparts are not necessarily better off. Indeed, many of the men are less qualified, but they are under less scrutiny nationally or internationally. There is no explicit expectation that they will be transformative leaders.

Liberia's Ellen Johnson-Sirleaf epitomizes the expectations of women's transformative powers. Two years into her tenure, she has not disappointed. Signaling the fight against governmental corruption, she appointed women to key ministerial posts, including the Ministries of Finance and Commerce, and as the chief of police. She has reined in governmental expenditures and joined regional efforts to bring peace to Côte d'Ivoire. But tensions remain high, and Liberia's need for international aid is stark. Yet by January 2007, international funding was at risk.

Speaking to the *Independent* (a UK newspaper), Johnson-Sirleaf said, "It will be catastrophic if aid is to be reduced. . . . If the promised aid does not arrive, especially for our health services, it will have serious consequences for Liberia."[32] The article notes that "the 66-year-old President remains widely admired, at home and abroad," but admiration alone does not enable her to rebuild the country.

In Latin America, with its machismo, history of military dictatorships, and related human rights abuses, the recent surge of women into key governmental posts is a clear indication of a shift away from the legacy that haunts them. Fifty percent of the ministers in Bachelet's cabinet in Chile are women, including the defense minister. Bachelet has pledged to appoint women to half of the additional 300 decision-making posts. Across the continent, by 2007 one-third of defense ministries were led by women. In Argentina, for example, left-leaning Nilda Garre is taking a firm stance against former military officers who have shielded themselves with state secrecy laws to avoid disclosing information about human rights abuses during the rule of the junta in the 1970s. Her counterpart, Vivianne Blanlot of Chile, was booed at General Augusto Pinochet's funeral in December 2006. The depth of anger was indicative of the continued presence and influence of the old guard. But Blanlot was not intimidated. An Associated Press article quotes her saying, "I'm the one who is in charge now."[33] Meanwhile in Uruguay, Azucena Berruti, another left-wing lawyer with a track record in defending victims of human rights abuse, fired her army chief for holding unauthorized meetings with the president's political foes. These women have certainly made their presence felt. The question is whether they can sustain a deep-rooted transformation.

In effect, it is a double-edged sword. Women claim to be, or are presented as being, different, transformative leaders, a force of moderation, and less corrupt, thus setting higher standards and expectations. But the inability to meet these expectations, to show change, regardless of their actions or the environment in which they are attempting to be active, is often deemed as *their* failure. In immediate postconflict settings, the external support provided to women is precarious. In some instances like Liberia, it is a function of the limited attention span of the international community as it runs from one crisis to the next. But often women have to prove their capacity to bring change before they get sustained support. The simple premise that gender equality or the inclusion of women in peace and security is mandated by international law and conventions holds little sway. Yet without sustained support (be it financial or technical), women have little chance of making a significant and irreversible difference in the short term.

Honor, Trust, and Corruption

"In an environment where people are disgusted with politics in general, who represents clean and change? Women."[34] Quoting US congressman Rahm Emanuel in 2006, *New York Times* journalist Robin Toner reported on a wave of women candidates emerging in the Democratic Party, running as outsiders against the "culture of corruption" in 2006. It is an effective strategy, as pollster Celinda Lake notes. "If you want to communicate change, honesty, cleaning up Washington, not the same old boys network . . . women are very good at communicating that."[35]

From Washington, D.C., to Phnom Penh, from Ramallah to Cape Town or Kigali, perceptions matter in politics. And women are perceived to be more trustworthy and less corruptible than their male counterparts. The universality of such perception prompted a 1999 study by the World Bank. Drawing on quantitative data across a range of countries, the authors of "Are Women Really the 'Fairer' Sex? Corruption and Women in Government" note:

> There exists a substantial literature in the social sciences which suggests that women may have higher standards of ethical behavior and be more concerned with the common good. Consistent with this micro-level evidence, we find that at the country level, higher rates of female participation in government are associated with lower levels of corruption. Increasing the presence of women in government may be valued for its own sake, for reasons of gender equality. However, our results suggest that there may be extremely important spin-offs stemming from increasing female representation: if women are less likely than men to behave opportunistically, then bringing more women into government may have significant benefits for society in general.[36]

In rural Rwanda in 2003, Powley documented the reactions of local officials and farmers, both men and women.[37] "Women are less prone to corruption than men; they offer services without embezzlement as men tend to do," says one village official in the Ruhengeri province of Rwanda. "Men in power tend to be corrupted," says another farmer. "[Women] render complete services, they are empathetic . . . and never corrupt," reflects a woman farmer.

The sentiments are echoed in rural Cambodia. "Women think about what children need. . . . Women do not cheat as much as men during food distribution," says a local official in Siem Reap.[38] Activist Pok Nanda recounted that during a 2003 call-in radio show, when asked if they would vote for women, the majority of callers said that "they wanted to see change, and they trust women more to make that change."

In postconflict states, the question of trust is often intricately bound up with experiences and perceptions of conflict. In Rwanda, where reconciliation was (and is) a critical issue, women were perceived to be "better" at forgiveness and reconciliation in the immediate aftermath of the genocide. They were trusted more, in large part because in general women were less implicated in the killings. They witnessed the massacres, and they may have aided them, but overwhelmingly the crimes were committed by men. Only 2.3 percent of genocide suspects were women. And, as noted earlier, the government and public also overwhelmingly acknowledged women's roles in bearing the burden of recovery.

In Cambodia the trust in women was partly tied to the endemic problems of political corruption and partly related to notions of responsiveness. Women were trusted to be less corrupt and outside the old boys' network. Additionally, reporting on interviews in rural and urban areas, Laura McGrew and her colleagues repeatedly point to people's perceptions of women as being better listeners, more available and willing to tackle the problems that people bring forth. In effect, they were also more trusted than men to prioritize the well-being of their constituency.[39]

Thus a dichotomy prevails: on the one hand women are seen as the weaker sex, subservient to men, but on the other hand, where they have emerged, they are perceived as symbols of trust and transformation. Women are scrutinized more heavily than the men, and as mentioned earlier, they are tested against a higher standard of behavior. Given prevailing sociocultural forces, any hint of misconduct can be immensely damaging. Thus for those who have entered politics, the pressure from within and without is palpable. The perception that they are being watched, judged, more readily criticized, and sanctioned is common among women in politics across conflict zones. Quite simply, as McGrew and her colleagues note, "Women are less likely to engage in corruption or other activities that could tarnish their credibility."[40]

Symbols of Change: Individuals or Critical Mass?

Does quality or quantity matter more? The debate continues about quotas and the belief that a critical mass of women—from 25 to 30 percent—is needed to enable women to leave their mark. Certainly there are instances in which individual women have had a profound impact. Even where the numbers are higher, performance depends on the skills and ability of the individuals involved. Moreover, the quota system can be easily gamed by all sides in a political system, so that the women who come forth are effectively mouthpieces for their male leadership.

But, says Bosnian Mirsad Jacevic, longtime peace activist and advocate for women's inclusion in peace processes, for the most part, women's sheer presence in these arenas has both transformative and profound symbolic value. At the very least, the affirmative action initiatives provide women—including those who have the skills and qualifications—a chance that is otherwise unavailable.

As Rwanda shows, where extremist politics leads to violence of such magnitude, the importance of a relatively peaceful path to reconstruction cannot be overestimated. That women make up 49 percent of the legislature is by no means the reason for Rwanda's recovery, but that women are active and involved in all aspects of public life at all levels and in all arenas, including reconciliation, despite their general lack of education and skills and a history of exclusion, cannot be ignored either. Similarly, despite the difficulties women face in Cambodia, Afghanistan, or Iraq, their presence, approaches, and voices signal the possibility of a different political environment. At the very least, they are indicative of how a more pluralistic and tolerant society could emerge.

Political Activism in Civil Society: Women's Space

A vibrant civil society capable of holding government accountable and providing choices for the public to express their identity and affiliations (for example, through trade associations, NGOs, etc., not only in political, racial, or religious terms) is a key pillar of good governance. Nonetheless, writes Roland Paris, "not all civil society associations are conducive to peaceful democratic politics, particularly those that espouse violence . . . or that reject the idea of democracy itself." He offers a spectrum: at one end are organizations dedicated to breaking down social barriers between formerly conflicting and warring parties, and at the other are those that reinforce the divisions. The difficulty for international actors intervening in postconflict situations is to support the "good" civil society while restraining the "bad" variant. "In particular," Paris says, "peacebuilding agencies should offer greater financial and logistical support to cross-factional associations . . . from political lobbying groups to trade unions and private social clubs."[41]

For all his conviction, it is noteworthy that even Paris makes no mention of the centrality of women to cross-conflict, civil society peace activism in war-torn societies. One of the world's oldest peace organizations, for example, is the Women's League for International Peace and Freedom (WILPF), which was formed in 1915 by a group of women from across Europe to prevent World War I. Today WILPF is active in over thirty-seven countries. Similarly, Women in Black, born from the Balkans crisis, is present across the Middle East, as well as in Europe and North America. Their message of peace and opposition to violence remains unchanged. Although it is not possible to quantify civil society organizations in many countries, there is no doubt that it is a growing sector, particularly where women are concerned. These organizations range from high-profile national entities to small, community-based, volunteer organizations. They are involved in a variety of activities from political lobbying and public consciousness raising to peace vigils, cross-community dialogue, and mediation and trust building. They provide social services, rehabilitate former fighters, support income generation programs, and promote peace in every other way possible, as shown by many of the 1,000 women Nobel Prize candidates. The issues they address may have profound political implications and can be easily politicized to create divisions. But they seek to depoliticize, address issues of suffering, promote reconciliation, and focus on the human face of the issue, which can resonate strongly with the public at large. In short, most epitomize what Paris calls good civil society.

Since the Beijing conference in 1995 and with the passage of Resolution 1325 at the Security Council, women have brought new energy, focus, and commitment to peacebuilding, working across warring communities, networking regionally, and finding a common platform globally. By 2004 in Afghanistan, the Afghan Women's Network comprised some seventy-two organizations and 3,000 individual members.[42] In Rwanda, Pro-Femmes/Twese Hamwe has forty member organizations.[43] In Colombia, 266 organizations have worked together for over four years to develop the Women's Emancipatory Coalition.[44] In Iraq, networks across the country with ties to activists outside continue to operate. These expanding networks of women indicate a trend toward increasingly active and sophisticated efforts among women's organizations to tackle issues of peace, security, rights, and development collaboratively and simultaneously at the global, regional, and local levels. Anecdotal estimates from places such as Palestine suggest that women run the majority of such organizations.[45] They also make up the staff of many organizations that are not overtly women-focused.

Particularly in war-affected countries, many women feel compelled to act, yet they see a formal political arena that is morally bankrupt and dominated by men who are typically unwelcoming of women. Civil society provides an alternative public space where they can address their issues of concern without compromising their beliefs, yet affect and influence the formal sector. This space between formal politics and traditional societal frameworks that convey identity—clans, tribes, religions—is a comfort zone for many women. They can break away from the social and political constraints to come together on issues of common concern. Moreover, the space women carve out in civil society is often not contested by traditional male leaders. For one thing, given that many of these organizations act voluntarily or with limited resources, it is of little interest to those seeking a significant source of income. Of course, that can change as resources increase, but by and large in conflict-affected countries women have a major presence in civil society. This presence can have negative consequences: the scarcity of funding, for example, can create competition among groups; political-, identity-, or class-based affiliations can be a source of tension. Generally, however, the emergence and presence of women's voices in civil society and the public arena is indicative of a more open society.

Through these efforts, many women also gain the confidence to venture into formal politics. In Iraq today, El Salvador, Guatemala, or South Africa in the 1990s, civil society, and particularly women's organizations, are and were the nurturing grounds for many women. In 1999, reflecting on her own political journey, former Cambodian minister of women's and veteran's affairs Mu Sochua said,

> I realized that our voices, as women, were not being heard at the higher level. There were almost no women at the top, and the ones who were at the top do not speak because they are so outnumbered by men. That was when I realized that I needed to join politics. It also exposed me to politics. Before that I thought of politics as a dirty game, as the game of men. Through my training in gender, through the different conferences, I realized that politics is not dirty unless you want to make it dirty. You can really clean up politics, and also giving ourselves the definition of politics. To me politics means having the power to change—and change can be for the best or the worst for the people. For me and for women who join politics in particular, when we change, we change so that people have a better life.[46]

Inclusivity and Participation: How Women Work

Inclusivity is another important trademark of women's political practices in postconflict arenas. Although a blanket generalization cannot be made, among those entering politics through civil society activism, ensuring an inclusive approach to their work is often a direct result of and reaction to their experiences of exclusion. It is evident in a variety of contexts. In Cambodia, South Africa, and Rwanda, for example, inclusivity was not only a principle that women sought to enshrine within the constitution, but also a mode of operation as they mobilized around the consultation and drafting processes.

The UN mission to Cambodia led the constitutional drafting process in the early 1990s, but local civil society groups played a pivotal role in organizing public discussions, meeting with representatives of the National Assembly, and making proposals for inclusion in the constitution. "We would . . . discuss what we wanted to see . . . and write down our ideas," said Thida Khus, an NGO director, in 2004. "Then we would meet with members of parliament every day and talk with them about our ideas . . . we focused on freedoms . . . expression, freedom of speech . . . democratic freedoms . . . and they listened to us."[47] Individual women and women-led NGOs and coalitions were the driving force behind civil society activism. They brought issues of equity to the table and reviewed constitutions from a variety of countries to articulate their own concerns. "We . . . had workshops and forums," says Khus, "and took several to the provinces and had dialogue." The group also mobilized the disparate peace movement to engage in the policymaking. "We moved in together," recalls Sochua. "We became issue-oriented, because the women started to define peace." The constitution that emerged reflects the diversity of issues and views. It is very liberal, says Khus. It provides for the protection of human rights and freedom from all forms of discrimination And though in the years since, Cambodia continues to struggle with the legacy of war, violence, corruption, and trauma, nonetheless, like the Guatemalan peace accords discussed in Chapter 3, the constitution also represents an ideal and a vision of a society toward which many Cambodians aspire.

In Rwanda, the new constitution unveiled in 2003 also resulted from extensive consultation at the local, provincial, and national levels. Like their Cambodian counterparts, the Rwandan women were active in the twelve-member constitutional commission that organized the consultative process. The women's movement, comprising civil society organizations and leading political figures in government and parliament, was pivotal in ensuring effective outreach to women at all levels. In November 2002, writes Powley, "Women from all social, economic and ethnic backgrounds participated in [a] national forum." In addition to parliamentarians and other national-level leaders, there were women farmers and "representatives of special interest groups, such as blind women, there on behalf of the physically handicapped, and students, including young women." The preparations prior to the national meetings ensured a level of confidence and knowledge among the representatives, enabling them to articulate a variety of concerns in the document. The women introduced issue statements pertaining to women's rights to inheritance and education, the inclusion of CEDAW in national law, and the establishment of a 30 percent quota for women in parliament. The farmers' representative, Powley says, inquired about loans and banking services for her constituency. The director of an orphanage recommended the "constitution establish a commission in charge of vulnerable young people."[48] A parliamentarian raised concerns regarding the church's jurisdiction over certain legal proceedings. Equality for all Rwandans, alongside the eradication of ethnic and regional divisions and the promotion of national unity, is among the most fundamental principles of the constitution, which was adopted by referendum in May 2003.

The constitutional process in Afghanistan was less lengthy, and women's activism there centered largely on gender equality. However, during the constitutional Loya Jirga of December 2003, women allied with minority ethnic groups such as the Uzbek. In supporting their efforts, they ensured that Uzbek gained status as an official language in regions where it was spoken widely. The willingness to recognize and reach out to minority groups strengthened the women's own stance, with wider recognition of the similarities between gender- and ethnicity-based discrimination. Sultan contends that even though not all Afghani women support minority group rights, the collective women's movement has "promulgated and been supportive of efforts to recognize the multi-ethnicity of Afghanistan and protect the rights of minorities."[49]

Key Afghan women were also leading voices in the struggle to promote human rights principles and practice across the country. Sima Samar, who gained prominence as minister of women's affairs, was appointed as the head of the newly formed Afghan Independent Human Rights Commission (AIHRC) in 2002. Its broad mandate included transitional justice, human rights education, and women's and children's rights. At its founding, five of the eleven commissioners were women. Writes Sultan, "In addition to symbolic leadership of the country's human rights instrument, Afghan women also have . . . proven valuable allies in efforts to recognize and manage the country's ethnic conflicts."[50]

A decade earlier in South Africa, women made their mark in the negotiations that led to the end of apartheid and a transition to democracy. As they unified across the political spectrum under the umbrella of the Women's National Coalition in 1992, South African women identified opportunities to ensure that not only issues of gender equality were enshrined in the agreements reached but that the constitution and legislative agenda embraced and supported the diverse nature of South African society. Reflecting on the process in 1999, Cheryl Carolus noted how the women's coalition lobbied hard to make the constitution and the government open and accepting of traditionally excluded constituencies. As a constitution, it firmly enshrines the rights of minorities and is explicit in banning discrimination based on a wide array of issues—from gender, race, and class to sexuality, pregnancy, physical and mental handicaps, and other conditions.

It is also unique in its articulation of the need to ensure participatory decisionmaking at the highest levels. The Women's National Coalition was the engine behind these principles. According to Carolus, "They successfully fought for participatory mechanisms in the Constitution that would require the government to consider input on policies from the population at large."[51]

Those principles came to the fore across the legislative agenda of South Africa's first fully democratic parliament, nowhere more so than in the debate about and development of a national security policy. Under most circumstances, national security issues are shrouded in secrecy and largely the domain of military and security experts. In the case of South Africa, as Nelson Mandela and the ANC moved toward victory over the apartheid regime, they faced the prospect of inheriting the white-dominated military and security services, which had been powerful key instigators of violence and oppression against the majority black population. Although the principles of civilian rule over the military and the creation of a multiracial force were central pillars of the ANC's policies, a larger question of defining new national security priorities was left open.

The ANC's leadership, in partnership with leading academics and anticonscription activists, many of whom were women, took the extraordinary step of revisiting accepted notions of national security. They reached out to civil society to ask simple questions such as, "What does security mean? And what are the threats facing the nation?" In this way, not only were notions of security broadened to include issues of health, education, environment, poverty, and other components of human- or people-centered security, but they also democratized the debate.

By 1994, South Africa had a new normative framework for national security policy in which principles of human security were central to the new paradigm. At the policy level, security was effectively demilitarized. The Parliamentary Sub-committee on Defence maintained strong ties with civil society groups, allowing for briefing and exchanges and public interactions. But the push-back from traditionalists was inevitable. By 1996, the committee was presented with a national defense review and recommendations for the nation's military needs.

The late General Rocky Williams recalled in a 2003 interview the initial push by the military and apartheid-era civil servants to manage a circumscribed consultative process within the defense and military sector. Again, women led the fight to reject the virtual fait accompli. Thandi Modise, chair of the parliamentary joint defense committee from 1999 to 2004, was a major force in demanding a national consultative process. "The Minister of Defence . . . asked the [parliamentary] committee to accept the review plan. . . . We said, 'go to the people.'"[52] Williams worked with Modise to ensure a broad-based consultative process.

The government sponsored town hall meetings and public gatherings nationwide. Using military equipment, they bussed and flew people in from rural areas. The women's movement brought forward the voices of women. The addressed a host of neglected issues, ranging from environmental degradation and military land usage to sexual harassment and gender inequality in the forces. There were questions raised about costs and expenditure. The security sector and those with related interests also had their say. The end result was not as utopian as the antimilitarists had hoped for. Yet the process was of profound importance. That people were given a chance to speak out, voice their opinions, and be included in the debate on a subject so sensitive resulted in renewed credibility and greater public trust in the security sector as a whole at a critical time. Arguably, without Modise's presence and adherence to the principles of participation and inclusion, the review would not have been as effective.[53]

Interdependence and Cooperation Across Party Lines

In the postwar reconstruction phase, Howard Wolpe and his colleagues write, "belligerent parties must come to an understanding that while some of their interests are in conflict . . . [they] have important interests in common and are fundamentally interdependent. . . . As a consequence they both stand to gain far more by collaboration than by military struggle."[54] This attempt to shift away from the zero-sum paradigm to a win-win solution is well understood and widely taught by the ever-expanding world of NGOs involved in conflict resolution, coexistence, and peacemaking. Although women are not always a specific target of such efforts, they appear more amenable to practicing it even at the highest levels.

In South Africa, Rwanda, Cambodia, and most recently Somalia and Iraq, women have led the way in forming cross-party caucuses around issues of common interest, typically matters that affect women most. In

South Africa, the Women's National Coalition paved the way for cross-party collaboration. In 1993, when the Transitional Executive Council (TEC) was established to work with local and national government entities to smooth the transition process, a subcommittee on the status of women was among the seven thematic committees formed to address critical issues. But it was unique in its reach across every other sector. The subcommittee was a venue for women across political parties to come together and move forward on a common agenda, and it had a formal mandate to review and ensure gender sensitivity across the works and reports of other committees.

In Rwanda, during the transition years, with start-up support from UNIFEM and other international agencies, women parliamentarians formed a cross-party caucus. Named the Forum of Women Parliamentarians, it was the first such caucus in Rwanda. Speaking in 2003, member of parliament (MP) Connie Bwiza Sekamana explained, "When it comes to the forum, we unite as women, irrespective of political parties. . . . [We think of] the challenges that surround us as women."[55] The forum reviews laws to ensure gender equality and offers amendments to discriminatory statutes. It also convenes meetings and trainings for women's groups to sensitize and advise them about legal issues.

Forum members see their contributions not only in terms of altering negative cultural attitudes toward women but also as affecting the "concept and thinking of Rwandan society." For example, the forum led efforts to revoke laws prohibiting women's inheritance of land. It was both an attempt at promoting women's rights and recognition that with the demographic imbalance and high percentage of women in the population, it was critical to Rwanda's long-term reconstruction that women—mothers, daughters, sisters, and their dependents—not be faced with eviction and further destitution. In approaching male colleagues, says one parliamentarian, "[We said,] OK fine, you think only men can inherit, not girls. But as a man you have a mother who might lose the property from your father because [your uncles] will take everything away from your mother. Would you like that? . . . When issues remain in the abstract . . . women and men become two distinct people. But the moment you personalize it, they do understand."[56]

By virtue of its existence in a difficult and ethnocentric political environment, the forum not only had to practice cooperation but also symbolized reconciliation for many, including other parliamentarians. "They worked across parties and ethnic lines. They are there as women leaders," writes Powley, quoting a male member of the labor party. "Their contribution is needed. . . . They are important to reconciliation."[57] Inspired by the forum's work, Rwandan MPs later created two other cross-party caucuses on population issues and regional peace.

In Cambodia, where political division and violence are rife even years after the peace agreement, NGOs such as Women for Prosperity, led by Pok Nanda, have successfully run programs that not only enable women's political participation but also encourage cross-party cooperation at the commune and provincial levels. Women for Prosperity focuses on difficulties facing women from all parties. It provides them with coaching and guidance on a variety of issues from public speaking to speechwriting, responding to constituents' demands and working with less than supportive male colleagues. Similar to Rwanda's parliamentary forum, it is both a means of strengthening women's political voice and a model of political cooperation for higher levels. In the run-up to the 2002 commune elections, Women for Prosperity trained over 5,500 women candidates.[58] A total of 954 won seats (8 percent of the total); two-thirds had received Women for Prosperity training and have continued their cooperation in the formal sphere. In Cambodia and elsewhere, the handful of women entering into a fraught political realm see cross-party cooperation as both a means of survival and a tactic for generating consensus around issues of common interest.

The cooperative strategy is one that UNIFEM and other international entities encourage and support in postconflict countries. Recognizing that women are in the minority even in cases in which quotas are imposed, UNIFEM sees the cross-party approach as a means of bringing synergy to their efforts; collectively they can be more influential than as individuals working their way through the system. One challenge they continue to face, however, is gaining and sustaining the numbers and presence across all decisionmaking structures.

Legislative Priorities: What Women Stand For

They tend to be inclusive and recognize the efficacy of cooperation, but what do women stand for? Their priorities vary across time and space and are typically in line with the issues facing their own countries. In Cambodia, as discussed earlier, where corruption is a key concern, women not only are symbols of anticorruption but also are among the leading anticorruption activists through their work in civil society organizations. In Rwanda, where reconciliation has been the focus, women in government and civil society have been at the forefront of the issue. In Afghanistan, they are engaged in education, health work, and development issues. Across Latin America and in South Africa, where defense and national security were among the most sensitive issues, they engaged directly.

In South Africa, for example, in the immediate post-transition years, women were the strongest advocates and defenders of the human security–centered national policy. Following the defense review, in 1999 the army's procurement program proposed the purchase of military equipment worth $4.5 billion from six contractors to the cabinet. Parliament had not approved the proposal. Civil society organizations, again women-dominated, protested the expenditure, arguing that South Africa faced no external threats. In parliament, women across the political spectrum spoke out. Suzanne Fos, MP for the Inkatha Freedom Party, recalls, "When [the women] spoke out, it wasn't about helicopters and dealing with obsolete equipment, it was about the amount of money being spent on the military when the country needed it so much more for development."[59] Key women resigned in protest of what was perceived as a whitewash of corruption among leading ANC figures. Pregs Govendar, a lifelong ANC member who was voted best parliamentarian of the year in 2002, was among those who resigned. "South Africa cannot afford such high military expenditure on arms while four million people living with HIV/AIDS have no access to treatment and care." In her official farewell speech, Govendar went further: "In this globalized world," she said, "war makes the profit margins that peace does not. We have to say loudly No! No! No! We will not accept that human life is so easily devalued and dispensable."[60]

In general, though, women entering politics pay less attention to security and defense, foreign affairs, or other seemingly gender-neutral issues or "hard areas." To be fair, a lack of knowledge and confidence can cause women to step away from these sectors. Yet if assistance is provided, and the issues are presented in such a way that women gain confidence, they do engage. For example, the South African experience resonated with women in Fiji, who were faced with a national defense review in 2004. Following just three days of workshop discussions, a group of women leaders met with governmental officials to question the review and offer concrete recommendations. The final review documents reflected a number of the concerns and actions noted by the women.[61] In 2003, Iraqi women were likewise keen to engage in security-related discussions. They sought to participate in the process of vetting candidates for the new army and police. Their approach was very pragmatic. Said one Baghdad-based politician in 2003, "In our neighborhoods we knew the men who had worked for Saddam and who hadn't. We could help select them. We tried to meet with the Coalition Provisional Authority to discuss this, but they didn't meet with us."[62] The women were not seen as contributors to the security situation, yet their proposal was efficient and potentially very effective.

Inevitably, new women politicians pay specific attention to structural factors, particularly legislation and customary laws and practices that impede women's lives. This is due in part to their personal convictions and their roots in women's rights activism. In addition, for many women private and public violence and discrimination are part of a continuum; as legislators, they feel compelled to act. International assistance (provided as part of major agencies' women's projects) reinforces this support *to* women *for* women's issues. Because available resources are limited, interventions often focus on an agenda of sociopolitical issues—those seen as most pressing to women's daily lives—instead of taking a more comprehensive approach; thus, issues relating to violence against women can become a priority. Yet questions of violence, trafficking, or prostitution not only touch on deeply rooted cultural norms and taboos, but are also linked to more complex issues of security, crime prevention, and economic development. If these issues are perceived as solely "women's issues," they are disconnected from the broader context, and neither the causes nor the consequences (e.g., prostitution as it links to HIV/AIDS and issues of public health) are adequately addressed.

The challenge for many women in politics is to gain sufficient support and understanding of the linkages. In other words, they have to see and show their colleagues that governmental policies that prevent equal access to health and education or laws and customs that perpetuate women's exclusion or enable violent perpetrators to act with impunity are related to the causes of conflict in society at large. Thus, attempts to change marriage laws and inheritance practices on one level not only benefit women directly, but can help dispel tensions that are fomented by sociocultural issues.

A 2005 World Bank study on postwar Liberia demonstrated the links. Traditional marital practices, including polygamy as practiced by tribal chiefs or "big men" and bride wealth payments, were among the root causes of the marginalization of young men and their propensity to join rebel and guerrilla movements. "Impoverished young men," says the report, "found it hard to pay bride wealth. 'Big men' allowed or encouraged their many young wives to sleep around, and assiduously pursued damages against any young man they caught. Court fines were often commuted to labor service in 'women damage' cases."[63] In effect, the young men became indentured laborers with little chance of ever accumulating their own wealth and saving enough to pay bride wealth, own land, or become "men." They remained perpetually oppressed by the traditional chieftancies. In this context, it is not surprising that many young men joined rebel movements that preached the rhetoric of equality and the promise of "manhood."

Demands for a ban on polygamy and the payment of bride wealth, which effectively make a woman hostage to her husband, are typically made by women's rights activists and perceived as women's issues. Yet as the World Bank study reveals, these social issues, seemingly of secondary importance, can be critical to either fueling conflict or, if addressed, can contribute to breaking the cycle of poverty and exclusion that young men are trapped in. As former US ambassador Don Steinberg says, issues often relegated as women's issues, deemed to be "soft" and of less relevance to "hard" security issues, are actually among the hardest to resolve. Even though they are directly relevant to the business of peacebuilding, they remain among the most neglected facets of that process.

Finally, the focus on inequality and women's discrimination in one sphere inevitably leads to discussions of other spheres. As in South Africa, the links between defense spending and the needs of the educational, health care, and welfare sectors can be easily drawn. Women-for-women is the door opener; it is a means of building relations, trust, and personal and collective confidence in taking an agenda forward. In Latin America it has been an effective stepping-stone toward women's involvement in the full range of political and governance issues. But the shift is not always visible or sustained. The reasons vary: many women are less interested or not at ease with the "hard" issues; they face pushback from male colleagues and leaders; and they receive less support, be it capacity building or technical assistance, from international actors for engagement in those sectors. There is also a significant generation gap. The first generation of politicians typically emerging from a conflict may seek to tackle the core issues, but if the momentum is not sustained by the next generation, any progress may be for naught. The danger is that women gain presence in politics, but they are effectively boxed into certain areas and voiceless in others.

Conclusion: Long-Term Impact or Flash in the Pan?

The immediate postconflict period provides a critical window of opportunity for women to enter and engage in the formal political arena. Where they have succeeded in gaining a foothold, women have not only symbolized change but also initiated it. They are often the first to develop cooperative and cross-party working structures. They tend to be more inclusive in their practices, particularly with regard to partnerships with civil society. They tackle many of the most deep-seated and difficult challenges facing their nations, from corruption to development and security sector reform. They expand the agenda to address the needs and concerns of socially excluded sectors of the population, particularly women. They also face significant challenges.

There is the inevitable question of which women. The fight for women's participation in politics, typically led by the educated, feminist, and often secular elite and increasingly resulting in the establishment of quotas for elections and parliamentary and even executive positions, has had varying results. The forces women activists struggle against, be they nationalists in Bosnia or conservative religious groups in the Middle East, have also learned to leverage and benefit from such measures. These developments create tension among the range of activists and advocates that may have supported the initiatives in the first place. For veteran peace activist Cora Weiss, for example, the issue of women alone is not enough. "We need to move away from the notion that ovaries alone qualify a person for participation."[64] It cannot be assumed that the women entering politics as a result of quotas or other mechanisms are naturally more conscious and supportive of human rights, equality, and other principles. Indeed, whether in Iraq, Bosnia, or the United States, the specter of women appointed to discharge the ideology of their political party to the detriment of social justice, peace, and equality is disturbing. So although the increased presence of women is important and can have both symbolic and actual value in promoting sustained peace, neither value should be assumed. Weiss points to the need to identify and support women who are proponents of human rights, peace, and equality.

Others agree in principle but note that in reality, the more conditions and expectations placed on women, the more they are excluded. The stories of conservative women shifting positions once they experience discrimination, or those in Iraq and elsewhere who appear more flexible and willing than their male cohorts to seek equitable solutions, are instructive. As Jacevic notes, their presence in and of itself is important, but it is not enough.

The push from civil society and the women-focused agencies and programs helps to open space for women. But sustained change comes through a combination of political leadership, deep societal shifts, and authentic women leaders at the national level. Few countries demonstrate all those conditions. In Iran, for example, conservative elements within the regime are resisting changes to laws that discriminate against girls and women. But society at large has moved forward. The average age of marriage is twenty-one for women, whereas the law allows for marriage at thirteen. By contrast, in neighboring Afghanistan legislation may espouse equality, but traditional values still run too deep. Alternatively, in Liberia, the authority and credibility of Johnson-Sirleaf is not questioned, but with literacy levels among women at approximately 15 percent and discrimination profound, the gains she makes may be short-term. Without delivering the services to improve the lives of ordinary people and make the necessary societal shifts, her tenure and impact may also be tenuous.

The underlying cultural forces that veer toward authoritarianism and patriarchy cannot be underestimated either. In a country like Rwanda, where the political reins are tightly held at the top, the genuine depth of commitment to women's participation in politics is difficult to gauge. Would the gains made since 1995 be sustained if President Paul Kagame left office? To what extent are political leaders exploiting women to further their own goals? What are the risks of backlash when women's political participation becomes overly politicized and is used in the power play between opponents and/or against international actors?

As the pendulum of society swings away from wartime to peacetime norms, the window for women can close. There is often an implicit collective desire to recapture a mythical past when life was good and societal norms were recognizable. It involves a return to traditional values, most significantly a reassertion of conservative gender roles. With men asserting their presence in the public sphere as decisionmakers and breadwinners, women with high public and political profiles suffer from a backlash and constraints on the issues they can address. The net result can be a reversal of gains made during conflict and a push back into the proverbial kitchen. A key challenge, therefore, is how to widen the inroads made during the transition years. Latin America offers critical lessons in this regard.

How women balance and integrate their peacemaking and political agenda with the inevitable agenda for the promotion of women's rights is also a key issue. It is not uncommon for women's groups supporting the candidacy of women to find that once in the system, their candidates do not automatically pursue or support gender equality initiatives. Many new politicians walk a fine line: the struggle to gain legitimacy and credibility among their counterparts (mainly men) and their local constituency can conflict with their interests in promoting women's rights (which is the interest of some or of a limited cross section of their constituency). They need to prove the linkages between issues of culture and discrimination and those of development and peacebuilding. In the words of a South African woman and ex-combatant turned politician, "Women cannot afford to stay out of politics because that is where decisions are made. . . . Women need to develop self-confidence to fight for their rights. Women should respect tradition and culture but never let it be used as a weapon against them. All issues are women's issues."[65]

On the substance of their political agenda too, women can face difficulty. They may be a moderating force, but if they also bring different legislative priorities and seek to reform the ways in which political business is conducted, they may and do shed light on complex issues and gaps in existing practices. That might put them at odds with the agenda of the international community, not to mention national counterparts that have entrenched interests. For example, in South Africa, the national security discourse has again tilted away from the ideals of human security, in part because of the reassertion of industrial and military interests in the political sphere. In Cambodia, the changes in attitude or struggles of women to transform the political setting go against the mainstream tides. Short-term gains are critical to longer-term sustainability, but too often the weight of business as usual or the fickle nature of international aid can slam the window shut.

What can or should be done to widen the space for women? First, women entering the political arena need support and capacity building. They (like their male counterparts) may lack the knowledge to pursue the full breadth of issues in economic, security, or foreign affairs. Often, women opt for (or are relegated to) the "soft issues" in the social sphere, which can be sidelined and thus receive limited resources. But effectiveness in health and education requires, at the very least, adequate financing. In turn, this means engagement in the decisionmaking of every area of government, especially big-budget areas such as defense and infrastructure. External actors can provide technical and financial resources to build women's knowledge and capacities. Global exchanges and networking among women politicians help bolster them. Encouragement from and interaction with women in civil society are also critical. This constituency can provide significant backup and technical assistance. Cross-party affiliations and women's caucuses are also essential.

Second, the collective expectations of women need to be tempered. Even where quotas are invoked to allow women's more effective participation, the actual numbers are still relatively few compared to men's participation. Yet there is an expectation that as 25 or 30 percent of the legislative body, they can and should have an influence over the majority. Without broader institutional and cultural changes, many women entering the arena are being set up for failure. Quotas are a means to an end, but too often they are perceived as ends in themselves.

Third, sustainability depends on a mix of political, economic, and social processes. It is not enough to educate girls and assume that they will bring change. The economic benefits and value that educated women can and do bring to society and their families must be publicized. Moreover, educational systems must also embrace and integrate principles of democracy, equality, and human rights, so that people value women and girls equally with boys and men from the outset. So long as women's second-class citizenship is considered as a norm and remains widely tolerated, women's access to and effectiveness in the political arena will be circumscribed.

The question of women's leadership also needs further exploration. Women in politics, as in other public arenas, are not fully aware of or utilizing their own gendered identity in the process of gaining power, negotiating, or wielding influence. Yet the question of what women bring remains important. They, more than the men, are under scrutiny to perform, make a difference, and prove their competence. In political environments dominated by men, unless women themselves are conscious of their approaches, the similarities across time and space, the difficulties they face and how others have overcome them, they can easily fail. It is also important for others to gain a better appreciation of what constitutes "feminine" leadership, its positive and negative implications, and how best to draw on the strengths of men and women and limit the weaknesses.

External support must move beyond the short-term, cosmetic, and technocratic to tackle the systemic and cultural factors that limit women's participation. For example, establishing women's affairs ministries or related posts is becoming common practice, but the outcomes and the effects of such institutions vary considerably from country to country. Too often they depend on the whims of the political leaders, the capacity of the individual running them, or the willingness of international donors to fund them. Quota systems are useful tools, but they need to have homegrown support. External support needs to be calibrated carefully to avoid a backlash. International actors should take their cue from local women in conflict areas. They understand their culture and know how best to navigate it.

Additionally, those in national or international institutions who readily embrace the rhetoric of women's participation are not always ready to support the potentially seismic shifts needed in the substance, process, and structure of governance. Thus on the one hand, the prevailing attitude is often the "add women and stir" formula. There is an implicit expectation that women will fit into existing structures and processes. On the other hand, women are heralded as change agents and transformative leaders. Yet the difficulty that existing institutions and norms (late-night voting, aggressive debating, old boys' networks, to name a few) present for women is an issue that is often neglected. These daily grind issues can be debilitating for women, most of whom, regardless of their political stature, still shoulder the responsibility of care at home.

Unless there is a willingness to address these underlying social and gender dynamics—what is deemed to be a man's or a woman's responsibility, how society and families perceive and treat women in politics, how the media portrays them, and so forth—the end result can be either women's failure or their withdrawal. In the words of South African Rocky Williams, organizational, political, and institutional transformations are essential, but cultural transformation is the most difficult. The environment, be it the military or the parliament, has to be more respectful of women, appreciating the values they add and supporting their progress. Said Williams in 2003, "Ultimately, if people are not going to feel at home in that [environment] or institution, you have not succeeded."[66]

Conflict opens the space and, despite the devastation wreaked by violence, provides an opportunity for profound societal change in its aftermath. Women entering politics bring a breath of fresh air. They can and often are transformative in their leadership, agenda setting, and commitment to peace. But they cannot do it alone. To succeed, they need a paradigm shift and deep-rooted change in social and political culture and institutions. The questions remain: Are international actors or national policymakers willing to acknowledge the potential contributions of women to peace and security? Will they help widen the opportunities afforded by the postconflict period or let the window shut?

Notes

1. "Female Heads of State and Government, Currently in Office," *Worldwide Guide to Women in Leadership.* The full list is available at http://www.guide2womenleaders.com, including nonelected heads of state such as monarchs.

2. *Women in Parliament,* World Averages, Interparliamentary Union, available at http://www.ipu.org/wmn-e/world.htm.

3. Ian Fisher and Stephen Erlanger, "Women, Secret Hamas Strength, Win Votes at Poll and New Role," *New York Times,* February 3, 2006, available at http://select.nytimes.com.

4. Thanassis Cambanis, "Islamist Women Redraw Palestinian Debate on

Rights," *Boston Globe,* January 21, 2006, available at http://www.boston.com.

5. Chris McGreal, "Women MPs Vow to Change Face of Hamas," *The Guardian,* February 18, 2005, available at http://www.guardian.co.uk, retrieved July 18, 2006.

6. Agence France Press, *Chilean Women Ready to Defy Macho Politics,* January 13, 2006, available at http://news.yahoo.com.

7. Interview with the author, New York, 1999.

8. Discussion with the author, Washington, DC, January 2006.

9. Presentation by the Democratization Department, Mission to BiH, OSCE, 2001, made available to the author by kind permission of Initiative for Inclusive Security, 2005.

10. Swanee Hunt, *This Was Not Our War: Bosnian Women Reclaiming the Peace* (Durham, NC: Duke University Press, 2004), pp. 140–141.

11. Milena Pires, *Enhancing Women's Participation in Electoral Processes Postconflict: The Case of East Timor,* January 2004, UN Office of the Special Adviser on Gender Issues and the Advancement of Women, Experts Group Meeting, EGM/ELEC/2004/EP.6, available at http://www.un.org, retrieved January 30, 2006.

12. Sally Armstrong, *Veiled Threat: The Hidden Power of Afghan Women* (London: Four Walls, Eight Windows, 2002), p. 178.

13. Masuda Sultan, *From Rhetoric to Reality: Afghan Women on the Agenda for Peace* (Washington, DC: Hunt Alternatives Fund, 2004).

14. Speech made by President Bush in honor of International Women's Day, March 2006. The full text is available at http://usinfo.state.gov.

15. USAID, *Agency Objectives: Governance,* available at http://www.usaid.gov/democracy/gov.html.

16. World Bank, "Measuring the Quality of Governance," July 14, 2003, available at http://web.worldbank.org.

17. UNDP, *Promoting Democracy Through Reform,* available at http://www.undp.org/governance/index.htm.

18. The Post-Conflict Reconstruction project is a joint initiative of the Center for Strategic and International Studies and the Association of the United States Army.

19. Roland Paris, *At War's End: Building Peace After Civil Conflict* (Cambridge, UK: Cambridge University Press, 2004), pp. 5–10.

20. Howard Wolpe et al., "Rebuilding Peace and State Capacity in War-Torn Burundi," *Round Table* 93, no. 375 (July 2004): 457–467.

21. Ibid.

22. Ibid.

23. Elizabeth Powley, *Strengthening Governance: The Role of Women in Rwanda's Transition* (Washington, DC: Hunt Alternatives Fund, 2004).

24. Ibid.

25. Catalina Rojas, *In the Midst of War: Women's Contribution to Peace in Colombia* (Washington, DC: Hunt Alternatives Fund, 2004).

26. *Cambodian Women Running for Peace,* E-journal, USAID, August 2005, available at http://usinfo.state.gov.

27. Name withheld, interview with the author, Tehran, Iran, 2003.

28. Sultan, *From Rhetoric to Reality,* pp. 21–23.

29. Author's discussion with workshop leaders involved in working with

political party members in Iraq, spring 2006.

30. Notes from the Iraqi Women's Movement Meeting, October 16, 2006, Baghdad, Iraq, available at http://www.wluml.org.

31. Ibid.

32. "Don't Turn Your Back on My Country," *Independent,* January 5, 2007, available at http://runningafrica.com.

33. Bill Cromier, "Women Come to South America's Defence," *Associated Press,* January 31, 2007.

34. Robin Toner, "Women Wage Key Campaigns for Democrats," *New York Times,* March 24, 2006.

35. Ibid.

36. David Dollar, Raymond Fisman, and Roberta Gatti, "Are Women Really the 'Fairer' Sex? Corruption and Women in Government," Policy Research Report on Gender and Development, Working Paper Series, No. 4 (Washington, DC: World Bank, 1999).

37. Powley, *Strengthening Governance.*

38. Laura McGrew, Kate Frieson, and Sambath Chan, *Good Governance from the Ground Up: Women's Roles in Post-Conflict Cambodia* (Washington, DC: Hunt Alternatives Fund, 2004).

39. Ibid.

40. Ibid.

41. Paris, *At War's End,* pp. 194–195.

42. Information provided on the Afghan Women's Network site at http://www.afghanwomensnetwork.org, retrieved July 20, 2006.

43. Powley, *Strengthening Governance,* p. 28.

44. Rojas, *In the Midst of War.*

45. Based on discussions with NGO leaders in Ramallah, Palestine, 2002.

46. Mu Sochua interview, 1999, part of which is published in Sanam Anderlini, *Women at the Peace Table* (New York: UNIFEM, 2000).

47. McGrew, Frieson, and Chan, *Good Governance,* pp. 8–9.

48. Powley, *Strengthening Governance,* pp. 26–27.

49. Sultan, *From Rhetoric to Reality,* pp. 22–23.

50. Ibid.

51. Anderlini, *Women at the Peace Table,* pp. 32–33.

52. Sanam Naraghi Anderlini, *Negotiating the Transition to Democracy and Reforming the Security Sector: The Vital Contributions of South African Women* (Washington, DC: Hunt Alternatives Fund, 2004), p. 23.

53. Ibid.

54. Wolpe et al., "Rebuilding Peace."

55. Quoted in Powley, *Strengthening Governance,* p. 27.

56. Ibid., pp. 28–29.

57. Ibid.

58. *Cambodian Women Running for Peace,* E-journal, USAID, August 2005.

59. Anderlini, *Negotiating the Transition,* pp. 27–28.

60. Ibid.

61. The author cofacilitated the workshop in Suva, Fiji, 2003.

62. Discussion with the author, Washington, DC, November 2003.

63. Paul Richards et al., "Community Cohesion in Liberia: A Post-War

Rapid Social Assessment," World Bank, Social Development Papers 31443, no. 21, January 2005, pp. 17–18.

64. Discussion with the author, New York, July 2005.

65. Quoted in Dyan Mazurana, *African Women in Armed Opposition Groups in Africa and the Promotion of International Humanitarian Law and Human Rights, Reports of a Workshop* (Geneva: PSIO and Geneva Call, November 2005), p. 46, available at http://www.genevacall.org/resources/publications .htm.

66. Anderlini, *Negotiating the Transition,* p. 25.

SIX

Transitional Justice and Reconciliation

Prisoners used to be afraid of even looking at victims. . . . But with time they came and asked for forgiveness because we encouraged them. Those who were released help us in fetching water, renovate our houses and to do our gardens. In return we give them food.
—Rwandan woman, widowed during the 1994 genocide

TRC Commissioner: Do you have any question to ask the commission?
Augusta Amara: I want to talk about my education, I want you to assist me with my education because I want to learn. I want you to assist my mother because I have lost my father.
TRC Commissioner: Do you want the government to do anything for you?
Augusta Amara: Yes, I want them to assist in my education.
—Extract from the Sierra Leone TRC transcript. As a young girl, Amara was abducted and raped by the RUF in Sierra Leone.

Cambridge, Massachusetts, 2003: "What kind of peace do we have if the men who raped and killed women now sit in the government?" Claudine Tayaye Bibi, a Congolese peace activist, asked the question at the start of a workshop on transitional justice. The participants were women peace activists—a Palestinian, a Bosnian, a Colombian, a Kosovar, a Rwandan, a Guatemalan, and a Burundian. Among them, her words resonated deeply. Drawing on their experiences, some personal, others based on their work and interactions with women in their communities, the group was well aware of the complexity and sensitivity of the issues. A Pandora's box was opening.

For those who had been victims themselves, the yearning for justice was palpable, not because they sought revenge, but because the experiences

153

never went away. "The memories come back in waves," said one woman. Yet they had learned to put aside their personal emotions to address the issues more broadly. On the one hand, political pragmatism was a driving force with which they were familiar; it was better to give blanket amnesties to end the war and tolerate the impunity than to watch the violence go on. On the other hand, they all agreed, ending impunity and bringing accountability for crimes committed during war would not only bringing justice but also helping to end the cycle of violence based on revenge and retribution. In other words, they argued, true peace is possible and sustainable only with justice. But in the context of modern wars, who are the victims? They are not just those killed or disappeared. Increasingly, they are among the ranks of the innocent, with limbs hacked off, born of rape, infected with the HIV/AIDS virus; in the eyes of many, they are the living dead. Who are the perpetrators? In Liberia, Sierra Leone, Nepal, and Uganda, to name a few, they include children; abducted, abused, often raped, and in turn forced to murder and maim. They are victims and perpetrators in one. The end of war brings no less clarity or solace. Rapist and victim, killer and survivor, have to live side by side again.

The demand for justice and accountability is almost visceral in nature, but those living with the reality of war recognize the complexity of the issues. They live in a shaded world of grays where the indictment of a war criminal does not suffice or address the very practical and daily needs of his surviving victims. In such contexts, justice is needed, but it can and must take many forms.

In this chapter I explore women's contributions to transitional justice processes, primarily tribunals and truth and reconciliation commissions (TRCs). I do not attempt to negate women's roles in perpetrating violence, acting as accomplices, or being passive witnesses to crimes. That is a fact of life in times of war. Nor do I deny women's victimization. That is amply dealt with in other works and raised below in the context of the tribunals noted. The discussion here draws attention to women's presence and activism in the development of the mechanisms that seek justice, promote national reconciliation, and bring a semblance of closure in the aftermath of conflict.

I reflect on how women expand and alter the substance of discussions, how they affect the processes and institutions, and what implications their involvement has on the outcomes of tribunals and commissions established to address crimes committed during conflict. In doing so, I highlight the limitations of existing international efforts, which tend to emphasize criminal justice and legal and judicial reforms. Through women's experiences, I also draw attention to the shortcomings of existing mechanisms in addressing the practical needs of victims—from reparations or support and care, to access to health care and education, to opportunities to become skilled and employed—which not only have direct implications for peacebuilding but also enable those people to move beyond their victimhood. I argue that the process of transitional justice must embrace and address the need for *social* justice, so that those most affected have a chance to live dignified lives, free of discrimination and ostracism.

Transitional Justice

Transitional justice is the term used to describe temporary judicial and sometimes nonjudicial mechanisms developed to address the legacy of war or dictatorial rule. Transitional justice has become a key pillar of the international community's postconflict reconstruction framework. In theory, it encompasses attempts at healing divisions within society resulting from human rights abuses and violence, provides justice for victims and brings accountability by perpetrators, enables "truth telling" to create an accurate historical record of events and allow individuals and society at large to get closure, restores or establishes the rule of law, reforms institutions with the goal of preventing human rights violations, and promotes coexistence and sustainable peace.[1] A tall order by any account. It is made more complex by the fact that transitional justice incorporates both justice and reconciliation, concepts that appear to be diametrically opposite each other, except for the fact that they share a goal of ending the cycle of violence and destruction.

In reality, much of the international community's engagement in transitional justice has taken place primarily through judicial processes such as the International Criminal Tribunals for the Former Yugoslavia (ICTY) and Rwanda (ICTR), the Sierra Leone Special Court, and the Iraq Special Tribunal. Within these processes, the focus has been primarily on retributive justice—in other words, trying and holding perpetrators accountable for past actions and meting out punishment or corrective actions for wrongdoing. By and large, the focus has been on leaders and the senior ranks of the various armed entities, as opposed to the foot soldiers and followers who are most directly implicated in the acts of violence.

From a distance, the reasons are understandable: war is a messy business, and attempting to convict every single person implicated in a crime is unrealistic. Close up, particularly for the victims and survivors, sanctioning impunity for the vast majority of perpetrators may not be so acceptable. But they have limited say. A driving force behind the establishment of war crimes tribunals is prevention. In supporting these institutions, the international community is intending to send a message to others engaged in carnage or would-be warlords that their day in court will also come.

Have the tribunals had the stated effect? The jury is hung. The ICTR and ICTY have featured on the global landscape for nearly a decade, yet they have not stopped the ravaging of Darfur. In Uganda, the International Criminal Court's indictment of Joseph Kony, leader of the notorious Lord's Resistance Army, received mixed responses among the locals who suffered most at his hands. A common refrain among local communities most devastated by the LRA was peace first, justice later. Some civil society groups reportedly favored amnesty provisions to bring the LRA out of the bush, but that goes against the ICC's provisions. In February 2007, leaders of the LRA hired lawyers to represent them at the ICC. At the time of this writing, the situation was not fully resolved. Although the Ugandan government and LRA have signed a cease-fire agreement and other protocols, the process is incomplete. Ultimately, if Kony were given amnesty by the Ugandan government, it could have a detrimental impact on the credibility of the ICC.[2]

The effectiveness of the courts is also questionable in terms of the specific conflicts they address. From 1997, when the first case was tried, to May 2005, the ICTR, based in Tanzania, handed down nineteen judgments.[3] The ICTY, although functioning at a better pace, has created a mix of frustration and ambivalence among citizens in the Balkans. As of March 2006, it had indicted 161 people. But the judgments passed are only half the story, if issues of peace and reconciliation hang in the balance. Writing in 2004, scholar and activist Julie Mertus noted the disillusionment and disappointment that Bosnians felt toward the court at The Hague. The trials, held in a distant country, mostly in an unfamiliar language, gave no sense of ownership to locals. Few connected to, accepted, or acknowledged their relevance. There was also anger at the perceived bias of the court because key leaders of the war remain free.[4]

In Rwanda the dissonance is starker. The accused wait in jailhouses in Tanzania, many with HIV/AIDS, receiving antiretroviral drugs courtesy of the international community. Meanwhile, their victims—mostly women and girls—are dying slowly in poverty, of the HIV they contracted while being raped. The hands and pockets of the international community rarely extend so long or deep as to assist them.[5]

Still, say human rights activists, warlords such as Charles Taylor are not getting away with murder like their predecessors. That is a major

step in the right direction. The courts have also made significant contributions to the development of international law, as discussed below.
By virtue of their existence, they have exposed many of the constraints
and complexities that hamper attempts to bring justice in a postconflict
setting. In Bosnia, for example, the dissatisfaction paved the way for a
War Crimes Chamber (WCC) located in BiH. The ICTY and Office of the
High Representative (OHR) established the WCC in 2005, but the objective is to make it Bosnian-led by the end of 2007. Those are positive
developments for the field.

Truth and reconciliation commissions are also gaining ground, offering an alternative approach, and are preferable to many national governments emerging from civil war. Although some TRCs have a judicial
mandate, they are better known for providing space to ordinary citizens
to come forth and tell their stories, in an attempt to bring out "the truth."
Perpetrators are also given the chance to admit to their past acts. In the
South African context, the TRC was able to offer amnesty, and explicit
efforts were made to promote reconciliation through its processes. The
"R" of reconciliation can, however, be akin to a whitewash, an easy
escape clause for governments, the military, or elites involved in the
shady business of human rights abuse. The lack of rigorous due process is
among the reasons for international bias toward formal judicial processes
as opposed to TRCs.

This bias is most noticeable in terms of the resources allocated for
such mechanisms, compared to those allocated for reconciliation or
even restorative forms of justice. The ICTR and ICTY have budgets of
approximately $90–$100 million per year and have been operating since
the late 1990s.[6] In Sierra Leone, the international community agreed to
a $25 million per annum budget for the Special Court, although initial
start-up costs in its first two years of operation resulted in increases to
some $34 million. In December 2004, the UN and the government of
Cambodia agreed on a $56 million budget over three years for the
establishment of a special court to try aging leaders of the Khmer
Rouge.[7] In comparison, the Sierra Leone TRC struggled with a budget
of some $5 million.

Ultimately, compared to the estimated $5 billion necessary for
international peacekeeping operations in 2005–2006, or the cost of a
single day of war in Iraq—$195 million, excluding amounts spent on
reconstruction—the sums spent on international tribunals are modest.[8]
But contrasted to the economies of the countries they focus on, the
livelihoods of the victims they aim to represent, or the amounts dedicated to TRCs or support to victims, the dollar figures can seem vastly
inflated.

These realities resonate across national and international boundaries. Reflecting on developments in transitional justice, journalist Helena Cobban notes that by 2005, the experiences of the ICTY and ICTR had led many pro-prosecution theorists to acknowledge that their tools may not be best suited for postconflict settings. There is a convergence of different disciplines. Nonviolent conflict resolution initiatives "from the ground up" are gaining ground, and development practices are broadening to address issues of impunity at the grassroots and the rule of law.[9] Cobban points to increasing recognition of the need to draw out the preferences of local actors, but like so much else in postconflict efforts, even that remains an imperfect work in progress.

Invisible Women and International Justice Mechanisms

The invisibility of women in transitional justice processes still needs to be addressed adequately. Prior to the ICTY and ICTR, war crimes tribunals or truth commissions were blind to the gendered dimension of political violence and war. The international tribunals in Nuremberg and Tokyo made no mention of rape, although thousands of Korean women—known as "comfort women"—were forced into prostitution by the Japanese military. In the Geneva Conventions, rape was originally recognized as an "honor crime." Even in the 1993 reports of the Salvadoran truth commission, rape was excluded because it was not regarded as a "politically motivated crime." In the case of Guatemala, rape was included under acts of torture.[10]

The general silence about sex-based crimes results partly from underreporting. Victims are faced with a difficult choice. Disclosure can result in shame and ostracism from their communities. Too often, women and girls are blamed for the violence inflicted on them and further victimized by their own families for bringing dishonor. In Iraq in 2006, for example, women's rights activists were concerned that the Special Tribunal is not addressing rape and sexual violence committed by Saddam Hussein's Ba'athist regime, although there is ample evidence of such crimes.[11] Beyond broader concerns about the legitimacy of the court and the ongoing violence surrounding it, the difficulty women face is largely cultural. Rape is considered to be the most shameful act that could be brought upon a family, and the female victim is held responsible. Coming forward can result not only in further trauma but reprisals and increased vulnerability to attack. Yet silence can mean that the crime remains invisible; perpetrators walk free, often in the same communities as their victims, with the latter having no means of legal redress, protection, or access to reparations.

In addition to the cultural barriers, there are pragmatic challenges. Where sex-based crimes have been pervasive—Peru, Guatemala, Sierra Leone, Bosnia, Rwanda, the DRC—the task of identifying and prosecuting every perpetrator is daunting. Encouraging victims to come forth and offering them protection in court and support in their communities afterward have also proven to be beyond the capacities of most international agencies. The difficulties also stem from a lack of sensitivity to women's experiences in international forums addressing peace and security issues, which is directly linked to the absence of women from the peace table, where issues of war crimes and amnesty provisions are often addressed. Women's rights activists often suggest that men are forgiving men for crimes committed against women.[12] The reality is more disturbing—in instances such as Iraq, for those at the table, sexual and other violent crimes against women are either not known or deliberately ignored. Thus the need for them to be acknowledged, addressed, or even forgiven does not arise. Willful ignorance wins the day.

Breaking the Barriers

There have been important developments nonetheless. In the 1990s, women made their presence known and felt in the development of transitional justice mechanisms in Africa and Europe. In 1992, women's rights groups, together with other human rights groups, agitated for an end to the overt targeting, systematic rape, and sexual abuse of women in the Balkans.[13] News of the notorious rape camps had made its way into the UN system. Mertus writes, "By December 1992 . . . the Security Council issued a declaration condemning wartime rape, and describing the rapes taking place as 'massive, organized, and systematic.'"

Did the rape camps and this vile form of ethnic cleansing catalyze international action for the formation of a court? In the minds of many who were involved in the processes at the time, the connections are clear. Gabrielle Kirk McDonald, the first American to serve as a judge at the ICTY, recounts how the international community decided to prosecute the perpetrators, even as it seemed unable or unwilling to stop the war, "when [it] witnessed the horrific method of ethnic cleansing."[14] Security Council Resolution 808 makes clear reference to the "treatment of Muslim women in Yugoslavia" as it declares the establishment of a tribunal to prosecute war crimes.[15]

The recognition of rape as a strategy of ethnic cleansing and war paved the way for Bosnian and international women's rights advocates to demand that sexual violence during the war be treated as a grave violation of international law, not just a by-product of war. By 1993, when the UN Conference on Human Rights was taking shape, the movement had gained global reach, through the Internet and networks of solidarity, says Mertus. As the UN Office of Legal Affairs was drafting the statute for the ICTY, women's rights activists were among key advocates shaping the institution.

Six issues were key: (1) the participation of women's rights advocates in the negotiations for the ICTY statutes; (2) inclusion of language on witness protection and equity; (3) prosecution of wartime rape and other forms of sexual violence in conflict; (4) ending impunity in cases of sexual violence and deterring perpetrators; (5) providing a model for addressing the gendered dimensions of war crimes in future international criminal courts; and (6) using the event as a means of educating the public about women's human rights and raising awareness of the horrific nature of crimes committed against women.[16]

Women's rights activists also pressed for the inclusion of experts with experience in gender-based violence and crimes within the structures of the ICTY. This pressure contributed to the appointment of some women with expertise in related areas. It also raised awareness of the gender dimensions of war crimes among the staff in general.

Working in parallel motion, but further away from the eyes of the world in Rwanda, women's grassroots organizations played a pivotal role in drawing attention to the experiences of women during the genocide, particularly the use of rape as a weapon. In 1998, the ICTR, under the presidency of a female South African judge, Navanetham Pillay, set a new international precedent not only by defining rape as a crime against humanity and an instrument of genocide, but also by making the first conviction on these grounds in the case of a former mayor, Jean-Paul Akayesu.[17] Speaking after the verdict, Judge Pillay said, "Rape had always been regarded as one of the spoils of war. Now it is a war crime, no longer a trophy."[18] This single case set the precedent for not only the ICTY but also the International Criminal Court statute, as discussed later.

As the ICTR was taking shape, the South African TRC, born out of the interim constitution and enacted through the 1995 Promotion of National Healing and Reconciliation Act, was also in place. On the surface, its mandate did not draw special attention to the experiences of women. There were no official quotas or earmarks for the inclusion of women among its leadership and the commissioners. Yet because the transition process in South Africa was marked by efforts to ensure the inclusion of every sector and women had mobilized an effective movement, they were present in significant numbers: 41 percent of the commissioners were women, of whom 43 percent were black, 29 percent white, 14 percent mixed race, and 14 percent of Indian descent. Writing in 2005, Pumla Gobodo-Madikezela celebrates the commitment to "transparency" that led to this progressive balance in numbers.[19]

By the late 1990s, it was clear that a sea change was taking place, and women were at the center of it. What did they bring? Did they succeed in bringing visibility to crimes committed against women? How did they contribute to the substance and process of these institutions and the loftier goals of transitional justice? The discussion below centers on key goals that transitional justice processes and mechanisms seek to attain, namely, revealing the truth about violations during conflict; reforms in judicial and institutional reform in legislation, procedures, and practices; and the promotion of reconciliation. It focuses on the impact that women's participation, as judges, lawyers, staff, witnesses, and civil society advocates, has had on the truth commissions and tribunals established since the early 1990s.

Revealing the "Whole" Truth: Women's Voices and Experiences

Revealing the whole truth and acknowledging the legacy of abuses is central to transitional justice mechanisms—tribunals or commissions. Yet oversight and ignorance in transitional justice mechanisms of the differential experiences of women and men (i.e., a gendered perspective) have, in many instances, resulted in the opposite. Julissa Mantilla, gender adviser to the Peruvian Truth and Reconciliation Commission, explains the implications most succinctly.[20] In the case of Peru, the commission operated on certain assumptions. Cases involved one victim, typically a man who was disappeared, and one crime—the disappearance or likely murder. Without a gender perspective, she notes, there is only one victim. But when the lens is broadened to view the crime from the standpoint of both men and women, we find that for every person who was disappeared, there is often a mother and a wife who searched for him. "These women were often subjected to sexual and physical assault, including rape. So instead of just one crime and one victim, we are faced with perhaps three victims and two or three forms of crime."[21] In the case of women who were themselves disappeared and killed as a result of their political activities or affiliations, in Peru, as in Guatemala, they were often subjected to rape prior to the murder. In Guatemala, indigenous women were also forcibly sterilized. These stark examples illustrate how gendered the issue of human rights abuse can be and how it can affect the scope of the investigation, the nature of expertise needed to pass judgment, and so forth.

Initially on a three-month contract to integrate "gender" into the workings and reports of the Peruvian TRC, Mantilla had her work cut out for her. The silence surrounding sexual violence and rape, typically against women but also men, was deafening. In addition to social taboos that made discussions of rape difficult for many, Mantilla found a dearth of information about sexual violence. National human rights organizations had not documented the cases. The commission had limited resources to address the issues. Knowledge of the potentially different experiences of men and women during the period under investigation was also limited. Mantilla and her team of two set out to fill the gaps. "Inevitably, we had to prioritize," she recalls. "Some issues, such as sexual violence against men, we just could not address with the resources we had." They were addressed under the framework of torture (Chapter 3 of the commission's report). But of the issues they did cover, namely women's experiences of abuse, the team developed innovative strategies for outreach to rural communities. They developed a cartoon booklet in which men discuss the need for addressing violence against women. They established gender focal points at the commission's local offices to help establish trust and enable the collection of testimonies. They also reached out to women's groups and NGOs, often formed by the mothers and relatives of those who had disappeared, to collect information. These organizations were not archetypal human rights groups, but they could provide much of the information that was missing. Their contributions to the investigations were critical to the airing of the "whole truth."

Mantilla's three months extended to two years, and still many gaps remained. But her presence and perseverance broke the silence about rape, exposing a vast and complex dimension of the truth, and contributed to Peru's acknowledgment of pervasive violence against women across the country. According to Peruvian feminist Marruja Barrig, the exposure of sexual violence during the conflict "helped draw the 'linkages,'" break the silence on "the daily sexual abuse women are suffering in their homes and in the streets," and open a window onto a "church-dominated discourse on sexuality."[22]

In South Africa too, despite the unprecedented balance of men and women in the structures of the TRC, recognition of the need to provide women with a space to describe crimes committed against them—sexual and otherwise—was an afterthought. Although the commissioners, particularly the women, were sensitive to the gender dimensions of human rights abuse and sought to include women's experiences, the forum neither was conducive to the revelation of forms of abuse that women felt were taboo subjects nor acknowledged the trauma and hardship that women endured as an integral and daily aspect of the apartheid experience. There was also criticism from women's rights activists, who argued that women witnesses were not coming forth to speak of their own experiences, but of their husbands, brothers, or sons, thereby reinforcing the notion that women were secondary victims, that they had been less affected, and thus their stories and contributions to the cause were of less importance than those of men.[23]

In response, the TRC created the Special Hearings on Women and used its outreach programs nationwide to encourage women to come forward. An all-women panel was formed, writes Gobodo-Madikezela, "in order to encourage women to speak freely about their experiences of human rights violations."[24] There were seventeen testimonies at the hearings, two provided by men. They focused on women's different experiences in the Johannesburg area during the apartheid years with a view, notes Gobodo-Madikezela, to creating a "more complete picture of the way in which both men and women . . . experienced human rights violations in South Africa." Implicit to the process, much like the TRC itself, the testimonies represented the lived experiences of thousands of others. They were the individual stories with universal reach.

The hearings sought not only to bring visibility and validation to women's experiences, but also to acknowledge that their contributions and suffering were equal to those of men. In effect, they recognized the ordinary and often daily forms of violence—the group removals, harassment, separation from families, and physical and sexual abuse in the private sphere (by black and white men)—alongside the extraordinary violence of torture, kidnappings, and killings. It was also about giving women their own identity and space. Reflecting on Sheila Masote, the first woman to testify at the hearings, Gobodo-Madikezela writes, "Her identity was defined by men as she grew up and when she was married." But at the hearings, Masote articulates the importance of being and speaking about herself. "I'm always either Zef's daughter . . . Mike Masote's wife . . . but now I feel I am me. And this is why I am here."[25]

Addressing and giving equal weight to the two dimensions—the extraordinary "gendered" violence and the less obvious but more pervasive forms—proved to be a difficult task for the Special Hearings. Many

*question of identity, everybody doesn't define their identity →
in the
same
way.*

women, especially fighters with experience of abuse, did not come forth. Those women had struggled to create an identity to protect themselves in the face of sexual abuse and harassment from men in their own ranks as well as those in the apartheid regime. Coming forward was risking their identity and losing credibility in the public sphere. One former fighter was unwilling to face her abusers and risk the trauma of returning to the state of powerlessness she had felt during captivity.[26]

In this context, the testimony of Yvonne Khutwane, a lifelong political activist, took on a new dimension, when she went forward to "tell the whole truth." She spoke of her activism and contributions to the struggle, writes Vasuki Nesiah, the interrogations and solitary confinement, the beatings and torture, and house burning, experiences that others mentioned too. But Khutwane also spoke of rape by a policeman. As it is elsewhere, in South Africa rape was a feature of the abusive landscape, yet few women spoke of it overtly. For the TRC it created a dilemma. On the one hand, the commissioners wanted to acknowledge that rape did take place widely; on the other hand, the testimonies and witnesses did not speak of it. Khutwane's story became the rape case to represent all the others. But in the retelling and reframing process it was distorted. Nesiah writes, "Khutwane's story to the commission was one of resilience, survival and continued political commitment to the struggle against apartheid—it would be tragic if this inspiring and courageous 'truth telling' regarding her experience of human rights abuse is reduced to the 'truth' about her rape."[27]

In her in-depth review of women's testimonies, anthropologist Fiona Ross also critiques the commission for its distillation of women's experiences into victimhood only.[28] By virtue of its limited mandate, victim-perpetrator dichotomy, and other factors, the commission did not embrace the complexity of experiences. Yet on the issue of sexual violence, the South African TRC, like its successor in Peru, was caught in a difficult position. To establish the fact of sexual violence, there is a need for cases to be brought forth, but few if any survivors are willing to take the risk. As a result, the handful of cases that are brought forward and that can be tried are framed as examples of those that remain unheard. Each individual story is used to represent a more general truth. By stripping the individual cases of their broader context, however, the commissions can inadvertently do disservice to the business of "truth telling" and the individual women who have the courage to come forth.

As Nesiah says, "The challenge for us is to assist future commissions to enable women's voices in the public sphere and represent women's experience of human rights abuse in more complex ways—recognize that they are not just points on a graph that will help us buttress statistics about sexual abuse, they are also activists with complex responses to human rights abuse."[29]

For all its flaws, some of the experiences gained in the South African case have resonated widely. The mandate for the Sierra Leone TRC explicitly addressed rape and sexual violence against women. The push by women inside and outside the Sierra Leone TRC process, as civil society actors and at the UN, shone a light on the vast extent to which rape and sexual abuse were used by all sides. As women's rights activist and scholar Binaifer Nowrojee writes, "Sierra Leone's conflict conjures up images of hacked-off hands and arms . . . yet sexual violence was committed on a much larger scale."[30] Quoting UN sources, Nowrojee notes that some 72 percent of women and girls were subject to human rights abuse, and 50 percent of them were subjected to sexual violence, rape, gang rapes, or rape with objects such as sticks and umbrellas.[31] Yet throughout the war, these crimes were largely invisible and underreported. The women's special hearings changed that, allowing women to come forward in a safe space, surrounded by supporters, to tell their stories. Although, as Nesiah notes, there is danger of distilling the full experience into the act of rape, in Sierra Leone the information and stories that came forth exposed not only the rape but the complexity of other traumas: witnessing the murder of relatives, of having pregnant bellies ripped open and babies slaughtered, of being kidnapped and forced into "marriage" with those who had killed your family, of the sexual slavery of young girls.

The Sierra Leone TRC report addresses the experience of women in its preliminary conclusions, as well as dedicating a full section to the issues. Similarly, in the Timor Leste Commission, the links between conflict and daily violence in the lives of ordinary people, particularly women, are noted. Says Nesiah, the TRC "report demonstrates how forced displacement resulted in a range of harms for women, from starvation to exacerbated vulnerability, to sexual abuse; from forced labor to denial of fundamental freedoms; the deprivation of women's civil and political rights were intricately tied here to the denial of their social and economic rights."[32]

In each case, women as advocates, commission staff, and perhaps most importantly as witnesses have been central to the process of exposing hidden truths about human rights violations in conflict. As Nowrojee says, recalling the first day of the Special Hearings on Women in Sierra Leone in March 2003, the chamber was packed, "gasps and tears could be heard throughout the session as rape victims, hidden behind a screen, recounted their harrowing experiences to the commissioners. The voices of victims were finally being heard by the nation."[33]

What Women Saw That Men Could Not

At the ICTY, the inclusion of women with expertise in women's rights and gender issues opened the door to more women as witnesses, who in turn provided valuable information to the court about incidents and individuals under investigation. Initially, many women accompanied their husbands, who were the key witnesses. Yet tribunal staff noted that the wives often provided more information than the husbands. In the words of one investigator, "women see things that men don't."[34] The implication is both metaphorical and literal. On the one hand, through their "lived experiences, social roles and gender-based distinctions," women saw or noticed things that men did not. On the other, in concentration camps, during the war, while men were blindfolded, forced to face the ground holding their head, or held in windowless rooms, women were kept in places where they could see things and recognize people involved. So, "they literally saw things that men could not," writes Mertus. Initially, women were brought in as witnesses in sexual abuse cases. But, says Nancy Patterson, "over time, [the court] learned that women can be central witnesses in all kinds of cases."[35] Despite the recognition of women's usefulness as witnesses, the ICTY still has its shortcomings: by 2004 only 21 percent of witnesses had been female.[36]

The experience also rang true for Rwandan women during the 1994 genocide: those who hid or were victims of rape and sexual slavery. In its early stages, the genocide targeted men more than women; thus not only did more women survive, but they lived to tell the tales. Says Bernadette, a woman who lost her husband and survived with three daughters, "They came and took my husband out, killed him and returned to the house to kill us. One of them said, 'Do not kill them; she only has daughters.'"[37] The importance of these women was recognized in the months and years following the genocide, when those who had committed the genocide made attempts to silence them.[38] The wives and female relatives of the genocidaires, who had witnessed the atrocities firsthand, also played an important role. Not only have some given evidence, but they also have sought forgiveness from the victims and even convinced their male relatives to come forward and face justice.

"Future tribunals," writes Mertus, quoting ICTY staff, "should think about women witnesses from the beginning, and remember that they have valuable information about a variety of crimes."[39]

Institutional Reform and the Rule of Law

"The involvement of women in the [ICTY] is a good example of a case where women's presence changed the course of history."[40] This observation, made in 2004 by Patricia Sellers, gender adviser to the Office of the Prosecutor, still resonates. The participation of women, particularly those within the structures of tribunals and commissions, has led to significant reforms in the processes undertaken at the tribunals and commissions and the substance of national and international law and jurisprudence. Women involved in the ICTR, ICTY, and the South African TRC broke new ground in many ways, but others in Peru, Sierra Leone, and elsewhere have subsequently built on these gains.

Changing International Criminal Law and the Course of History

If a woman had not been on the ICTY in the early years, there might not have been any indictments for gender-based crimes, recalls former chief prosecutor Richard Goldstone.[41] And if women's rights advocates had not been pressing for changes in international jurisprudence, using multiple strategies, the changes may not have come about.

The key issue for the women's human rights movement at the time of the ICTY's formation and the writing of its statute was recognition of rape as a direct violation of international law and a serious crime, not just a by-product of other crimes, nor merely bundled as an "honor crime" or an attack on personal dignity. The difference is critical on many levels, notes Catherine Niarchos, not least because when rape is considered as an injury to one's reputation or honor, it is treated as less serious and not as worthy of prosecution as physical injuries to the person.[42] It is also considered as an offense against the family, clan, tribe, or community, which implicitly reinforces notions of women as property rather than as individuals with rights.

The strategies adopted by women's groups varied; some chose to fight for the designation of rape as a form of genocide, torture, or mutilation, whereas others pushed for the recognition of rape as a form of violence. There were also discussions about "genocidal rape"—with some advocates actively pursuing the formulation, whereas others were more cautious, warning against the difficulty of proving intent and the loss of focus on individual victims, who may have been raped outside a broader strategy of genocide. Ultimately, the differences were tactical, with many believing that to ensure rape was addressed, every possible angle and approach must be covered. They also pressed for an expanded notion of liability for rape and sexual violence, writes Mertus. Not only those who planned, ordered, and committed the act but also those who aided and abetted in the planning, preparation, and execution of the crime would be liable. In addition, commanders who knew or "had reason to know" were also liable. That in itself was groundbreaking, as senior figures could no longer shield themselves on the basis of ignorance.

As Mertus says, these provisions in the ICTY statute were the basis for a number of landmark decisions that expanded "the understanding of sexual violence under international law." And "each case bears the imprint of women . . . as judges, prosecutors, investigators, and witnesses, as well as behind the scenes as advocates."[43] The case of Serbian café owner Dusko Tadic, who had "aided and abetted" the sexual mutilation of a man, resulted in the recognition of sexual assault as inhumane treatment and a breach of the Geneva Conventions. It also set the precedent for rape by nonstate actors as being recognized as a war crime. Other decisions included holding commanders responsible for knowing about, but failing to stop, incidences of rape; recognition of rape as a form of torture; and recognition of the rape of one person as a violation of international law. Although the ICTR brought forward the first case of rape as a war crime, the ICTY was the first tribunal to bring forward an international criminal case exclusively based on sexual crimes. It was also the first tribunal to try cases of sexual violence against men.

In addition to placing rape and sexual assault firmly in the terrain of war crimes and crimes against humanity, under Article 15 of the ICTY statute, the court adopted Rules of Procedure and Evidence. Judge Gabrielle Kirk McDonald was pivotal in the formulation of the rules that protect victims of sexual abuse and have largely benefited women witnesses. Mertus notes that Rule 96, for example, provides that in cases of sexual assault no corroboration of the victim's testimony is needed; consent as a result of threats or coercion is not admissible by the defense, nor is the victim's prior sexual history. Other rules that were adopted with more general application, but of specific importance to women and in rape cases, included maintaining the confidentiality of a victim's identity during investigations; using deposition-based evidence to spare victims and witnesses the difficulty of traveling to The Hague; and allowing the tribunal to take extra measures to protect the identity of witnesses and victims, including through nondisclosure of records, closed sessions, and the use of image- and voice-altering devices.

Finally, Rule 34 calls for the creation of a Victims' Support Unit to provide services and counseling to witnesses and victims, particularly those involved in sexual assault and rape cases. Specific mention was made of the need for qualified female staff to run the unit, and the provision of care to children, dependents, and accompanying persons, as well as relocation assistance to witnesses and flat fees for costs incurred while they were away from home.

The precedence set by the ad hoc tribunals of Rwanda and the former Yugoslavia were used by international women's rights advocates, particularly the Women's Caucus for Gender Justice, to influence the design and statute of the International Criminal Court.[44] Among them, the ICC statute recognizes rape, sexual slavery, and forced prostitution, pregnancy, and sterilization, as well as other forms of sexual violence, as crimes against humanity and as war crimes. Trafficking is included under the category of sexual slavery, and gender-based persecution is included as a crime against humanity.

These developments also influenced the establishment of the transitional justice mechanisms for Sierra Leone. The statute of the Sierra Leone Special Court not only lists rape, sexual slavery, enforced prostitution, forced pregnancy, and any other form of sexual violence as crimes against humanity and violations of the Geneva Conventions, but also explicitly considers the abuse of girls under fourteen and the abduction of girls for "immoral purposes" as crimes that the court would prosecute.

Improving Practice and Protection: Victims, Investigations, and Witness Support

The writing of the statute and establishment of procedural rules set the stage for how cases were approached, investigated, and adjudicated. Again, the presence of women as staff of the ICTY and in the South African, Peruvian, and Sierra Leonean TRCs each resulted in significant changes and development in the treatment of victims and witnesses, as well as in investigative procedures.

At the ICTY, Patricia Sellers, as mentioned earlier, was charged with developing the ICTY's approach to the investigation and indictment of gender-related crimes, notably sexual crimes, and she led the way in innovations. For example, investigative teams were initially assigned to specific towns or detention camps. Although they were mandated to investigate sexual crimes, the teams, overwhelmingly male, had little access. Interviewed in 2003, Judge Richard Goldstone explained the dilemma. "We had tremendous difficulty staffing women investigators, because we were insisting that [they] have ten years of experience."[45] Yet only a handful of countries have female police investigators with such experience and, in the meantime, few of the male investigators had experience in investigating sexual crimes. To overcome the problem, the tribunal established "sexual investigation teams" made up exclusively of women. They worked in tandem with other teams, ensuring that rape and sexual violence were not overlooked. Speaking in 2004, team leader Nancy Patterson recalled that after a couple of years, awareness of how to investigate and try sexual crimes had grown considerably among the investigators, so the specialized team was no longer needed.[46]

The differential impact of having women among the judges, lawyers, and staff has also been noticeable. Male witnesses speak more freely to women judges, and male defense attorneys are more respectful of female witnesses when a woman judge presides, notes Mertus, following interviews with key staff. The treatment of witnesses altered as a result of women's involvement in the tribunal's processes. In particular, witness protection and victim support programs have improved. Recounting the experiences of staff, Mertus writes that in its early days, the ICTY received witnesses "without anything in place with regard to their physical or psychological comfort and security." For the protection staff, the task of identifying witnesses, fitting the bulletproof vests, flying them to Croatia to prepare the necessary paperwork and travel authorization, and transporting them back to Bosnia for delivery to The Hague was challenge enough. But once they arrived, the few waiting rooms that did exist had no access to bathrooms, food, or drinks. In sum, there was little recognition of the needs of witnesses or their sense of dignity.

Over time and with the involvement of trained staff in the Victims' Support Unit, however, changes were put in place. From a logistical standpoint, simple initiatives such as the provision of child care and other family care allowances have resulted in more female witnesses coming forward. More substantively, there is greater recognition of the trauma that witnesses and victims have and continue to experience and thus increased attention to their needs. There is also better understanding of the motivations of many witnesses who agree to come to the court, and acknowledgment that regardless of what motivates them, witnesses need as much information as possible about the procedure before their appearance. There are, of course, a host of other factors that affect witnesses, including the risk of being retraumatized, of lacking protection once home, and so forth. There is still much that needs to be done, but acknowledging the practical and emotional complexities that witnesses endure is an important step.

In South Africa, the TRC Act specified that the process be victim-friendly but did not provide further guidance. Says one former male commissioner, "Our interpretation of 'victim-friendly,' I mean . . . us male commissioners, . . . was that we simply had to provide the setting that would allow witnesses to testify. . . . But the women on the commission said no, the TRC . . . had to provide emotional support for witnesses at all times."[47]

The sentiments are echoed by women commissioners themselves, who recognized that many of the witnesses would be speaking of their traumas for the first time. A system of "briefings" was set up in which TRC counselors met with witnesses prior to and after they had given testimony. The thread of caring was woven through the entire process. As witnesses completed their testimonies, the comments and thoughts that commissioners conveyed to them infused a deeper level of connection and understanding. Says Commissioner Glenda Wildschut, "I observed that women did this well. Their statements and questions, even if they were searching for clarification . . . they always tried to connect with how the witness was feeling."[48]

Others suggest that men were concerned about witnesses' feelings, but that they did not focus on this aspect in the way that women did. Women were not just interested in the bare facts of a case but recognized the need to allow witnesses to speak of their feelings about the situation, unburden themselves, and know that they were being heard. Says another committee member, women were "the embracing" arm of the TRC.[49]

Gobodo-Madikezela was the TRC's coordinator in the Western Cape. Women, she reflects, balanced the quasi-legalistic nature of the process by bringing a more human touch. Her own responsibility was outreach to communities. "We had a problem on the TRC: public hearings had been in session for two months . . . and white people were simply not visible." Her challenge was to engage them in the process. Recognizing the ways in which black women had come forth to speak about their sons, Gobodo-Madikezela approached white women, mothers of conscripted soldiers, in the hope that they too would want to tell their sons' stories. Bringing a story from the other side, she reflects, was quite radical at the time. But the impact enhanced the credibility of the TRC and brought visibility to the experiences of white people under apartheid. They came forth to tell their stories and to attend hearings. The situation was by no means perfect. There was concern that on the one hand, the victimization of white people was overly represented, and on the other, too few came to the hearings. Nonetheless, the outreach effort enhanced the notion of bringing the whole truth, as discussed above, by acknowledging the pain and trauma of the other side. That the TRC held public hearings in predominantly white communities made it a symbol of the bridge building that was needed.

In Sierra Leone, the lessons of South Africa were applied widely, particularly with regard to highlighting women's experiences. Women advocates also drew on international developments to shape the Sierra Leone transitional justice mechanisms (i.e., the court and the TRC), pressing for the creation of a special unit to investigate war crimes from a gender perspective. A woman's task force was created to bring together representatives from the police, media and legal professions, civil society actors, and the UN to foster greater women's participation in the institutions, as well as keeping a tab on gender sensitivity in the context of the truth commission. The effect was notable. Section 6(2)b of the TRC's enabling Act in Sierra Leone mandated that the commission pay special attention to the "subject of sexual abuses and to the experiences of children within the armed conflict."

Here again, the involvement of international and national activists paved the way for not only substantive changes but also critical procedural changes needed for these crimes to be considered and, more importantly, to enable women to come forward. In part, that resulted from the involvement of UNIFEM, which hosted a three-day fact-finding mission for international leaders to draw attention to the plight of women, and released a report on the issues. It was an effective means of generating wider attention for the often-marginalized question of women. The participation of Yasmin Sooka, one of the South African commissioners who brought the lessons of South Africa to Sierra Leone, was also critical. Sooka not only raised the issue of the gendered dimensions of the TRC process but also called for staff training on understanding the different experiences of women and men and increasing sensitivity to witnesses and victims, particularly those who had suffered sexual abuse. UNIFEM and Urgent Action Fund (UAF), a small NGO, provided financial and technical support for the training of commissioners and staff.

Recognizing the social pressures and trauma women were facing in terms of coming forward, the TRC was cautious in gathering testimony. The entire process of statement taking was reviewed. The principle of being victim-friendly was embraced, and investigators worked to create an environment of trust and comfort for witnesses and victims. UNIFEM funded specialists to support statement takers in coping with the harrowing tales they were hearing, developed guidelines on how to take statements, and tested them in two regions. Among the issues the guidelines addressed were the conditions under which interviews would be conducted. For example, meetings had to be one-on-one with the victim; the participation of fathers and husbands was discouraged, unless the victim explicitly demanded their presence; and rape victims automatically spoke with female statement takers, unless they were willing to speak to men. Some 40 percent of statement takers were women, and they were trained in working with sexually traumatized women.[50]

At the hearings, those who wanted to come forward during the public hearings did so. Others spoke openly but anonymously behind a screen. Interestingly, despite initial assumptions that women would not come forward to speak of the violence they had endured, hundreds did. They wanted to tell their stories, be acknowledged, and when possible, hear the apologies. The participation of women counters stereotypical notions and arguments based on cultural norms of women's reluctance to speak about rape or violence. Given the right conditions, many do come forward. Others, perhaps the vast majority, may choose not to, and that is their right.[51] The challenge is creating the conditions that give women and other survivors a viable choice.

These debates and developments surrounding the treatment of witnesses that came to the fore with the ICTY and South African TRC and influenced other country-specific processes have made their mark at the ICC. Its statute addresses a number of institutional and procedural issues that should, if implemented, improve the treatment of witnesses and victims. They include witness protection programs (encompassing security and protective measures) and counseling through the creation of a victims and witnesses unit. The unit's staff must have expertise in managing trauma, including trauma related to sexual violence. Another provision of the court relates to the protection of witnesses in the presentation of evidence, particularly in cases of sexual or gender-based violence. In an effort to protect the physical, emotional, and psychological well-being and dignity of witnesses, evidence can be provided through electronic means or "in camera" (in judges' chambers or other private settings). The court can also award reparations, either as restitution, compensation, or rehabilitation.[52] In recognition of the need for victims to speak out and the value of the TRC process, the ICC statute and rules also allow victims to tell their stories as they wish, rather than as witnesses being cross-examined in an often stressful court setting.[53]

Judges at the ICC are required to have gender expertise (i.e., awareness, experience, and an understanding of the differential nature and impact of crimes committed against men and women). There must also be fair representation of men and women on staff and as judges. One provision that could have significant impact is that states that ratify the ICC statute are, as Amnesty International notes, "bound to investigate and prosecute genocide, crimes against humanity and war crimes."[54] If they are unwilling or unable to do so, the ICC can assert jurisdiction. This obliges state parties to the ICC statute to amend or enact new laws to conform to international standards. It is particularly important in the context of violence against women, as often national legislation regarding the criminalization of such forms of violence is lax, ineffective, or nonexistent.

In sum, the involvement of women in the structures of transitional justice mechanisms since the early 1990s has resulted in significant developments in the substance and the practice of international criminal law and justice. The lessons from one case have been incorporated into subsequent structures, each aiming to improve on the last. Much of it has culminated in the ICC statute. The question now is whether the provisions will ever be fully resourced and implemented.

Reconciliation as Transitional Justice

"Reconciliation," writes scholar Payam Akhavan, is "beyond a mere recital of objective facts, however, reconciliation requires a shared truth—a moral or interpretive account—that appeals to a common bond of humanity."[55] Gobodo-Madikezela echoes that idea. "[It] focuses on the human factor, on factual information as well as on emotional content. For reconciliation to take place, both of these components of people's stories must be acknowledged."[56]

This idea of shared truths and acknowledgment of the other is essential to the process of building peace and steps toward reconciliation in every context. Reflecting on the "micropolitics of reconciliation" in a small community in Peru, anthropologist Kimberly Theidon notes that "villagers differentiate between 'forgiveness' and 'reconciliation.'" Forgiveness is a more personal and emotional matter: perpetrators must request "perdon" in front of a community, and it must, she writes, "come from the heart or the mouth outward." No one can be forced to forgive another. Reconciliation, however, is seen as a matter of coexistence, "restoring sociability and the trust necessary to cooperate with others on collective life projects." But the two are intertwined. Theidon quotes villagers speaking in 2001 (at the start of the Peruvian TRC process): "If the soldiers want to reconcile with us, then let them come here and apologize and repent for what they did."[57]

The inclusion of and attention to reconciliation as a key element and outcome of transitional justice processes gained prominence through the South African case. Earlier commissions, notably those in Latin America, were focused on the truth, uncovering the facts and events relating to the disappearances, tortures, and deaths of civilians and dissidents. The assumption was that truth was needed to allow for recovery and perhaps reconciliation, but the latter was not given much attention, either in the commissions or as a matter of national policy. Similarly, although after South Africa, the "R" of reconciliation is included in the commissions that have been formed, it is often more a question of political expediency than a genuine and concerted effort at reconciliation and, by extension, the more complex business of forgiveness.

In South Africa, laying the foundations for national reconciliation was among the key goals in the TRC's mandate. The interim constitution and the TRC Act make reference to the indigenous philosophy of *ubuntu,* which is a widely held value among South Africans. *Ubuntu,* writes Gobodo-Madikezela, is a principle of community, morality, and group solidarity and suggests that "a person is a person through other persons." In the context of the TRC, it was used to promote understanding, not vengeance; reparations, not retaliation; empathy, or "putting yourself in the others' shoes"; acknowledging their roles and actions in the wider social context; but not victimization. *Ubuntu* and the principle of reconciliation infused the workings of the TRC in a variety of ways, particularly in terms of giving equal time and space for people to express emotions and tell their stories as they wished, rather than relaying a series of facts or responding to the demands of a lawyer or prosecutor.

Observers have criticized South Africa's top-down approach to reconciliation and forgiveness, pointing out that people cannot be ordered or forced to reconcile or forgive and that it is more a matter of personal choice. Nonetheless, Nelson Mandela's willingness to forgive his persecutors and captors after twenty-seven years in prison, together with Archbishop Desmond Tutu's moral credibility and call for forgiveness, serve as important symbols and inspiration to the nation. As the reflections below indicate, the personal nature of the issues at hand and the agency and power they gave men and women were of importance to many who participated in the TRC.

Women and Reconciliation

Gobodo-Madikezela quotes Tiny Maya, a regional committee member who explicitly sought to recognize the emotional aspects of testimonies. "What was of concern to me when a witness testified," recalls Maya, "was how to get her or him to feel that this was his or her moment, that we did not just want the facts, we were also concerned about how they *felt.*"[58] Her views are reflected by other female staff of the TRC across the nation. "There was a gentleness in the way that we worked together

and with members of the public. I'd say this is the 'feminine consciousness,'" recalls Marcella Naidoo, director of the TRC in Cape Town and
responsible for the public hearings in the Western Cape. "It was a kind
of mission for me, to try and make others feel comfortable about themselves, rather than making them feel guilty. . . . It's just part of caring.
. . . It's women's ethos of care."[59]

The nature of the interaction between TRC commissioners and witnesses, suggests Gobodo-Madikezela, created a space not only for the
transformation of victims and survivors—of being heard and being able
to unburden themselves—but also for those who caused the suffering
and loss. Men, notably Archbishop Tutu, also fostered the space for
empathy, but it was a discerning feature of women's active presence in
the process. Women were more ready to show their compassion and be
empathetic. "Part of the reason that some conflict resolution interventions don't lead to any significant dialogue about reconciliation,"
reflects Gobodo-Madikezela, "is that there is little focus on how to create an environment in which perpetrators can acknowledge wrongdoing.
That acknowledgement is what invites the victim to engage and reach
out with forgiveness."[60] The fear of breaking down, crying in public, or
showing emotion is stronger among men; for the environment to be
conducive to forgiveness, empathy toward victims and perpetrators is
essential.

Women witnesses played a critical role in sustaining the atmosphere that allowed for emotional expression and steps toward reconciliation, through personal yet highly symbolic acts of forgiveness.
Men who appeared typically spoke of their own experiences of human
rights abuse, whereas women typically spoke of the suffering of their
children—often sons—and husbands. As mentioned above, the media
and many women's rights advocates were critical of the TRC in this
regard, suggesting that the women were represented in stereotypical
images, as the "crying team," and as secondary objects, as if their own
experiences did not matter. Yet interviews with former female witnesses, white and black, reveal a very clear understanding and agency
on their part. Many saw their participation in the hearings as the
opportunity to speak out and about people that mattered to them. They
also saw it explicitly as an opportunity to reach out to other women,
black and white, to share their experiences, bring back the humanity
of their children, confront the reality of the past, and move forward
together.

Gobodo-Madikezela quotes Nomsa, a black woman whose son was
tortured and murdered. "When I went up there I didn't want to talk about

me," says Nomsa. "How would that bring out my son's story? How would it help me heal this void of silence? How would it get other mothers to hear what our children went through, especially those mothers who had a normal life, and whose children had a normal upbringing?" Nomsa continues, "You invite others to participate in . . . remembering your child . . . this kind of putting yourself behind others, that's something that women can do, to put others first, for the greater good. That's what we were able to do."

Her views are mirrored by Anne-Marie, the mother of a white soldier who also died. "What good would it be to talk about myself? . . . I want to talk about my son so that all white women who lost their sons in the army can know that the time for silence is past and gone. So that they can realize that the truth commission was not just for blacks, but also for whites. Ja, men spoke about themselves . . . that's how men are . . . but women are able to step back and say: how can we make this story ours?"[61]

Nomsa and Anne-Marie also symbolized different aspects of how women engaged in the TRC. For Nomsa it was a means of reaching out to women as mothers, regardless of their race. In Anne-Marie's case, her single testimony and willingness to speak as a white mother resulted in "tremendous response, with whites turning up in greater numbers," thus giving the TRC credibility and a more inclusive sense of public ownership. They, as well as other women, were deliberate in the choices they made and the words they spoke. They believed in the principle of reconciliation and the need to "bring others along" through the TRC forum.

This willingness to reach out and belief in *ubuntu* and the humanization of the "other," particularly perpetrators, were also evident at the Special Hearings on Women. Even though they recalled their own experiences of violence, in their testimonies many also spoke of the small acts of kindness by prison wardens and policemen that reflected their humanity and compassion in the midst of an inhumane institution and state. One witness testified that a policeman smuggled in asthma medication for her. "I will never forget his name, Taljaard," she recalled in 2004. Remembering his name is valuing his humanity, says Gobodo-Madikezela. Acknowledging that perpetrators can show compassion is important in the process of transitional justice, "because it overtly encourages victims of politically motivated violations to demonstrate tolerance and compassion, when dealing with people who have acted on behalf of undemocratic governments."

Other witnesses demonstrated their willingness and desire to forgive those who had assaulted and even raped them. "I would really like to see him coming to apologize. . . . I would like to see him coming to ask for forgiveness," said one woman; "I forgave him on that very day, but I still want him to come out." Another woman who was beaten and raped echoed the sentiments. "[He] never came to ask for forgiveness. . . . I can forgive him. I so wish he could come to me, where I stay and ask for forgiveness." Others spoke of wanting to forgive those who violated their families, but not knowing whom to approach.

For perpetrators, asking for forgiveness can be a means of reclaiming a part of their humanity that was lost or suppressed by the brutality of the system. For victims, the act of forgiveness is in itself empowering, a means of emerging from victim status and moving toward healing. Reflecting on the experiences of one woman, Gobodo-Madikezela writes, "her aim was not to dehumanize the perpetrator through retributive punishment; her primary aim was to engage him in order to find peace within herself."[62]

As in so many other arenas, Rwanda offers some of the most striking examples of reconciliation, with women at the helm. The 1994 genocide affected the country on a level incomparable to other cases of conflict in recent years. Some 10 percent of the country's total population was decimated, mainly Tutsis and moderate Hutus. In the aftermath, the Tutsi-dominated Rwandan Patriotic Front won control of the country. Some 110,000 people, almost exclusively men, were arrested and imprisoned on charges relating to the genocide. But the nation's judicial system could not cope; of its 785 judges practicing prior to the genocide, only twenty were left. Almost a decade after the genocide, only 5,000 had gone to trial. The ICTR worked too slowly.

In the meantime, women across the country literally picked up the pieces, rebuilding communities, giving homes to some 500,000 orphans, and coming together to build a future. Publicly, men and women openly speak of their trust in women's leadership in the aftermath of the genocide.[63] The Government of National Unity in power from 1994 to 2003 recognized the importance of women and not only initiated efforts to draw them into politics, but appointed women to lead the Unity and Reconciliation Commission (URC).

Many of the most prominent women were members of different political parties but collaborated through the umbrella organization Pro-Femmes/Twese Hamwe, mentioned above and in Chapter 5. One of the conditions for membership in Pro-Femmes in the aftermath of the genocide was peace-related activities. Through the Forum of Women Parliamentarians and the Women Leaders' Caucus and Unity Club (women leaders and wives of leaders), the first groups to formally cross ethnic and political lines, women led reconciliation efforts, linking the personal with the political.

The most striking symbols of reconciliation were women at the grassroots. In 1996–1997, when the GNU was still fighting extremist Hutu insurgents in northern Rwanda, local women, relatives of anti-government fighters, became intermediaries, on the one hand cajoling and convincing their sons and husbands to lay down weapons, and on the other warning security forces of impending attacks and seeking guarantees that their menfolk would not be harmed.[64]

But it was the most impoverished women who came to embody and personify reconciliation. At the community level, widows of victims and wives of genocidaires, trying to cope with the pressures of poverty and social ostracism as women heading households alone, joined together across ethnic lines, first as individuals and gradually under organizational umbrellas. Interviewed in 2004, one woman reflected on her work.

> Our association is for women heads of households: genocide widows, women whose husbands are in prisons or refugees outside the country, children heading families and we also have some men about two or three. . . . What brought us together was poverty, most of us knew each other before the war. . . . [But those of] us who were working had no peace of mind when our neighbours were starving because they had no parents or husbands to provide for them. So we came together as women sharing the same problems to be able to help one another by lending each other some money. . . . We [started] income-generating projects and were funded by the Swiss who bought secretarial materials for us. We offered secretarial services which employed some of us who were not working. We also started a bakery which also employed others, we make little money but no one sleeps hungry.[65]

Victims have been willing to forgive, and the wives of alleged genocidaires have played a particularly important role in not only seeking forgiveness on behalf of their husbands but also encouraging them to confess. Interviewed in July 2003 in the Mirenge Kibungo province, one former prisoner whose wife had encouraged his confession spoke of how "women help prisoners overcome shame and fear in order to confess." The views are shared by others, notably representatives of the Genocide Widows Association (AVEGA-Agahozo). "Prisoners used to be afraid of even looking at victims," recalled one widow. "But with time they came and asked for forgiveness because we encouraged them. Those who were released help us in fetching water, renovate our houses and to do our gardens. In return we give them food."[66]

These initiatives took place across the country. Interviewed in 2003, a Catholic priest in Gitarama province with responsibility for the Peace and Justice Commission of the Kabwayi Diocese recalled the interactions of rural women. "In Butare women whose husbands killed the husbands of other women, came together, about 20 [of them], they went to the women and they said, 'Please, we are sorry, we know our husbands killed your husbands. We are really asking for pardon. We can give you physical support in any way you need.' After some time, the genocide survivors sat together and said, 'These women [wives of genocidaires] are coming to collect food every day; their children have dropped [out of] school. What can we do?' They collected money and gave it to those women and said, 'We are sorry that every day you and your children have to come so far to get food. We hope this money can help you.'"[67] Without women, say many observers, reconciliation in Rwanda would be impossible.

Women's NGOs and Civil Society

As mentioned above, women's civil society groups at the national and international levels have been key contributors to the changes and developments seen in formal transitional justice structures. They have also been important partners in the pursuit of justice and reconciliation. From Bosnia to South Africa, Peru to Sierra Leone, women's NGOs—those investigating disappearances, documenting human rights abuses, raising awareness among women in communities, or providing psychosocial support to victims and witnesses—have been an important backstop to the institutions. In many instances, the initial outreach to women was almost accidental. In Peru, as Mantilla notes, more often than not it was the mothers, wives, and daughters who collected the data and were able to pass them to the TRC, not the traditional human rights organizations or governmental bodies. Elsewhere a combination of local ownership and limited funding resulted in collaborative relations between the structures and civil society. In Sierra Leone, the general lack of funding for the TRC resulted in innovative partnerships with international and civil society organizations. UNIFEM and the UAF funded workshops for Sierra Leonean women's organizations to inform them of the processes and seek their views on the best ways to bring women's experiences to the TRC. These organizations played a critical role in reaching out to victims and helped prepare women to give testimony. They also assisted UNIFEM in formulating guidelines for the commission.

In Bosnia, women's organizations, particularly those working with victims, also created a direct channel between the tribunal and the witnesses, providing information and supporting investigations. According to Mertus, ICTY investigators "made [it] clear that were it not for the work of local NGOs, there would have been few, if any, witnesses on sexual violence cases and many other cases."[68] In 2003, for the first time, a group of Bosnian psychotherapists and psychologists received private funding (outside the ICTY's own budget) to visit the tribunal at The Hague. The group comprised many women who had spent years providing counseling to victims of war crimes and preparing many as witnesses. The visit revealed enormous missed opportunities and potential for partnership. It alerted the group to the reality of the victims' experiences as witnesses. It also provided them with ideas on how to improve protection for witnesses, including changes needed in national laws. Finally, the women who returned were themselves ambassadors for the ICTY in Bosnia itself. Over the years, poor communication had resulted in disillusion and unrealistic expectations among the Bosnian population. But, notes Mertus, the group's visit was an indication of how increased contact with civil society can enhance the effectiveness and legitimacy of such tribunals among the populations they seek to serve.[69]

The numbers and impact may be difficult to ascertain, but, says Mirsad Jacevic, women are often at the forefront of reconciliation. Reflecting on his own experiences in Bosnia, Jacevic notes that women were the first to get together, to speak and reflect. They did so as individuals and through forming NGOs. When the atmosphere is charged, the smallest effort is a courageous act. Similarly, the initiatives of women in their local communities, if recognized and strengthened, can be the window to and effective conduit for promoting reconciliation and coexistence value more broadly.[70] Yet their potential is still not fully valued by outsiders.

Transitional Justice:
From International Efforts to Local Practices

The involvement of women in transitional justice processes, formal mechanisms, and the efforts of civil society has profound symbolic, legislative, judicial, and even social value. They have broken taboos and ensured that the cloak of invisibility and silence surrounding gender-based crimes in war will gradually be removed. In doing so, they have also drawn attention to the vast and previously underacknowledged complexity and reality of victims' lives in the aftermath of war and violence. Put simply, the victims are not just the dead or their relatives; they are also those who have been maimed and raped. They are also those born of rape and living with HIV/AIDS or other deadly diseases. They are the socially shunned and traumatized. They are those who have to continue living with the past.

Promoting the rule of law and a culture of human rights as measures to prevent and break a cycle of violence is essential to the process of building peace. Transitional justice mechanisms can be catalytic in this regard. Still, for the most part these institutions have had limited impact on the immediate lives of the majority of the actual victims and the most vulnerable. Tribunals and commissions tend to individualize guilt, often focusing on the most powerful figures or those deemed to have greatest responsibility. Yet while the prosecutions of Saddam Hussein and Charles Taylor and others of their ilk represent a significant step in criminal justice, they also represent impunity for the hundreds of less important figures. In the words of an Iraqi woman who witnessed her son's murderer being designated as town mayor by US military officials in 2003, too often the "little Saddams" remain at large.[71] Courts and commissions that are the primary vehicles of transitional justice cannot tackle mass public involvement in human rights abuses. The effect, therefore, is that the majority of people who rape and terrorize civilians do so with impunity.

The sheer numbers of perpetrators make it virtually impossible. In Bosnia, European Union estimates indicate that some 20,000 women were raped.[72] In Timor Leste, during the Indonesian occupation, some 200,000 men were killed, leaving 45 percent of women as widows.[73] Rape and sexual assault were widespread throughout the conflict, and as in other conflict-affected countries, HIV/AIDS is the latest deadly threat. Similarly, in the DRC, Amnesty International estimates that some 40,000 women were raped from 1999 to 2005, and up to 30 percent of rape survivors may be HIV-positive.[74]

No judicial system can cope with such figures. And no society emerging from war, attempting to heal, reconcile, and move toward peace, is able to consider prosecuting the thousands (overwhelmingly men) who would be implicated in such crimes. Even victims are often willing to live with impunity for their attackers, either for fear of reprisals or because they believe that trials would jeopardize the fragile peace. So the question remains, how can the chasm between outright impunity for perpetrators and the need for justice for victims be bridged?

From a more pragmatic standpoint, what could or should be done to enable the victims of war crimes—be it rape, forced impregnation,

mutilation, or other physically or psychologically debilitating experiences—to live normal lives again and have access to services, without
being marginalized, discriminated against, and violated? What role can
international peacebuilding and postconflict reconstruction programs
play in enabling people to attain a level of basic security and dignity? If
that is too idealistic a goal, what are the risks to the long-term sustainability of peace processes if such groups, and particularly their children,
live and grow up on the margins of society?

Beyond the formal structures, community-based or traditional
efforts at forgiveness and reconciliation can be important in bringing
closure. In northern Uganda, where the Lord's Resistance Army has
waged a violent war against civilian populations, traditional forgiveness rituals are being used to cleanse former combatants and enable
them to return to society.[75] In Sierra Leone too, traditional rituals have
been used to cleanse and forgive former child soldiers, particularly
girls, whose acts of violence are considered strictly taboo. In some
instances, people are opting for traditional practices that are more
attuned to "forgiving and forgetting," as opposed to the mantra of
"revealing is healing" that came with the South African efforts.[76] That
is born out of necessity. On the one hand there is an implicit understanding that in the context of these wars, in which children were
abducted and forced to fight, the lines between victim and perpetrator
are blurred. On the other hand, people—directly or indirectly victimized by violence—know only too well that justice will not be done and
that they have to coexist with their erstwhile abusers. Resignation, fear
of retribution, and the desire to move beyond their victimhood are
among the driving forces.

Reflecting on the reaction of local communities in Sierra Leone,
anthropologist Rosalind Shaw suggests that there was overwhelming
support for the prosecution of the "big big ones who sent the children to
do bad things."[77] But, she adds, the inability of the national structures
and even the NGO community to embrace the alternative healing and
forgiveness rituals or desire for silence contributed to rejection of the
TRC by some.

In Rwanda, the government took a different, ambitious, and highly
controversial approach by seeking to address the mass public involvement and impact of the genocide. Since 1994 some 110,000 people have
been in jail, under the worst conditions, on charges relating to the genocide. With the national courts lacking the capacity to try cases and the
ICTR being even slower, in 1998 the government proposed an alternative
solution in the form of traditional, community-based *gacaca* courts.
Gacaca jurisdictions offer a participatory form of justice, bringing

together survivors, perpetrators, and witnesses to establish the truth of events. The guilty are charged with forms of community service as a means of giving reparations and assisting their reintegration into the community. A key caveat: people accused of "category one" crimes (i.e., the most serious criminals, such as planners and leaders of the genocide, well-known murderers, and those guilty of rape or sexual torture) cannot be tried by these courts.[78] As a mechanism though, the *gacaca* courts seek to create a mix of restorative justice, reparations, and reconciliation.

The government rolled out the *gacaca* courts over a period of time. Since July 2006, they have expanded from 106 tribunals to enough to cover the entire country. Some 40,000 people have been tried already, and information has been gathered from villages nationwide. The data indicated that, together with those already in jail, a total of 766,489 people have been named as suspects and are complicit in the genocide to some degree. Among those named, 72,539 fell into category one, 397,103 into category two, and 296,847 into category three. By January 2007, there were over 9,000 *gacaca* courts operating at the cell (smallest administrative) level and over 1,500 at the sectoral level. According to media reports, the Rwandan government plans to end the process by the end of 2007.[79]

There is, of course, plenty of criticism of the *gacaca* system, ranging from those who argue that it is politically motivated and the victor's form of justice to those who voice concern about the lack of international standards, the lack of protection for witnesses (a number were murdered prior to giving testimony), the propensity to give false testimony in exchange for lighter sentences, the risk of making new arrests, and the reopening of the wounds of genocide. Additionally, the fact that rape and sexual torture are recognized as serious crimes beyond the jurisdiction of *gacaca* has both positive and negative connotations: positive in that they are being acknowledged as heinous acts that must be tried in criminal court, but negative in that many victims may not benefit from the potential reparations and other mechanisms that the *gacaca* system provides. Finally, the tightening of political space in Rwanda and the government's sidelining of opposition parties are fueling criticism and could exacerbate ethnic tensions again.[80] The system may well backfire, but the need to bring perpetrators of the genocide to some form of justice is widely acknowledged.

For all its weaknesses, *gacaca* also acknowledges that thousands were implicated in the violence; that each victim has a right to justice; and, perhaps most significantly, that justice must be broadened and made accessible to all in their own communities. It should encompass not only truth telling, but elements of social justice, community service, and reparations to a broad swath of victims, not just to a handful that are able or willing to appear in court.

The promise of reparations, although controversial in the eyes of many, can be critical in bringing psychological closure and offering pragmatic assistance to victims who live with the consequences of violence. For many survivors, punishment of perpetrators is one element of justice, but not necessarily the priority. Reflecting on rape survivors in Peru, for example, Mantilla notes how many of them preferred to receive child support and acknowledgment of paternity for the children born of the rapes they endured. Similarly, access to physical and mental health care, employment, and education is essential for enabling victims to rebuild their own lives.

Testimonies from the Sierra Leone TRC point to similar issues. Augusta Amara, a young victim of abduction and rape who spoke to the commission in Freetown, exemplifies the desires of victims. "I want to talk about my education," she says after the court offers her a chance to add to her testimony. "I want you to assist me with my education because I want to learn. . . . I want you to assist my mother because I have lost my father." Commissioner Sooka indicates that the commission has a limited mandate but asks, "Do you want the government to do anything for you?" Augusta reiterates her demand, "Yes, I want them to assist in my education."[81]

There is a noticeable gap between the international community's treatment of victims of war crimes, be they men or women, and the attention paid to the perpetrators of those crimes. The resources channeled into the creation of tribunals and commissions stand in stark contrast to those directed to victims. In Sierra Leone, for example, in August 2005 the TRC report called on the Sierra Leone government to establish a national reparations fund for victims. It called on the international community to support that fund. A year later, the fund was not in existence.[82] By April 2007, the UN's Peacebuilding Fund had contributed just $3 million to begin reparation payments for the thousands of war amputees and other victims.[83]

Moreover, as discussed in Chapter 3, resources are also more readily channeled toward former fighters as disarmament and demobilization benefits than toward those who were victimized by them, or indeed those who are involved in the arduous business of trust building and reconciliation. Changing judicial practices and promoting human rights values are important steps. Unless, however, the notions of human rights and justice are broadened to address the survival needs of people, encompassing issues of health, welfare, and access to education and employment—in effect, the promotion of social justice and the resolution of the root causes of conflict—transitional justice mechanisms, tribunals, TRCs, or otherwise, will remain flawed.

Conclusion

Can there be peace without justice? Yes, it happens every day. Is it a lasting and positive peace? Certainly not for the survivors of violence. Justice is essential, but not courtroom justice alone. The tribunals and the ICC signify real progress in the struggle to bring attention to war crimes, even if they cannot end all impunity. TRCs have come some way in recognizing the blurred lines between survivor, victim, and perpetrator. The attention to reconciliation and issues of forgiveness, however fraught and flawed, is an important development. The acknowledgment of rape and sexual violence as strategies of war is also an important marker of progress. So too are attempts at capturing the fullness of people's experiences, not just focusing on physical violence but giving space to those who wish to speak of their traumas in displacement, lost childhood, and dreams of the future. Acknowledging and giving space to mechanisms and rituals of reconciliation that exist across traditions are also important steps.

Throughout this process, women have played a central role in enhancing the effectiveness of institutions substantively and procedurally. As judges and lawyers, experts on the staff of tribunals and witnesses, they have individually and collectively contributed to the theory and practice of transitional justice. As civil society activists, they have engaged the international community and national governments, infusing a human-centered approach to the work, through the provision of care, support, and protection to victims. They are also focused on the long-term community-based reconciliation efforts. Perhaps most importantly, they have also drawn attention to the existing gaps, particularly with regard to the long-term needs of victims.

If the goal is to promote sustainable peace and justice, the international community, including states and NGOs, academics and activists, supporting and funding transitional justice mechanisms, must hear and respond to the voices of victims and survivors. The indictment of war criminals does not address the immediate and long-term needs of the maimed, the raped, the orphans, and the AIDS carriers. Even the provision of symbolic reparations is not enough. The international community must move beyond the limits of criminality and the law to embrace social justice. For the women, men, boys, and girls who live with the memories "like waves," justice must include acknowledgment of their future needs, their humanity, the provision of support and care, access to health care and education, and opportunities to become skilled. At the very least, justice means to be free of discrimination and ostracism, so they, like others, can care for themselves and their dependents, beyond their labels and experiences of victimhood, and have hope for a dignified life.

Notes

Parts of this chapter were published in Sanam Naraghi Anderlini, "Women and Peace Through Justice," *Development* 48, no. 3 (2005): 103–110.

1. For a more detailed description, see Sanam Naraghi Anderlini et al., "Transitional Justice and Reconciliation," in *Inclusive Security, Sustainable Peace: A Toolkit for Advocacy and Action* (Washington, DC: Hunt Alternatives Fund, International Alert, 2004).

2. For an overview of the situation, see Amy Ross, "Catch-22 in Uganda: The LRA, the ICC, and the Peace Process," *Jurist,* July 17, 2006, available at http://jurist.law.pitt.edu/forumy/2006/07/catch-22-in-uganda-lra-icc-and-peace.php.

3. Information available at the International Criminal Tribunal for the former Yugoslavia website, available at http://www.ictr.org/default.htm, retrieved July 26, 2006.

4. Julie Mertus, *Women's Participation in the International Criminal Tribunal for the Former Yugoslavia (ICTY): Transitional Justice for Bosnia and Herzegovina* (Washington, DC: Women Waging Peace Policy Commission, 2004). Much of the discussion about women's participation in the ICTY is drawn from Mertus's work. The issue is also discussed in Adam Smith, "Trying War Crimes Locally," *New Republic,* April 2006, available at http://www.global policy.org.

5. For a detailed discussion, see Human Rights Watch, "Struggling to Survive: Barriers to Justice for Rape Victims in Rwanda," *Human Rights Watch* 16, no. 10(A) (September 2004), available at http://hrw.org/reports/2004/rwanda 0904/2.htm.

6. According to the US House of Representatives Committee on International Relations, the ICTY 2001 budget was $96 million and the ICTR's 2000 budget was $86 million. Committee on International Relations, US Congress, *How Well Are International Criminal Tribunals Working?* News Advisory, February 2002, available at http://wwwc.house.gov, retrieved July 26, 2006.

7. Anthony Dworkin, "Cambodian War Crimes Tribunal Given Go-Ahead," *Crimes of War Project,* available at http://www.crimesofwar.org, retrieved June 27, 2006.

8. For more information, see *The Real Cost of the Iraq War to American Taxpayers,* available at http://www.democrats.org, retrieved July 26, 2006.

9. Helena Cobban, UNU Conference on Transitional Justice, *Just World News,* January 30, 2005, available at http://justworldnews.org/archives/001104.html.

10. Anderlini et al., "Transitional Justice."

11. Issues raised by Iraqi women's rights activists, including relatives of victims, in discussions with the author, London, November 2006.

12. This point has been raised in various discussions with the author by Congolese, Cambodian, and Nepalese women involved in human rights work.

13. Mertus notes that the Women's Coalition Against Crimes Against Women in the Former Yugoslavia was a key player. The coalition does not exist in that form any longer.

14. Mertus, *Women's Participation,* p. 4.

15. Security Council Resolution 808 (1993), available at http://www.ohr.int.

16. Mertus, *Women's Participation.*

17. More information on the case and its implications can be found in Kelly Dawn Askin, "Gender Crimes Jurisprudence in the ICTR," *Journal of International Criminal Justice* 3, no. 4 (2005): 1007–1018.

18. Quoted in Emily Newburger, "The Bus Driver's Daughter," *Harvard Law Bulletin,* spring 2006, available at http://www.law.harvard.edu.

19. Pumla Gobodo-Madikezela, *Women's Contributions to the South African Truth and Reconciliation Commission* (Washington, DC: Women Waging Peace Policy Commission, 2005).

20. Mantilla spoke about her experiences at the Initiative for Inclusive Security and in personal conversations with the author, Washington, DC, April 2005.

21. Ibid.

22. Vasuki Nesiah, *Gender and Truth Commission Mandates* (New York: International Center for Transitional Justice, 2005), available at http://www.ictj.org.

23. This point is noted by Gobodo-Madikezela with reference to unpublished submissions to the TRC by Sheila Meintjies and Beth Goldblatts.

24. Gobodo-Madikezela, *Women's Contributions,* pp. 16–17.

25. Ibid., p. 18.

26. This point was raised in conversation with the author by at least one former fighter, Cape Town, 2003.

27. Nesiah, *Gender and Truth Commission,* pp. 4–5.

28. Fiona Ross, *Bearing Witness: Women and the Truth and Reconciliation Commission in South Africa* (London: Pluto, 2003).

29. Nesiah, *Gender and Truth Commission,* p. 5.

30. Binaifer Nowrojee, "Making the Invisible War Crime Visible: Postconflict Justice for Sierra Leone's Rape Victims," *Harvard Journal of Human Rights* 8 (Spring 2005): 87–105.

31. The full extent of sexual violence and rape is always difficult to measure, particularly in conflict-affected areas. A 2000 study by Physicians for Human Rights and the UN's Assistance Mission to Sierra Leone found that, of 991 households of internally displaced populations surveyed randomly, in 94 percent of the cases there was at least one household member who had experienced serious abuse. One of

every eight household members (13 percent) had experienced sexual violence. The report is available at http://www.physiciansforhumanrights.org.

32. Nesiah, *Gender and Truth Commission,* p. 3.
33. Nowrojee, "Making the Invisible War Crime Visible."
34. Mertus, *Women's Participation,* pp. 11–13.
35. Ibid., p. viii.
36. Ibid., p. 15.
37. Unpublished interview, Kigali, May 2004, courtesy of Initiative for Inclusive Security (formerly known as Women Waging Peace).
38. The vulnerability of witnesses has been reported in the media since the genocide in 1994. It is discussed in Aimable Twahirwa, "Rwanda: Justice Eludes Many 1994 Genocide Survivors," Inter Press Service, July 31, 2006, available at http://www.peacewomen.org.
39. Mertus, *Women's Participation,* p. 15.
40. Ibid., p. viii.
41. Ibid., p. 13.
42. Ibid., p. 17.
43. Ibid., p. 19.
44. The ICC statute is available at http://www.un.org/law/icc/statute/romefra .htm.
45. Mertus, *Women's Participation,* p. 12.
46. Ibid.
47. Gobodo-Madikezela, *Women's Contributions,* p. 10.
48. Ibid.
49. Ibid.
50. Pumla Gobodo-Madikezela, "Sierra Leone's TRC: Contributions and Gains Made by Women" (working title), unpublished mimeo (New York: UNIFEM, 2006). The author thanks UNIFEM for providing access to this document.
51. For a discussion about the willingness of victims to come forward and Sierra Leonean attitudes toward forgiving and forgetting, see Rosalind Shaw, "Rethinking Truth and Reconciliation Commissions: Lessons from Sierra Leone," *US Institute of Peace Special Report No. 130* (Washington, DC: USIP, February 2005), available at http://www.usip.org.
52. For more information about the workings of the court, see http://www .iccwomen.org, retrieved May 9, 2005.
53. Human Rights Watch, "International Justice for Women: ICC Marks a New Era," *Human Rights Watch Backgrounder,* July 2002, available at http:// www.hrw.org.
54. Amnesty International, *International Criminal Court Guidelines for Effective Implementation of the Rome Statute—An Introduction,* September 2004, available at http://web.amnesty.org.
55. Payam Akhavan, "Justice in The Hague, Peace in the Former Yugoslavia? A Commentary on the United Nations War Crimes Tribunal," *Human Rights Quarterly* 20, no. 4 (1998): 737–816.
56. Gobodo-Madikezela, *Women's Contributions,* p. 11.
57. Kimberly Theidon, "Justice in Transition: The Micropolitics of Reconciliation in Postwar Peru," *Journal of Conflict Resolution* 50, no. 3 (June 2006): 1–25.

58. Gobodo-Madikezela, *Women's Contributions,* p. 10.

59. Ibid., p. 11.

60. Ibid., p. 15.

61. Ibid., pp. 14–15.

62. Ibid., p. 20.

63. Elizabeth Powley, *Strengthening Governance: The Role of Women in Rwanda's Transition* (Washington, DC: Hunt Alternatives Fund, 2003), pp. 24–26.

64. Ibid.

65. Unpublished interview, courtesy of Initiative for Inclusive Security (formerly known as Women Waging Peace), 2006.

66. Ibid.

67. Unpublished interview, conducted on behalf of the Women Waging Peace Policy Commission, provided to author, courtesy of Initiative for Inclusive Security, 2006.

68. Mertus, *Women's Participation,* p. 22.

69. Ibid., p. 23.

70. Discussions with the author, Washington, DC, May 2006.

71. Discussion with the author, Washington, DC, April 2003.

72. For more information, see Bosnia and Herzegovina country profile at http://www.womenwarpeace.org, retrieved July 26, 2006.

73. For more information, see Timor Leste country profile at http://www.peacewomen.org.

74. Amnesty International Democratic Republic of Congo, country profile at http://web.amnesty.org, retrieved July 26, 2006.

75. Marc Lacey, "Victims of Uganda Atrocities Choose a Path of Forgiveness," *New York Times,* April 18, 2005.

76. For a more detailed discussion, see Shaw, "Rethinking Truth and Reconciliation Commissions."

77. Ibid.

78. For more information about the *gacaca* courts, see *Gacaca Courts in Rwanda,* available at http://www.penalreform.org/english/theme_gacaca.htm, retrieved July 26, 2006.

79. Godwin Agaba, "Gacaca Courts to Change Structure," *Kigali Times,* January 7, 2007, available at http://allafrica.com.

80. Stephanie Wolters, "The Gacaca Process," *African Security Review* 14, no. 3 (2005), available at http://www.iss.co.za.

81. Augusta Amara, transcript of testimony, *Appendix 3—Transcripts of TRC Public Hearings,* 2004, pp. 103–113, available at http://trcsierraleone.org.

82. The World Organization Against Torture, *Sierra Leone Victims of War Remain Without Reparations,* June 26, 2005, available at http://www.crin.org, retrieved July 27, 2006.

83. "Sierra Leone TRC Receives $3M to Pay Reparations," *Panapress,* April 24, 2007, available at http://www.panapress.com.

seven

How the International System Lets Women Down

I know only that this world is off its rocker when it comes to women. I must admit that I live in such a state of perpetual rage at what I see happening to women in the pandemic, that I would like to throttle those responsible, those who've waited so unendurably long to act, those who can find infinite resources for war but never sufficient resources to ameliorate the human condition.
—Stephen Lewis, UN Special Representative of the Secretary-General on HIV/AIDS in Africa, 2005

"While welcoming the progress achieved so far, the Security Council stresses the importance and urgency for accelerating the full and effective implementation of Resolution 1325 (2000)."[1] So reads paragraph three of the October 2005 Statement of the UN Security Council President, epitomizing the state of international efforts regarding women's protection in war, and their participation in peace processes.

Just months later, reporting to the Security Council on his return from Sudan in June 2006, Emyr Jones Parry, UK ambassador to the UN, reflected,

We could only admire the courage of women confronting the immense burdens of life in Darfur and in the camps of Chad. With quiet dignity, they have to carry water, search for firewood, face attack and violation, not just from the Janjaweed, and at the same time bring up families, often without male support. SCR 1325 was much quoted. So it should be. It was a landmark Resolution which addressed the role of women as the particular victims of conflict. . . . At the same time, they lack the empowerment to play the role in political life which is not only their right, but would introduce a degree of sanity into much of the activity in the region. So the need for full implementation of 1325

191

is obvious. . . . Sudanese women have already identified a series of actions to help achieve these goals.[2]

Year in and year out, progress is made and women's resilience, creativity, and dignity in the face of adversity are noted and applauded in multilateral organizations and international conferences. Resolution 1325 was indeed a landmark. It is the legal and political framework under which national governments, the UN, EU, African Union (AU), other regional organizations, and the bureaucrats who run these systems are obliged to address the situation of women in war—their empowerment and protection. Few question the catalytic role it has played since 2000, and certainly changes are taking place. Within the UN system and governmental institutions, many have units or individuals dedicated to the task of "mainstreaming gender" or (more accurately) focusing on women, not only in traditional developmental issues but also in the ever-expanding field of peace and security.

In 2004, the Security Council requested "action plans" from the UN system to demonstrate implementation of the provisions of its resolution. The agencies produced a system-wide plan. Busy officials, many reluctantly, sat through workshops, hearing about the provisions of 1325 for the first time. Research papers and reports were written, speeches made, trainings provided, conferences attended, handbooks developed, and limited budgets allocated. Yet the council itself has not set a high standard. From 2000 to 2006, the council referenced SCR 1325 in just 25.52 percent of its country-specific resolutions (69 out of 239).[3] Since the advent of the resolution, international entities (the UN, EU, and others) have done little to promote women's involvement as mediators. A 2005 review concludes that, of the range of peace processes ongoing or recently concluded at the time, including those in Sudan and Aceh, only the Ugandan process was mediated by a woman, Betty Bigombe.[4] By 2007, she was no longer directly involved. This paucity is often couched in terms of expertise. Attempts to redress the situation are window dressing. The terms *qualified* and *suitable* often precede the word *women*. Yet as Cora Weiss says, "Are men ever asked to be qualified for these jobs?"[5]

Nationally, peace talks continue to exclude women; peacekeepers, militaries, and rebel groups continue to exploit women sexually; and post-conflict reconstruction programs and funding, by and large, continue to bypass women. Progress on 1325 is being made, in much the same way that there is progress on the Universal Declaration of Human Rights, the Convention on the Elimination of All Forms of Discrimination Against

Women, and other international human rights instruments that honor and uphold women's rights. On average, however, women, particularly those living in conflict-affected areas, activists or not, rarely see, touch, or feel it.

In this chapter I move away from the contributions and limitations of women's activities to focus on the weaknesses of the international system in fulfilling its obligations to women. I touch on normative and conceptual challenges; institutional and structural issues; and the triple-A syndrome of apathy, ad hoc practice, and amnesia that is manifested across international institutions. In concluding the discussion, I consider some key steps for moving beyond the current limitations to secure a sustainable commitment to women in peace and security.

A Normative Conundrum

The participation of women in peacemaking and security-related issues, although simple enough on one level, strikes at the very heart of the Westphalian system and principles of noninterference and state sovereignty in international relations. The women, peace, and security discourse is not the first to do so. The Universal Declaration of Human Rights set a strong precedent. Nonetheless, the United Nations is an organization of member states, with a mandate to preserve *international* peace and security. From its earliest inception the United Nations system was beset by minimalist notions of peace—between states—and maximalist notions of peace with development and respect for human rights between and *within* states.

Speaking in 1999, then UN Secretary-General Kofi Annan tackled this dichotomy head-on. He said:

> As long as I am Secretary-General, the United Nations as an institution will always place the human being at the centre of everything we do. . . . No government has the right to hide behind national sovereignty in order to violate the human rights or fundamental freedoms of its peoples. Whether a person belongs to the minority or the majority, that person's human rights and fundamental freedoms are sacred. . . . This developing international norm will pose fundamental challenges to the United Nations. . . . Of this there can be no doubt. . . . But nor can there be any doubt that if we fail this challenge, if we allow the United Nations to become the refuge of the "ethnic cleanser" or mass murderer, we will betray the very ideals that inspired the founding of the United Nations.[6]

His comments placed him squarely among the ranks of human security advocates who recognize the changing realities in global security in the aftermath of the Cold War, the increase in intrastate conflicts, genocide in Rwanda, and a host of other factors (including the structural development policies of the 1980s) that wrought havoc and increased poverty in many countries. This evolving and complex world of conflict involving nonstate actors, fought in villages and towns and with civilians as targets, was prompting closer examination of the nature of warfare. Together with the emerging nontraditional security threats, such as HIV/AIDS and environmental degradation, that cross national boundaries, it was fueling a new discourse that linked development to peace and security under the broad umbrella of human security. It was a paradigmatic shift away from traditional state and military-oriented notions of security to one that was more people-centric and looked to the internal conditions of states.

The concept of human security, first coined by the UN Development Programme and later elaborated by former Canadian foreign minister Lloyd Axworthy, provided the framework in which politics and security issues on the one hand and development issues on the other could be brought together. "In essence," wrote Axworthy also in 1999,

> human security means safety for people from both violent and nonviolent threats. It is a condition or state of being characterized by freedom from pervasive threats to people's rights, their safety, or even their lives. . . . It is an alternative way of seeing the world, taking people as its point of reference, rather than focusing exclusively on the security of territory or governments. Like other security concepts—national security, economic security, food security—it is about protection. Human security entails taking preventive measures to reduce vulnerability and minimize risk, and taking remedial action where prevention fails.
>
> The range of potential threats to human security should not be narrowly conceived. While the safety of people is obviously at grave risk in situations of armed conflict, a human security approach is not simply synonymous with humanitarian action. It highlights the need to address the root causes of insecurity and to help ensure people's future safety. There are also human security dimensions to a broad range of challenges, such as gross violations of human rights, environmental degradation, terrorism, transnational organized crime, gender-based violence, infectious diseases and natural disasters. The widespread social unrest and violence that often accompanies economic crises demonstrates that there are clear economic underpinnings to human security. The litmus test for determining if it is useful to frame an issue in human security terms is the degree to which the safety of people is at risk.[7]

As noted in Chapter 1, the concept of human security was adapted and further articulated by Kofi Annan in his 2005 report. *In Larger Freedom: Towards Security Development and Human Rights for All* articulates the rights of people to live in freedom from want and poverty, freedom from fear and oppression (including threats of terrorism or use of force), and freedom to live in dignity. "At no time in human history have the fates of every woman, man and child been so intertwined across the globe. We are united both by moral imperatives and by objective interests,"[8] states the report, calling for member states of the UN to step up to their responsibilities.

The human security paradigm also resonated with the challenges and limitations of international law relating to internally displaced persons (IDPs). In accordance with international law, refugees (i.e., people fleeing across state boundaries) have rights to protection by the international community, but IDPs (those remaining within their state boundaries) have no legal recourse internationally. IDP populations were on the rise in 1992 when Sudanese statesman Francis Deng was appointed as the UN Secretary-General's Representative on Internally Displaced Persons. Over the years, he spearheaded the development of the Guiding Principles on Internal Displacement and sought to shift the focus of state sovereignty and the right to noninterference toward a discourse of states' responsibility to protect citizens. Deng highlighted the relevance of the human security paradigm in a speech at a ministerial meeting in 2000. "Human Security provides a compelling conceptual framework for confronting the global challenge of internal displacement. . . . [It] provides the umbrella for the stipulation of sovereignty as responsibility under the watchful eye of the international community to hold states accountable and to offer them a helping hand in ensuring the physical, psychological, moral and material well-being of all those under their jurisdiction." He also pointed out that "human security . . . provides an appropriate framework for bringing non-state actors into parameters of accountability."[9]

Deng's reference to nonstate actors was in relation to armed or other opposition groups. But by going beyond state structures, the framework also allows for alternative, substate civil society voices to have a space in dialogue and decisionmaking.

For women in particular, the human security paradigm resonates strongly on two counts. First, as discussed in Chapter 5 in the South African context, the security issues that can be raised and addressed under that paradigm are ones to which women relate. No amount of military hardware can resolve the problems of poverty or HIV/AIDS. Military might can do little to stop environmental degradation and land loss. Even crime in communities, domestic violence, human trafficking, drug abuse, unemployment, or shifts toward religious extremism cannot be tackled by security forces alone. The state can and must lead the efforts to solve these problems, but it cannot do so without the input and participation of its own population. Second, the paradigm opens space for a more inclusive discourse where women can participate directly.

Despite the benefits of this approach, the normative shift has not been made. Human security has gained many proponents and traction at the conceptual and policy levels, spawning a field of study and high-level attention, but it has not replaced traditional state or national security paradigms. The September 11, 2001, attacks in the United States and subsequent military interventions by the United States were a setback to the field. The UN system (and affiliated regional organizations) is still driven by the will of its member states, not the needs of their citizens per se. As a result, for the same reasons that the UN's political division cannot interfere in the Zimbabwean crisis or weigh in strongly on human rights abuses in Iran or elsewhere, it cannot compel its member states to take actions regarding the inclusion of women in peace-related processes.

Resolution 1325: A Trojan Horse?

Resolution 1325 is a proverbial Trojan horse in this context. It comes from the Security Council and calls on member states to take action. It explicitly calls for consultation with and the inclusion of civil society–based women's groups in the implementation of peace agreements. It also calls on member states to appoint more women to decisionmaking posts relating to conflict prevention, resolution, and reconstruction. It makes explicit references to women's needs in the context of elections, judicial processes, and other institutions. Detractors will argue that even though it was unanimously adopted, the resolution comes under Chapter VI of the UN Charter, as opposed to Chapter VII. Its implementation, therefore, cannot be enforced, and noncompliance cannot be penalized. Nonetheless, in accordance with Article 25 of the Charter, "Members of the United Nations agree to accept and carry out the decisions of the Security Council in accordance with the present Charter." SCR 1325 is a bridge, albeit a slim one, between the minimalist state-centric paradigm and the more inclusive people-focused paradigm of security.

Its significance was perhaps not entirely acknowledged at the time it was passed, in 2000. Countries such as Canada, Namibia, Bangladesh, and Jamaica supported it, much as they supported resolutions on children and armed conflict, protection of civilians, and the idea that HIV/ AIDS was a threat to security. But others, notably Russia, pushed back, arguing that such issues were not the purview of the Security Council. In the end, the message of women as peacebuilders and women as victims giving a human face to new conflicts resonated with the council. The victimization of women (a considerable challenge) was balanced by women as peacebuilders, a positive message and partial solution to the messy wars the council was facing. Namibia's attention to the gendered dimensions of peace support operations and interest in promoting the Windhoek Declaration was timely and linked directly to the council's general review and assessment of peacekeeping and support operations.

The advocates acknowledged and, at times, drew on the perception that women are not considered to be threatening to the status quo and world order. "Women are women," smiles one activist, evoking images of the (anything but) "simple mothers" of Argentina, Sri Lanka, and elsewhere. Talk of women as peacebuilders did not (and still does not) raise alarm bells among member states in the same way as a mention of civil society or human rights groups might.

The resolution had four distinctive but wide-ranging themes: (1) women's need for protection in conflict-affected situations, (2) women as participants in peace processes, (3) gender mainstreaming in peace operations, and (4) gender mainstreaming in the UN system and reporting. But in all likelihood, council members were not fully aware of the way in which women's groups in civil society, governments, and the UN system would keep Resolution 1325 alive.

At a normative level, therefore, the question of women's inclusion sits firmly at the center of the tug-of-war between opposing notions of peace and security. On the one hand, there is the minimalist, state-centered view in which international interventions are limited and governments are king. On the other, there is the maximalist, people-centered approach involving ideals of development and human rights and inclusivity. The lack of clarity at the normative level contributes to the lack of effective implementation.

Stated or unstated, the negligence regarding protection of women in conflict-affected areas and their participation in peace processes is also due to an overt rejection among some actors and institutions of the basic premise regarding women's rights and roles in matters of peace and security. Some argue that peacekeeping is about bringing security, not about women's rights. The question of security and peace for whom is often left hanging. Others point to the proliferation of issues that have to be addressed. In the words of one senior UN official, "One day it's women; the next day it's endangered species."[10] There is a tendency to take a cafeteria approach to the range of seemingly soft issues, with individuals selecting the elements they deem important, regardless of the policies and mandates that direct them.

Finally, there is an overwhelming attitude that the promotion of women's involvement is akin to social engineering and imposition of Western values on non-Western societies. That is doubly ironic. First, the spirit and demand for Security Council Resolution 1325 came from non-Western societies and women who were resisting war. It was not driven by a Western country. Second, the international system's drive toward democracy and market liberalization in poor countries, and its presence in postconflict states, have profound social impact. And yet, accusations of social engineering on this front would be met with much denial, qualification, and head shaking.

Still, slow as it may be, change within the international system is coming. By 2006, the United Kingdom, Sweden, and other countries had formulated their own plans and policies vis-à-vis the implementation of the resolution. In Israel, the Knesset amended the Women's Equal Rights law, mandating that the government include women in any negotiation on peacebuilding or conflict resolution. Across the world, island states of the Pacific, led by Fiji, are taking up the issues in their own realm. Over the years, the EU, Organization of American States (OAS), and other regional bodies have either adapted the provisions of the resolution or adopted their own policies that capture the spirit of the resolution.

Within the UN system too, plans and programs are afoot for more effective attention to the needs of women in humanitarian and emergency crises, peace processes, during peacekeeping, and after conflict. For example, the UN Department of Political Affairs plan includes measures for the effective engagement with women's groups in conflict-affected countries and production of gendered situation analyses. If implemented, it would also ensure that where the UN acts as mediator in peace processes, it sets a high standard with regarding to the protection and participation of women.

In practice its steps have been slow but critical. For example, a partnership with the West African Mano River Women's Peace Network was beneficial to all. Founded in 2000 and winner of the 2004 UN Human Rights Award, the network has a diverse membership of women from the grassroots to the elite in Sierra Leone, Guinea, and Liberia. Their mission is to prevent and end war in the subregion. Precisely because of their local and regional identity and their presence on the ground, MARWOPNET has been an effective partner for the UN in sensitizing the public against violence in Guinea and promoting peace in Sierra Leone and Liberia.[11] They can say and do much that outside actors could not. By supporting them, the UN not only pursued its mandate of promoting regional peace but also helped enhance the network's credibility and amplify its voice.

The action plans and directives compel departments and agencies to focus on the provisions of the resolution, which not only generates greater awareness and support among staff, but also allows for implementation of targeted initiatives. The partnership between the UN Department of Political Affairs and MARWOPNET helped set a precedent within the department in terms of what and with whom the UN's political arm can and cannot engage. The outreach also shows that cooperation with civil society does not threaten a state's authority. More importantly, using Resolution 1325 as an entry point, the UN system is able to engage with sectors of society that are committed to and working for peace without hidden political agendas. Where the partnerships are effective, civil society groups can also be strong advocates for the UN system, thereby enhancing its credibility and legitimacy in the eyes of the public at large. The international peace and security paradigm cannot be changed overnight, but through the policy discourse and such initiatives, it is being transformed gradually.

The challenge is to make the implementation of SCR 1325 part of business as usual within the workings of the UN in the longer term. Doing so brings the focus back to national governments and their willingness to embrace and implement the resolution, yet another catch-22 situation. The UN can and should set the tone and standard of practice, and it can prompt or encourage member states to comply and adhere to higher standards and principles of human rights and equality. Yet it remains constrained if its members are unwilling to take ownership of these principles, to root them in their own national legislation, discourse, policies, and leadership on the international stage.

Conceptual Confusion:
Gender-ology Versus Common Sense

Lack of consensus about normative issues is not helped by the confusion caused by gender terminology. Although Resolution 1325 is clearly about women and issues of peace and security, it joins a cacophony of policy directives, conventions, and broader discourse that is littered with phrases and concepts related to the word *gender*. The term appeared on the international development policy scene in the 1980s following the failure of the "women in development" (or WID) approach. WID programming largely focused on bringing women into the economic and productive sphere, but without a parallel shift in redressing the structural inequalities, such as women's lack of political power, inequality in the law, and cultural norms that hindered women's progress. The shift to gender and development (GAD) was an attempt by women's rights proponents to draw attention away from biological factors and refocus on the socially constructed identities of men and women that determine their roles, capacities, constraints, and opportunities for development. It was also a means of acknowledging women's heterogeneity (i.e., issues of race and class that affect women), while simultaneously shedding light on power inequities between men and women. A focus on gender issues was seen as a way of understanding the division of labor and the distribution of political, economic, social, and cultural power that enhance or curtail women's and men's lives.

Gender terminology expanded and seeped into international development discourse in the 1990s, gaining credence at the 1995 Beijing conference. By 1997 the Economic and Social Council of the United Nations (ECOSOC) had issued its definition of *gender mainstreaming:*

> Mainstreaming a gender perspective is the process of assessing the implications for women and men of any planned action, including legislation, policies or programmes, in any area and at all levels. It is a strategy for making the concerns and experiences of women as well as of men an integral part of the design, implementation, monitoring and evaluation of policies and programmes in all political, economic and societal spheres, so that women and men benefit equally, and inequality is not perpetuated. The ultimate goal of mainstreaming is to achieve gender equality.[12]

"Mainstreaming," declares the International Labour Organization, "includes gender-specific activities and affirmative action, whenever women or men are in a particularly disadvantageous position. Gender-specific interventions can target women exclusively, men and women together, or only men, to enable them to participate in and benefit equally from development efforts. These are necessary temporary measures designed to combat the direct and indirect consequences of past discrimination."[13]

For all the talk of gender mainstreaming being about addressing discrimination and the differential experiences of women *and men,* in reality it was, and still is, predominantly about women. Where achieving gender equality is a stated goal, the continued focus on women is somewhat understandable, given the discrimination that women endure in all walks of life. Without sufficient attention, however, to the drivers of inequality, why and how patriarchy is perpetuated, or the societal pressures, threats, and vulnerabilities that men face, the roots of the problem will not be tackled adequately. As discussed in Chapter 5, in conflict-affected situations in particular, attention to the status of men is essential in tackling discrimination against women, and both can be related to the causes of conflict.

The same trend is evident in discussions of gender perspectives. Inevitably, they concern women. For example, it is not uncommon for a female political leader, particularly one coming from a conflict area, to be questioned not only on issues relating to her portfolio but about her personal experiences as a woman leader, and the situation, status, and experiences of women more widely. Similarly, consultations with women in conflict areas—regardless of whether they are lawyers, doctors, community workers, or otherwise—will point to their needs and roles as women. That is considered gaining a gender perspective—but it is women's perspectives. A male political leader is rarely asked about the situation or needs of men in his society, and when men are consulted, it is typically about general issues, not about men's experiences of the conflict or peace process as men.

Although conceptually the differences between the terms *gender* and *women* are clear, the terms are often used interchangeably. The situation is not helped by women's rights advocates and others who have jumped on the gender bandwagon. If *gender mainstreaming* and *gender balance* were not enough, terms such as *gender justice* and *gender architecture* have appeared in policy documents and discourse. The politically correct even speak of *gender groups* and *gender rights* as if mention of women's groups, women's rights, or equal access to justice for women were somehow unsavory.

This conflation and expansion of terms has turned what should be obvious and fundamentally good practice into a seemingly incomprehensible set of issues. In the process it has created confusion across institutions and has often gotten lost in translation across languages and cultures. Recalls one former UN staff member, "During a workshop in Cambodia, each time the English term 'gender mainstreaming' was used and translated into Khmer, the participants fell about laughing."[14] It soon became apparent that the translator's closest approximation for the term *gender mainstreaming* in Khmer was "men and women jumping into the stream together."

The terminology is no less problematic among the development practitioners, political analysts, peacekeeping experts, and others, English speakers or otherwise, who are bound by policies to mainstream gender but are not sure what it means or how to do it. A 2005 independent evaluation of UNDP's gender mainstreaming program is unequivocal in this regard: "Differing interpretations of 'gender mainstreaming' create confusion and impede progress."[15] To some, talk of gender has to do with increasing the numbers and status of women in the workplace. Others conceive of gender as relating to women and reproductive issues or domestic violence.[16]

In reality it is about ensuring that the projects and programs are executed effectively. It can be explained in four basic steps.[17] First, mainstreaming a gendered perspective is one way to avoid doing harm. In other words, the intervention—be it provision of basic food supplies or an assessment of conditions—should in no way inadvertently harm either men or women. Second, it is a means of ensuring that intervention does not inadvertently perpetuate harmful practice. In other words, out of ignorance of local contexts and cultures, outside actors should take care not to reinforce and empower groups or individuals who perpetuate exclusion and heighten vulnerabilities and violence against others, notably women. While this sounds obvious, it happens all too often. Outsiders consult with village or community leaders (typically men) who may have no knowledge or no interest in highlighting the needs of women. Third, it is simply about good programming. Gendered analysis and mainstreaming help identify the beneficiaries and their needs as well as the potential opportunities and constraints they face. It has relevance in every sector, whether it is planning and implementation of elections, the provision of supplies for camps, distribution of food, or investigation of war crimes. Women and men have different needs and different levels of access. If this information is not integrated into program planning, the outcome is invariably flawed. Thus, if the job at hand is the provision of medical supplies, gender mainstreaming can help ensure that the differential medical needs of women and men are accounted for and the relevant supplies provided. It can also highlight the most effective ways of reaching the broadest cross section of the population. For example a mobile clinic staffed with female medics is more likely to reach women in a traditional Islamic community than would a fixed facility staffed by men. Finally, mainstreaming also contributes to the promotion of equality, basic human rights, and internationally sanctioned values.

Inevitably, when the clarification is given and the relevance of gender analysis to peacekeeping, conflict prevention, or other issues is presented, most practitioners respond positively. "This is common sense. It is about good programming."[18] But they also point to the disingenuous nature of the gender proponents. If gender is about men and women, they say, why is gender work always focused on women?

Ironically, the conflation of terms and the assumption that gender issues are about women only have led to both—women and gender—being relegated to the edges of peace and security discourse. Yet, as discussed elsewhere, gender analysis is profoundly important in the context of peace and security. Attention to societal norms and the changing or deteriorating situation of men and women can give detailed insight into the dynamics of conflict and peacebuilding and point to opportunities for preventing, mitigating, and resolving crises from the bottom up. As noted throughout, women also have significant contributions to make to peace and security issues. As academics, policymakers, and practitioners, we need clarity in the vocabulary and terms we use. If we are focusing on women, we should talk about women. If we are addressing the gendered dimension of issues, we should ensure that men and women are taken into account. For people—women or men, girls or boys—living in conflict zones, there is too much at stake. Their needs and concerns, their strengths and willingness to build peace, cannot be ignored or set aside because of frustration or confusion around the terms being used.

Institutional and Operational Complications

The normative and conceptual inconsistencies are reinforced through and by institutions. At the operational level, various factors contribute to the continued marginalization of women in programming related to peace and security. First, to the extent that there is attention, issues relating to women have been integrated overwhelmingly into the development work of multilateral and bilateral institutions. Second, integrating conflict-sensitive perspectives into development initiatives generally, let alone with a gendered lens, remains a challenge. Third, there is insufficient qualitative and quantitative information available. What exists at the field level is often edited into oblivion. Fourth, leadership is still sporadic, and fifth, there continues to be a lack of effective coordination within and among agencies and donors, which perpetuates the slow pace of change.

Passing the Buck and Ghettoizing Women

On the one hand, policies dictate that gender perspectives are to be mainstreamed throughout the work of every sector of the UN family or bilateral donors and others. On the other hand, the invisibility of this approach and the particular lack of attention to women have led to a haphazard mix of entities within the system, charged with attention to and the advancement of women. Within the UN system, on development-related issues, UNIFEM takes the lead at the field level. It is part of the larger UNDP structure, yet operates independently too. UNIFEM

> is the women's fund at the United Nations. It provides financial and technical assistance to innovative programs and strategies to foster women's empowerment and gender equality. Placing the advancement of women's human rights at the centre of all of its efforts, UNIFEM focuses its activities on four strategic areas: (1) reducing feminized poverty, (2) ending violence against women, (3) reversing the spread of HIV/AIDS among women and girls, and (4) achieving gender equality in democratic governance in times of peace as well as war.[19]

Second, there is the Division for the Advancement of Women (DAW). It "aim[s] to ensure the participation of women as equal partners with men in all aspects of human endeavour. . . . The Division promotes women as equal participants and beneficiaries of sustainable development, peace and security, governance and human rights. As part of its mandate, it strives to stimulate the mainstreaming of gender perspectives both within and outside the United Nations system."[20] DAW works with the Office of the Special Adviser on Gender Issues, whose "main objective is to promote and strengthen the effective implementation of the Millennium Declaration, the Beijing Declaration and the Platform for Action of the Fourth World Conference on Women (FWCW) held in Beijing in 1995 and the Outcome Document of the special session of the General Assembly on Beijing+5."[21] Third, there is the International Training and Research Institute for the Advancement of Women. It claims to be "the only United Nations entity mandated at the international level to promote and undertake research and training programmes to contribute to the advancement of women and gender equality worldwide."[22] Fourth, UNICEF and the UN Population Fund (UNFPA) also consider women as among their primary constituency or beneficiaries. And finally, as the UN's development agency, UNDP is clearly of immense importance.

The disparate (yet clearly overlapping) nature of these entities not only creates confusion and the inevitable turf battles but also gives the impression that much more is being done for women than is really the case. Moreover, although the mantra is of gender mainstreaming across the UN system, the existence of the women-focused entities often results in the gender (i.e., women's) buck being passed to them. Yet the requisite funding is never available. As Stephen Lewis, the UN's Special Representative of the Secretary-General (SRSG) on Africa and HIV/AIDS, puts it, "Here's what festers in the craw: the funding for implementation is not yet available. The needs and rights of women never command singular urgency."[23]

Recognizing this dilemma, some donor countries have at times suggested the disbanding of UNIFEM and company and their integration into larger bodies. But given the poor record on addressing women's needs in general, the fear is that without the dedicated women's agencies, even the limited focus on women now would be lost entirely. Others, notably Stephen Lewis, have pointed out the dearth of leadership by and support for women. "Within multilateralism, that is within the UN system, wherein lies the best hope for leadership, there must be a change in the representation of women," said Lewis in April 2005, calling for the creation of a new major entity with increased resources that places women firmly at the center.[24] The idea of a superagency dedicated to women has gained ground during the UN reform process and may well become a reality. In November 2006, the High-Level Panel on UN Reform endorsed the idea. But could doing that compound the existing ghettoization of women and result in further neglect on the part of others? What guarantees will there be that the agency will be funded sufficiently? On paper and bureaucratically the agency may have stature, but in practice, on the ground, how will it coordinate its efforts with those of others? The question remains: How do we ensure that the international system provides comprehensive support and opportunities to ensure that women's participation, needs, strengths, and perspectives are addressed systematically, in every area of work, by everyone?

The system-wide structure is mirrored internally within institutions. Gender units, gender advisers, and gender focal points are now commonplace within the UN system and among bilateral donors and regional institutions. Their mandates may speak of gender issues, but by and large their programs are almost entirely dedicated to women—their empowerment, protection from violence, participation in elections, and so forth. The reasons for this emphasis are obvious. Proverbial playing fields have been, and still are, heavily weighted against women. To bring equality, significant attention, intervention, and affirmative action are needed. Arguably, however, if the focus of work is on women or the provisions of Resolution 1325 or issues of equality, then the labels and titles should reflect that more accurately.

The existence of a dedicated unit or staff person is, however, a double-edged sword. In many instances, without them, attention to the situation of women would be entirely missed. Yet the danger is that, where there is a dedicated gender officer or unit, the interpretation across agencies (among staff and management) is that gender issues (i.e., women's issues) are being dealt with by someone else. Thus although in theory, staff with responsibilities for political affairs, human rights, or development must take account of the differential needs and circumstances of men and women (i.e., a gendered perspective), in reality, they either do not understand that or consider the gendered dimensions to be neither their priority nor their responsibility.

The Development and Security Nexus

The stovepiping of issues relating to women is similar to the ways in which political, developmental, human rights, security, and other issues have also been separated.[25] In the years since the end of the Cold War, the development community has become increasingly aware of the complex and inextricable relations among conflict, peace, security, human rights, and development. By definition, development programs aim to alleviate poverty and improve livelihoods. But if misconstrued, development initiatives can also exacerbate existing societal or political tensions that ultimately lead to conflict. Clearly, conflict, particularly armed conflict, is extremely detrimental to development efforts. As a result, over the years the principle of "do no harm" coined by Mary Anderson has been widely embraced by the community.[26] More recently, however, attention has also been paid to ensuring that development efforts not only do no harm but play a positive role in helping to alleviate tensions, address structural sources of conflict, and promote sustainable peace.

The "do no harm" approach weaves into the rights-based approach to development, which places international human rights instruments at the center of the development paradigm. The premise is that people everywhere have a right to social, political, and economic development. They have a right to be empowered and participate in decisionmaking, rather than be passive recipients of choices made for them. This approach is about promoting active citizenship, such that people have rights, expectations, and responsibilities. In 1998 Kofi Annan stated that such an approach obligates society to "respond to the inalienable rights of individuals . . . empower them to demand justice as a right, not a charity."[27] Writing in 2002, scholar Hugo Slim took it further.

> Rights-talk has the ability to finally politicize development between the muddy low ground and the moral high ground. Human rights give

a language of political contract to matters of poverty, injustice, and armed violence. Rights-talk keeps people from being perceived as needy, as victims, and as beneficiaries. Instead, it enables these same people to know and present themselves as rightful and dignified people who can make just demands of power and spell out the duties of power in terms of moral and political goods.[28]

In effect, human rights, peace, and security issues are seeping into the operations of traditional development agencies. The stovepiping of efforts is being challenged by the need for more holistic approaches that take account of conflict and rights issues. Major development agencies are, for example, attempting to integrate conflict sensitivity into their assessment and operational procedures. They have developed an array of conflict-analysis and early warning tools to meet this objective. But the impact and implementation vary.

Situation analyses that include an assessment of security, political, economic, and sociocultural variables inevitably point to new issues that require attention. Such analyses can rarely be done in a vacuum, however. Typically, agencies have established programming priorities using alternative means of assessment, or the programs under way are multiyear efforts that cannot be altered or stopped unexpectedly. Moreover, given the relative newness of conflict perspectives to development work, most agencies have not yet fully integrated conflict expertise into their mainstream areas of work. As a result, a team of conflict analysts may offer guidance to their development colleagues, but they do not always have the resources (technical, financial, or human) to follow through with their assessment and recommendations. Entrenched practices and sensitivity to the politicization of development issues—an occupational hazard among development practitioners—compound the challenge. In effect, the rhetoric of conflict-sensitive development is still not fully matched in reality.

As discussed earlier, women and men experience conflict and cope (or don't cope) in very different ways, which poses important challenges to development actors working in conflict-affected societies. Gender roles need to be understood throughout the phases of conflict, in order to obtain a comprehensive assessment of the situation and to respond adequately through programming and policy. Yet if the integration of conflict and development issues is not tricky enough, then adding gender perspectives is certainly proving to be difficult. Ideally, development practice should already be gender-sensitive. Since that is not the case, the challenge is to mainstream conflict and gender sensitivity into development practice simultaneously. But, in the words of one practitioner, it is "too much to ask."[29]

Various factors contribute to the cycle of invisibility. First, analysts can overlook or ignore information through benign neglect and lack of understanding of the linkages among conflict, peace, and men's and women's experiences. Second, although the frameworks for analysis aim to provide a balanced assessment of conflict causes and mitigators, too often the emphasis is on the former. Since gender and women are confused, there is a tendency to disregard the gendered dimensions of the causes of conflict. In other words, unemployment among male youth may arise as a contributor to conflict, but it is not seen as a gender issue. By the same token, women's experiences are rarely the cause of conflict, and thus they are invisible in the assessments. The dynamics of gender relations and notions of masculinity and femininity that can fuel or exacerbate conflict are also largely disregarded.

Equal attention to conflict mitigators would provide a more accurate assessment of the situation in-country and, where relevant, point to alternative forces and positive agents. In many instances, those are women. In the Solomon Islands, for example, women play a key role in targeting alcoholism, which is a catalyst for much communal violence. As scholars Caroline Moser and Cathy McIlwaine have discovered in their participatory community-based research in areas experiencing gang and other forms of violence, such as in Colombia, women's associations emerge as the most positive institutions in terms of violence prevention.[30]

In efforts to address the gaps in existing frameworks, some institutions, notably the World Bank and UNDP, have reviewed and produced additional documentation with specific guidelines to draw out the gendered dimensions of analysis and practice.[31] But the question is whether such institutions pursue the agenda systematically, or if the guidelines join the reams of other reports neatly stacked on office shelves, to be used by the cluster of "gender experts" alone.

The Information Gap and Invisibility Trap

The lack of data about the gendered impacts of development, conflict, poverty, or crises compounds the institutional weaknesses. For example, although assertions are made about the "feminization of poverty" in conflict situations, there are insufficient quantitative data to confirm it fully. Even the definition of the phrase is unclear. There are countless qualitative examples, anecdotes, and significant information about the factors that link poverty, conflict, and women, but quantitative data are limited. Without the statistical information, institutions such as the World Bank and many donor countries are unable and unwilling to focus attention and resources to the question of women. It is often a catch-22 situation, however: countries need the assistance and funding to develop effective means of capturing the quantitative data. Without the data, however, they are unable to generate the funding needed. In a 2007 donors meeting on Liberia, the Norwegian government sought to break this cycle by pledging funds for data collection.[32] It remains to be seen how sex-disaggregated the statistical data will be.

Similarly, there are significant anecdotal and country-based studies that point to women's empowerment during conflict. The impact of women's activities, their changing status vis-à-vis men, and their potential leadership capacities in communities are not widely known, understood, or drawn upon in programmatic planning. Mainstream multilateral actors make limited use of the information that does exist.

The information gap is also apparent across the reams of country reports that international agencies produce for internal or external consumption. Time and again, information about the differential security, human rights, and governance implications of a crisis on women and men is not documented. Similarly, the efforts of ordinary women and men or organized civil society entities to withstand the spread of violence are not mentioned or analyzed effectively. There is still a tendency to insert a paragraph on gender at the end of reports and say it is mainstreamed.

To be sure, in the midst of crises, detailed information or quantitative data are not always readily available. But there are plenty of sources—especially women's human rights and peace-oriented NGOs and research centers—that collect and analyze information. These sources can contribute to gaining a more accurate understanding of the situation at hand. Using their information is critical to every aspect of policymaking, emergency relief, and long-term programming. As a 2006 UN handbook on humanitarian responses advises, "Unless we know who the affected population is, men or women, girls or boys, young or old, and who among them is the most vulnerable or the strongest, the responses we develop may be off target."[33] Similarly, those involved in setting up elections and providing security and other aspects of postconflict peacekeeping and peacebuilding acknowledge that sex-disaggregated data—and situation analyses that highlight the differential roles, capacities, and vulnerabilities of men and women— would benefit their programs. Yet the information either is not captured or, worse, is collated and reported by the gender unit/adviser and then edited out by others as the report moves upstream. The exclusion is

explained in a variety of ways: it was poorly written; we needed space
for other issues; or, simply, we forgot.[34] "Time and again, information
about women seems to evaporate," says Sarah Maguire, consultant and
former senior human rights adviser to the UK's Department for International Development.[35]

Whatever the reasons for the exclusion or oversight of information
regarding women, the net result is perpetuation of the cycle of invisibility. If the information is not available, it will not be considered when
policies are made and programs planned. At best a side project may be
developed, but it will be separate from the major programming efforts.
The exclusion of women from policies and programs in turn leads to
their invisibility in reporting and assessments. So the cycle continues,
and the parallel universes remain disconnected.

The women, peace, and security (WPS) agenda creates a bureaucratic conundrum. It comes from the real world where development and
politics, security and social issues, human rights and culture merge and
flow together. But within bureaucracies such as the UN, no single agency
can take the lead on the WPS agenda in its totality. To date no one has
been appointed to take the lead on coordinating the issues and entities
either. Unlike the children and armed conflict agenda or issues relating
to internally displaced persons, WPS does not have a dedicated senior
representative with the means and credibility to conduct research, advocate policies, and convene others. Such senior representatives are not
always effective at pushing the agenda and the envelope and may be the
cause of more competition. But they can be an important focal point.
The alternative is that the issues are everyone's responsibility and therefore no one's.

Of course, there is an advantage to dispersing responsibility: as
interest spreads across and within agencies, a sense of ownership also
emerges. For example, UNFPA was not a key player in the WPS discourse in its early years, yet by 2006 it had emerged as a major force in
the UN system. Increasingly, more NGOs and donor agencies are developing projects related to the provisions of Resolution 1325. But there is
a disadvantage too: efforts are disjointed. Although there is overlap in
some areas, such as women's leadership and governance, other issues
receive little or no attention. There is little monitoring of activities, no
concerted way in which key actors (including the Secretary-General,
major agencies, or UN member states that hold the purse strings and
influence senior appointments) can be held accountable for their areas
of responsibility. With apathetic and at times resistant national governments, the UN system can easily point to member states as the reason

for lack of implementation. The buck is easily passed from one to the other.

Once-a-Year Leadership

The situation is not helped by the lack of systematic commitment from organizational leaders, donors, and others. The involvement of high-ranking personnel can make a difference. If they prioritize the WPS agenda, allocate the resources, and demand accountability and information, the message filters down and across agencies. If they do not, the issue is diluted and set aside. Too often, those individuals and units dedicated to ending discrimination against women or promoting the provisions of Resolution 1325 find themselves isolated, marginalized, and at times mocked.

The once-a-year speeches do not and cannot replace sustained focus and attention to the situation of women in each conflict. Leadership is not the responsibility of one nation or senior UN personnel. It must come from all levels of management, country teams, and SRSGs, showing through action that women's protection and participation matter. It involves taking the lead to make the links: for example, if a 1999 World Bank study indicates that women's involvement in decisionmaking lessens corruption, why hasn't women's empowerment become a systematic priority in the good governance and anticorruption agenda?

Similarly, if the sexual exploitation and abuse of women by international peacekeeping and humanitarian personnel is deemed intolerable, why does it still occur? If increasing the numbers of women in peacekeeping missions is a concrete means of stamping out such exploitation, why are there still so few women associated with peace operations? A lack of qualified women in security forces is the excuse often given. But it is a tired excuse. With pressure from the NGO community, the UN Department of Peacekeeping Operations (DPKO) convinced India, a key troop-contributing country, to deploy an all-female police unit to Liberia in 2006. Women across Africa, Europe, and Latin America are interested in serving on peace missions, not least because of the attractive financial packages offered and career enhancement that results. If the system is sincere in its commitment to the deployment of women and to the protection of host communities, then its recruitment efforts have to alter accordingly. It may mean advertising in alternative arenas, working with women's organizations to raise awareness, identifying countries with strong contingents of women in military and police forces, or providing incentives to troop-contributing countries that include higher percentages of women in their peacekeeping units. A variety of initiatives can be put in place. The talk is still not matched by the walk.

At times, the simplest yet profoundly symbolic steps are not being taken. For example, Resolution 1325 calls on the UN system and member states to appoint more women to senior posts. Speaking to the Security Council in 2000, UN Secretary-General Kofi Annan appeared decidedly supportive.

> We know that conflict resolution, peacekeeping and peace-building call for creative and flexible approaches. In all these areas, we have seen examples of women playing an important role—not least on my own continent, Africa. And yet the potential contribution of women to peace and security remains severely under-valued. Women are still grossly under-represented at the decision-making level, from conflict prevention to conflict resolution to post-conflict reconciliation. . . . We are here today because we are determined to change that. . . . I am here today to ask you to do everything in your power to . . . help ensure that women and girls in conflict situations are protected; that perpetrators of violence against women in conflict are brought to justice; and that women are able to take their rightful and equal place at the decision-making table in questions of peace and security.[36]

Five years later on International Women's Day, he reiterated his commitment. "At the 2005 World Summit, world leaders declared that 'progress for women is progress for all.' On this International Women's Day, let us rededicate ourselves to demonstrating the truth behind those words. Let us ensure that half the world's population takes up its rightful place in the world's decisionmaking."

Yet throughout this time, Annan appointed only two women as SRSGs to conflict-affected countries, notably Georgia and Burundi. At the end of his tenure, out of eighteen SRSGs in conflict-affected areas, none was a woman. Year in, year out, when the opportunities arise, women are bypassed. Whether it is willful or benign negligence, the result is the same. The message sent and received is that, regardless of what women need or do, or how they might "bring a degree of sanity" to the situation, there are always more pressing issues.

Poor Coordination

Despite the existence of interagency working groups and coordination mechanisms within bureaucracies, the ongoing lack of coordination is notable. A 2007 evaluation focusing on potential synergy between the DPKO and the UN High Commissioner for Refugees (UNHCR), for example, commends both entities for their progress in raising the profile of gender issues in policies and tools as they relate to conflict and emergency situations. Yet the report states that "it is unclear the extent to which the resolution [1325] is being incorporated into UNHCR's programmes and activities."[37] It calls for greater cooperation, information sharing, and coordination between the two entities. The key recommendations emerging from the report call for increased joint planning, common strategies to tackle gender-based violence, and sharing of tools and action plans.

The disconnect between policy and practice, between headquarters and field offices, and between rhetoric and resources, which is so prevalent in international agencies, is affecting women on the ground. At the policy level, major actors endorse the inclusion of women in planning and implementing programs. There has been a proliferation of policy directives, guidelines, and handbooks across international entities. For example, the World Bank's policies state that its aim is "to reduce gender disparities and enhance women's participation in the economic development of member countries." The bank claims to design gender-sensitive policies and programs in a variety of ways, by identifying barriers women face, assessing costs and benefits of strategies to address these barriers, ensuring effective program implementation, and establishing effective gender-disaggregated monitoring and evaluation systems.[38] Yet there is no systematic approach to or understanding of issues relating to women in postconflict situations, despite the fact that the bank has been heavily involved in postwar processes.

Even major agencies that recognize the need to support women's groups in conflict areas have not developed adequate means of disbursing and monitoring small grants, and thus even if there is some will to support women's groups, inertia gets in the way. The World Bank's Conflict Prevention and Reconstruction Unit, which was a key proponent of gender sensitivity, managed the Post-Conflict Fund until 2007. According to researchers Andrea Zuckerman and Marcia Greenberg, however, "between 1997 and 2004, an estimated 3 percent of the Fund's grants (approx. 5 percent of the total funding) targeted women as a specific group."[39]

The Triple-A Syndrome

To observers and women activists working outside these structures, the normative and conceptual issues, coupled with the inertia that often characterizes bureaucracies, manifest themselves through the triple-A syndrome of apathy, ad hoc practice, and amnesia.

Apathy

Regardless of the policies and the seemingly heartfelt speeches, the inaction and the lack of leadership within major institutions set a tone that women are not important. The 2005 evaluation of UNDP's gender-mainstreaming efforts points to the inconsistency. "In 2001 the [UNDP] Administrator reaffirmed that gender equality remained a core commitment of UNDP. . . . However the global gender programme budget for 2000–2004 was a fifth of its earlier budget. . . . In 2002 . . . UNDP did not emphasize gender mainstreaming or the promotion of gender equality as its priorities in its change management process."[40]

Addressing women's protection and certainly their participation in decisionmaking is still perceived as an optional extra, a good idea if the time, context, or situation allows for it. It is rarely taken as an issue of sufficient importance. This apathy seeps down to all levels of practice. It is evident in the ways in which information about women is collected or edited; whether meetings with women's organizations are included on the agenda of international missions'; how women's needs are addressed in peace accords and other documents; if mainstream policies and programs take account of the differential circumstances of women; and how resources are allocated. To make a comparison with other areas of practice: there are no ifs, ands, or buts in the need for accurate financial management. It is not up to individual managers or staff to determine if budgeting standards will be maintained or not. It is mandatory. The same principle should apply to the question of women's protection and participation and the broader goals of gender mainstreaming and equality in conflict-affected settings.

Apathy often hides behind a disingenuous veil of cultural sensitivity. "Women are very important, but in this culture, under these circumstances, we cannot" is the way of many a conversation with senior staff, especially men in national and international structures.[41] The "culture card" is an effective means of avoiding the question of women and continuing work along a well-trodden path that not only excludes them but also is detrimental to society. It is an excuse that arises consistently in the context of negotiations, disarmament and demobilization programming, transitional justice initiatives, governance, and other aspects of peacebuilding. As noted earlier, cultural sensitivity is rarely a concern when democracy promotion (i.e., elections) or market liberalization is being promoted.

Moreover, women—particularly those emerging from grassroots and community activism—are the most sensitive to their own cultural context. They are also more discerning about the ways and means in which issues must be addressed to avoid a backlash. For example, as noted earlier, Afghan women were alarmed when the lifting of the burkha became synonymous with their struggle for rights and equality. It not only deflected from more critical issues, but was also an easy target of the more traditional elements in their society. This is not just an issue in Islamic societies. In Cambodia, former minister Mu Sochua recognized that by dressing and conducting herself in accordance with Cambodian culture she was able to initiate policies that otherwise would be deemed culturally unacceptable.

A common message from many women activists is that the environment in which they are operating and the issues with which they are grappling are far too important to be discredited simply because of imagery, dress code, ignorance of social mores, or apathy on the part of outsiders. If these women are willing to step into the fray, then the very least that international actors must do is to acknowledge, respect, and support them.

Ad Hoc Practice

Those who become indignant about charges of widespread apathy often point to the areas of progress. Inevitably, in every institution, pockets of innovation and good practice can be found. But there is no systematic practice or integration of the issues into the mainstream activities and programs of the institutions. As mentioned above, there is little coordination, but the ad hoc practice makes itself evident in a number of other ways.

Always pilots, never programs. There are often small-scale initiatives or projects in place run by various agencies with a focus on women. They are rarely scaled up or implemented more broadly. For example, the UNIFEM/UNDP project on the involvement of women in weapons collection in Albania (discussed in Chapter 4) is often cited as an example of good practice, yet there is no indication that the elements of the project were ever replicated, adapted, or integrated effectively elsewhere.[42] Similarly, despite the endless calls for participation and the precedence set in various countries, the involvement of women in peace negotiations is still not a matter of course. The wheel is invented over and over again. One-off initiatives never seem to take off.

We have a very capable [young] woman, a.k.a. crazy gender woman. The efforts of major institutions can often be traced to individual personnel who have an interest in or dedication to the issues. Typically they are women—either young and in junior positions or veterans of the system, bruised by the glass ceiling, and branded as too outspoken or difficult. In many instances the people taking on the task of mainstreaming gender become focal points. In other words, an individual (typically a woman) is tasked with an additional set of responsibilities but is not given additional compensation or time to do so. They do two jobs for the price of one. There are focal points for other issues too, but it is absurd to think that one person should be responsible for ensuring (and has the requisite expertise) that every policy, program, and document produced by her department addresses the differential needs of women and men.

Since 2000, with support from more progressive donors, gender advisory posts have been established in some UN agencies and across regional and multilateral organizations. They give space to the handful of professionals, predominantly women, who have developed expertise in women, peace, and security issues. Yet the contradictions prevail. The posts exist, but staff often face a dual challenge of having to prove the significance and benefits of gendered perspectives or women's inclusion, while at the same time being marginalized by the institution for being overly focused on the issues. This isolation and the perception that the institution does not value the expertise can result in self-censorship by personnel, especially women, who may be concerned about a dead-end career path. At times it seems that for every person who enters the fray, another is stepping aside, burned-out, exhausted, and disillusioned with the immobility and hypocrisy of the systems and institutions.

Of course, when there are success stories, as in the case of the UN Transitional Authority in East Timor, the departments in charge are quick to take credit. The uphill battles that individual staff face to get women on the agenda, to ensure that the resources are available for them to get the work done, are brushed aside. The lack of sustained follow-through is also left unmentioned. And the departure of an individual can typically result in the slowdown or even closure of programs relating to women, peace, and security.

Wall-to-wall paper. Publications, policy statements, and printed speeches such as those quoted above have a long shelf life. They give the impression of clear priorities and commitments to women's rights and gender equality. Yet it is more likely that the reports are commissioned and produced by typically small gender units and the speeches are given on particular occasions—notably International Women's Day or the annual anniversary of Resolution 1325. They are singular initiatives, contained within the context of the day they were spoken, with little impact on or relevance to the mainstream work of the institutions in question.

Fickle funders and shoestring theory. Funding practices and donors perpetuate ad hoc practice in many cases. A government may be a leading proponent of Resolution 1325 and a keen supporter of entities dedicated to the advancement of women. Yet the same donors do not apply their own policies systematically in their interactions with other agencies within the UN system or in their bilateral interactions. Thus, with one hand they may espouse the need for women's political participation, and with the other they provide significant funds to major agencies or governments with a mandate to support good governance or reconstruction, but do not specify a focus on the promotion of equal opportunities for women in politics as a criterion for the provision of funds or in the overall priorities of the major players.

Similarly, at international donors' meetings, national governments are asked to set priorities, and then donors make their pledges. Yet in the scramble to prioritize, the needs of women are among the first to be taken off the table. In part because of a lack of understanding, the stated priorities are rarely, if ever, framed with a full gender lens. In other words, a government may support security sector reform as a key peacebuilding priority, but in identifying the concerns they are more likely to focus on the perceived threat of male ex-fighters or the needs of their military personnel than to tackle the challenges of ensuring women's equal access to the sector. Similarly, economic programming or poverty alleviation strategies do not systematically integrate the differential needs and capacities of women and men in all sectors of the economy. The rhetoric of gender equality or mainstreaming is not put into practice where it counts.

The lack of systematic funding for gender advisory posts also perpetuates the ad hoc practice. Multilateral and bilateral agencies can achieve a great deal if there is staff commitment. Typically, the gender advisers or, more often, the gender focal points drive much of the progress. Yet these advisory positions are often not included in regular agency budgets. The funds allocated to staff training or regular programming are minimal. This shoestring approach to broader gender mainstreaming or even the specific focus on women's protection and participation belies the stated goals of the international community writ large.

Women in conflict areas are being let down severely when rhetoric is not matched with the necessary resources.

The cake and the egg. Ad hoc practices are perhaps best exemplified by the odd projects and last-minute attempts that are sometimes apparent. The temporary appointment of a gender adviser to put gender into the work of the Peruvian TRC, as described in Chapter 6, is a classic example. Similarly, the project to support women's political participation, the small fund, the odd workshop, and the now obligatory gender paragraph in reports feed the feel-good notion of something being done. But these initiatives cannot make a difference if the major players have not absorbed important lessons about the important roles women can play. As one practitioner put it, it's like baking a cake. You can't add a whole egg when the mixture is in the oven. You have to mix it from the beginning. Doing that changes the very nature of the cake.[43]

Amnesia

Finally, there is pervasive institutional amnesia. Good practices get lost, are not well documented, or are transferred. In El Salvador, for example, the DDR program involving a range of international actors addressed women to some extent. Ten years later, many of the same institutions were operating in Sierra Leone, yet they failed to implement the same policies.

The lack of strong documentation and codification of experience—successes and failures—is a major hindrance in this field, within and between institutions. In many cases field offices and headquarters communicate poorly. Thus lessons from one place are not readily available to the staff in another place. The lack of documentation is compounded by the assumption among some practitioners that initiatives cannot be replicated or adapted across regions. For example, in the case of Rwanda, many international practitioners and former USAID personnel who were involved in the aftermath of the genocide readily acknowledge the work and contributions of women. They point to the success of the Rwandan Women's Initiative, a small fund dedicated to supporting women's recovery. Yet when asked why similar funds were not created in other contexts, they are quick to classify it as unique to Rwanda,[44] despite the fact that the Rwandan Women's Initiative was a close replica of a similar fund set up in Bosnia just a year earlier in 1996.

Lack of institutional memory is not helped by a reliance on short-term consultants. Oftentimes they come to assist with planning or programming, yet may not have access to past information or the impact of other initiatives. As short-term staff they also take away much of the knowledge upon their departure. In other words, initiatives targeting women or aimed at ensuring the equitable treatment of women appear not to be monitored, reviewed, or collated in a systematic manner to enable exchange of experience and improvement.

Evaluations, onetime workshops, and action planning on gender issues help to draw management attention to those issues. But if the results and recommendations made are not followed through comprehensively or in a timely manner, the net effect is minimal. Veterans of international bureaucracies sometimes argue that these problems exist in all areas. But that is neither a good enough excuse nor entirely true. Where there is leadership or donor commitment, systematized efforts are more in evidence. But on women, the reluctance to stop, review, and revamp, means that ad hoc practice and amnesia can prevail.

Moving Forward to Make a Difference

Have things changed since October 2000? The answer is undoubtedly yes. Internationally there is more awareness not only of the specific challenges facing women but also of their role in and contributions to reconstruction. Some agencies are beginning to revise their programs to ensure sensitivity to women earlier on in their processes. More staff are being trained on such issues, and analytical tools developed to assess needs and the impact of conflict are being reconfigured to highlight the differential experiences of men and women.[45] But the normative and institutional challenges remain. National governments—donors and recipients of assistance—which are the members of multilateral entities and collectively make up the international community, are arguably the main offenders. Lack of consistent leadership means the burden of ensuring visibility is still shouldered by a handful of NGOs and smaller entities within multilateral institutions. The major actors in postconflict reconstruction, multilateral agencies, and even major international development and humanitarian NGOs have been slow to take the issues on board comprehensively and systematically. The resources available are still far too limited. Progress has been made, but it is far from sustainable or institutionalized.

Conceptual confusion and gender-ology are still obstacles. Institutions need to review and revise their use of terminology and labeling. More clarity is needed in terms of mandates and job descriptions. Distinctions must be made between women-focused (and men-focused) programs and those that are seeking to mainstream women into traditionally male-oriented areas. If gender equality is the goal, then its implications must feature in all policies, budgets, and programming. Staff must receive training, and their performance reviews must assess their knowledge and practice of gender-sensitive analysis and programming.

It is also not enough to insert a paragraph on gender in reports or to fund a handful of projects and claim that "gender has been mainstreamed" or that women are being fully integrated. There needs to be a shift away from the notion that attention to women is a luxury and toward the recognition that genuine gender analysis is integral to the success of work in postconflict areas. Quite simply, if the breakdown is not done to ensure that the needs of men and women are being met, how can agencies ensure that their programs are targeted correctly? In many instances, meeting that goal will require the integration of gendered perspectives into existing program areas, as well as specific projects tailored to or targeting women or men only. Such changes have implications for resource allocation, the expertise needed, the nature of partners in-country, and so forth. In other words, there may be a need for significant redirection of programming. In turn, that will require demonstrated leadership and commitment.

Recognition of the existing work that women do is also a critical step. With assistance and capacity building, their initiatives could be scaled up to have a broader impact and become more sustainable. It has to start early. From the time that international actors are considering "structural prevention," or when the low-profile talks-about-talks are taking place to sound out possibilities for negotiations, women's voices must be heard and included. The international community, through the UN, can be the standard-bearer, committed to upholding its own values, principles, and policies. If the UN or other international entities send in teams made up of predominantly men, they have no credibility asking local parties to have 30 or 50 percent female representation.

In negotiating the language of peace accords, the UN and its regional partners can again set the standards and uphold the values they espouse and the resolutions they are obliged to follow. Including the language of equality for men and women or ensuring that texts being negotiated reference women's needs in peace and postconflict processes is not that difficult. There are far more contentious issues. Yet too often, the multilateral system holds back; instead of aspiring and being greater than the sum of its member states, it takes the lowest-common-denominator position.

International actors and agencies involved in peace and postconflict processes could take a few simple steps, at little financial cost, to ensure women's inclusion. For example, targeted outreach to women's groups can shed light on their work and identify a cadre of women with knowledge and access to grassroots communities who can enhance needs assessments, planning, and implementation processes. Ensuring that missions and team members with expertise in political, security, or other areas are aware of the implications of their work for both women and men can be catalytic in terms of the information that is gathered and resultant programming. For example, in 2006, the UN's Technical Assessment Mission to Nepal recognized the critical disadvantage that women, particularly those in lower castes and ethnic minorities, faced in accessing information about elections. Through interactions with women's civil society networks, they explored partnerships for alternative modes of information dissemination to remote communities and the range of targeted materials needed.

Proactive efforts to bring women's representatives to international donors' meetings can ensure that their voices are heard at the highest levels and that consideration of gender issues is not only part of the agenda but specifically mandated by donors. Above all, major actors can ensure that such efforts (many of which are already being undertaken in some circumstances) are coordinated and institutionalized, so that the onus is not on a handful of small organizations like UNIFEM or individual NGOs.

Financial support for women's groups is another key means of acknowledging their work. But it is not enough to provide organizations with the guidelines developed in New York, London, or Washington, D.C., and expect them to fulfill every criterion. For example, language is a major stumbling block for many smaller and rural organizations. Donors should allow for proposals to be presented in national languages. They should develop partnerships to help strengthen the administrative capacities of smaller organizations, so that they can continue their fieldwork without being overwhelmed with paperwork. In situations in which local NGOs do not have the means to access international funds directly, field-based representatives and international NGOs can be more effective conduits, setting up funds, disbursing grants, and bridging the divide between major donors and small, highly effective organizations. This decentralization is taking place among many bilateral donors and multilateral agencies, but without a requisite awareness of and attention to women's grassroots initiatives, women's groups can be, and often are, marginalized from funding initiatives.

The appointment of women to senior positions has important symbolic value. In the case of the UN, for example, in taking the helm of the UN in 2007, Secretary-General Ban Ki-moon appointed women to three out of five key leadership posts at the UN's New York headquarters. Are these appointments window dressing or an indication of a genuine commitment to women's leadership in the system? From the standpoint of countries affected by conflict, one test will be the number of women appointed as SRSGs and to senior field posts.[46] Of course that depends on the candidates put forward and endorsed by UN member states. It also has implications for the ways in which international entities (the UN and others) recruit, train, retain, and value the skills, capacities, and often diverse experiences that women may bring. In other words, it may require a significant overhaul of human resource management.

The bureaucratic obstacles exist, but ultimately, giving attention to women and, by extension, a more nuanced and fully gendered analysis is not difficult. It is largely about asking the questions, having the will to see conflict-affected societies through different eyes, and acknowledging that each person—regardless of status or circumstances during a conflict—has a voice and an understanding of what she or he needs to survive and move on in life. It is about making the invisible visible. It is also about looking beyond the stereotypical images of women's victimhood, respecting their desire and commitment to live in peace, recognizing that this commitment is among the most important ingredients of sustainable peacebuilding, and ensuring that interventions are designed to strengthen their capacities.

When alerted to these factors, few disagree with the fact that women's needs should be addressed or that women should be included. There are, of course, detractors who argue that the overt focus on women and the conflation of gender terms has failed women *and* men. Moreover, the advocacy of and attention to women have antagonized many people and have resulted in a backlash or implicit intransigence in many institutions. It is helped neither by the stereotyping of gender roles for men and women nor by the fact that both collude in perpetuating the norms. A change of tack and paradigm is needed; perhaps a focus on "excluded groups" is a more inclusive approach. Ironically, however, discussions of class, caste, disability, or other forms of identity can tend to overlook gender issues. Attention to women, however, tends to draw attention not only to men but to other cross sections of society—the elderly, children, traditional leaders, and so on. It introduces a level of nuance and texture to the analysis and understanding of societies changed by and emerging from conflict. If taken into account, women's experiences can help us address the sources of conflict and contribute to genuine peacebuilding.

Overt opposition is rarely the challenge; inertia, misunderstanding, lack of leadership, apathy, and the resultant ad hoc practices and amnesia are. The women, peace, and security agenda has been raising the volume and challenging the status quo for many years. Simple awareness and concern, however, are not enough. The reams of policy documents are necessary but not sufficient. Practice needs to change. The onus should be on all professional staff, not lone advisers, isolated units, or NGOs alone. Systematic technical and financial resources are needed. National governments must be held accountable for raising the issues. Bilateral and multilateral donors must respond and demonstrate their commitments. Perhaps then the women of Somalia, Sudan, Cambodia, and Colombia will finally feel the progress being made.

Notes

1. UN Security Council Presidential Statement, S/PRST/2005/5, October 2005, available at http://www.reliefweb.int/rw, retrieved July 26, 2006.

2. Emyr Jones Parry, *Report to the Security Council on the Council's Mission to Sudan, Addis Ababa and Chad,* June 15, 2006, available at http://www.darfurpeaceanddevelopment.org, retrieved July 26, 2006.

3. See Peacewomen 1325 Monitor, 1325 Resolution Watch, Country Index, available at http://www.peacewomen.org.

4. Antonia Potter, *We the Women: Why Conflict Mediation Is Not a Job for Men* (Geneva: Center for Humanitarian Dialogue, 2005).

5. Personal correspondence with the author, February 2007.

6. Kofi Annan, "No Government Has the Right to Hide Behind National Sovereignty in Order to Violate Human Rights," *Guardian Unlimited,* April 7, 1999, available at http://www.guardian.co.uk.

7. Lloyd Axworthy, *Human Security: Safety for People in a Changing World* (Ottawa: Canadian Ministry of Foreign Affairs, 1999), available at http://www.securitehumaine.gc.ca.

8. Kofi Annan, *In Larger Freedom: Towards Security, Development and Human Rights for All* (New York: United Nations, 2005), paragraph 220.

9. Francis Deng, "Human Security and the Global Challenge of Displacement," speech, Ministerial Meeting on Human Security, May 11, 2000, available at http://www.brookings.edu.

10. Discussion with the author, UN, New York, June 2006.

11. For more information, see Modem Lawson-Betum, "Women and Conflict Prevention in West Africa," in *Conflict Prevention and Transformation: Women's Vital Contributions,* Jolynn Shoemaker (ed.) (Washington, DC: Hunt Alternatives Fund, 2005), pp. 29–32.

12. International Labour Organization, *Definition of Gender Mainstreaming,* available at http://www.ilo.org, retrieved July 26, 2006.

13. Ibid.

14. Discussion with the author, Fiji, June 2006.

15. UN Development Programme, *Evaluation of Gender Mainstreaming in UNDP* (New York: United Nations, 2005), p. ix.

16. The discussion in this section is based on the author's interactions with personnel from a cross section of agencies, 2004–2006.

17. This reflects a similar format provided in the OCHA/IASC's "Gender Handbook," to which the author contributed. United Nations Inter Agency Standing Committee, *Women, Girls, Boys and Men: Different Needs, Equal Opportunities* (New York: United Nations Office for the Coordination of Humanitarian Affairs, 2006).

18. Discussions with UN personnel, New York, September 2005.

19. UNIFEM, *About UNIFEM,* available at www.unifem.org.

20. Division for the Advancement of Women, *About DAW.* For more information, see www.un.org/womenwatch/daw.

21. Office of the Special Adviser on Gender Issues and the Advancement of Women, *About OSAGI.* For more information, see http://www.un.org/women watch/osagi/aboutosagi.htm.

22. UN International Research and Training Institute for the Advancement of Women, *About INSTRAW.* For more information, see http://www.un-instraw.org.

23. Stephen Lewis, "Text of a Speech by Stephen Lewis, Delivered at the University of Pennsylvania's Summit on Global Issues in Women's Health," New York, April 26, 2005, available at http://www.realizingrights.org, retrieved July 26, 2006.

24. Ibid.

25. Sanam Naraghi Anderlini, *Mainstreaming Gender in Conflict Analysis: Issues and Recommendations,* Social Development Papers, No. 33, February 2006 (Washington, DC: World Bank, 2006).

26. Mary B. Anderson, *Do No Harm: How Aid Can Support Peace—or War* (Boulder, CO: Lynne Rienner, 1999).

27. Quoted in *Background to the Rights-based Approach to Development,* Australian Council for International Development, available at www.acfid.asn.au/campaigns.

28. Hugo Slim, "A Response to Peter Uvin, Making Moral Low Ground: Rights as a Struggle for Justice and Abolition of Development," *PRAXIS, Fletcher Journal of Development Studies* XVII, 2002.

29. Discussions with the author, July 2005, Washington, DC.

30. For more on this, see Caroline Moser and Cathy McIlwaine, "Violence in Colombia and Guatemala: Community Perceptions of Interrelationships with Social Capital," paper prepared for the International Conference on Crime and Violence: Causes and Policy Responses, Bogotá, Colombia, 2000, available at http://lnweb18.worldbank.org.

31. The author was involved in assessments and the development of guidelines for the World Bank and UNDP, 2005–2006.

32. The information was shared at a public event, "Priorities for Liberia's Reconstruction," at the Woodrow Wilson Center for International Scholars, Washington, DC, February 14, 2007.

33. United Nations Inter-Agency Standing Committee, *Women, Girls, Boys and Men.*

34. These comments and observations arose during the author's personal discussions with personnel at the UN and other entities regarding the exclusion of information about women from analyses and reports.

35. Discussions with the author, London, June 2006.

36. United Nations, Press Release SG/SM/7598, October 24, 2000.

37. Women's Commission for Refugee Women and Children, *Room to Maneuver: Lessons from Gender Mainstreaming in the UN's Department of Peacekeeping Operations* (New York: WCRWC, January 2007).

38. World Bank, Gender and Development, http://www.worldbank.org /gender/module/overview/bank.htm.

39. Marcia Greenberg and Andrea Zuckerman, "The Gender Dimensions of Post-Conflict Reconstruction: An Analytical Framework," *Gender and Development: An Oxfam Journal* 12, no. 3 (2004), available at http://www.genderaction .org.

40. UN Development Programme, *Evaluation of Gender Mainstreaming in UNDP*, p. vi.

41. The author has had numerous conversations with staff from multilateral and bilateral donor agencies. The intolerance of local culture (in Afghanistan, Nepal, etc.) was used as an excuse for not including or engaging women directly in postconflict programming.

42. For a summary of the project, see UNDP, "From Recovery to Transition: Women, the Untapped Resource," *Essentials,* no. 11, available at http:// www.undp.org.

43. Comment made during a presentation at the Center for Strategic and International Studies, 2004.

44. Author's discussion with former USAID senior staff, Washington, DC, 2006.

45. Examples of attention to staff training include the following. Within the UN system in 2005–2006, the Departments of Political Affairs and Peacekeeping Operations held workshops for some 300 staff in total. The UK's Post-Conflict Reconstruction Unit has also held trainings for some fifty-five personnel across government agencies. UNDP developed training modules. UNFPA also initiated workshops.

46. For a more detailed discussion on the recruitment and appointment of women to peacekeeping operations, see *United Nations Reform: Improving Peace Operations by Advancing the Role of Women* (Washington, DC: Stanley Foundation and Women in International Security, 2007), available at http:// www.stanleyfoundation.org.

eight

Conclusion

We showed our commitment through our peace advocacy.
We showed it when we went into the cantonments to disarm the boys.
We said it through the elections.
We say it on behalf of women everywhere. We are capable.
Hold on to our hands, and let us walk this walk together.
—Leymah Gbowee, executive director,
Women, Peace, and Security Network Africa, 2007

June 2007: The death toll in Iraq is mounting. In Darfur, the killing and rape go on, as international actors quibble about the nature and number of peacekeepers to be deployed. The peace deal signed in May 2006 is no more than a piece of paper. In Afghanistan, the 2006 spring offensive extended into the summer and beyond. Lebanon, bombarded by Israel in 2006 in the name of peace and security, is ever more tense. Sri Lanka is in another tailspin of violence. Palestine is splintering. In Nepal, hope reigns as the ten-year conflict with a Maoist movement ends, but the postconflict recovery process is daunting. Peace is still fleeting and fragile for much of West Africa.

Year in, year out, billions of dollars are being spent, the budget for peacekeeping operations seems to bloat, but sustainable peace remains elusive. The international community continues to struggle with crisis after crisis: Bosnia in the mid-1990s, Kosovo in 1999, Afghanistan in 2002, Iraq in 2003, and so forth. It is ambulance chasing on a global scale, but with an approximate 50 percent patient survival rate. Its attention span is limited, and the focus remains on the spoilers, those who shout loudest and threaten most. The war makers are still trusted to bring peace. Regardless of the evidence or the logic, the international community seems unable to change tactics and adopt alternative approaches: ones that are inclusive of local populations and supportive of the men and women who, amid the violence and attacks on their own communities, are preserving a slice of normalcy, reaching across the crossfire to reconcile, transform, and genuinely make peace.

In this book I focus on women as a cross section of these stakeholders. Whether by choice or necessity, conflict brings women to the fore. It changes social and gender relations. Devastating as war and conflict are for women, they are also a time when women step into the fray and empower themselves. They get a glimpse of how their roles in the family and society at large can be different. They are also a time when men's reliance on women increases. They learn to respect women for their abilities to cope, survive, protect, and recover. Thus, in conflict the seeds of transformation are planted. They can be easily crushed when peacetime norms return. But the international community should not lead that charge. It must not revert to old status quos and support the failed leadership and systems that led to war in the first place. It must not box women as victims only.

The international community has a responsibility to uphold the core values of human rights, equality, and respect by recognizing and building on the diversity that emerges from conflict. With respect to women, it can be a fine line to tread as external intervention can lead to backlash. We, as international actors, must not ignore them because the purported wisdom is that attention to women's voices, rights, and needs is "culturally insensitive." On the contrary, we should listen more closely and consult more effectively with a cross section of women. As practitioners and academics, we can bridge the gaps in knowledge and information, bring the experiences of one country to the other, and explore the successes and the failures to help avoid the pitfalls. As noted, however, the women activists of Afghanistan, Nepal, Liberia, or Somalia are the best navigators of their own cultural and political terrain. They know which issues are most important. They also know how to frame the issues in order to improve the lives of the people in their communities and to instill and demonstrate the universality of human rights values. This is not cultural relativism; it is realism.

I framed the discussion in this book around five of the pillars that international practitioners consider important: prevention of conflict; peace negotiations processes; disarmament, demobilization, and reintegration; governance; and transitional justice. There are others, notably socioeconomic development and trauma healing, that were beyond the scope of this book. Peace is not built on these pillars alone. It requires time and patience, involving myriad mundane issues. The 1,000 women Nobel Prize nominees can attest to that. But my goal has been to bridge the divide between the world of women's peacebuilding and that of the international peace and security community, to show how and why women's presence, activities, opinions, approaches, and resilience matter in precisely the areas that they are often ignored. In every area of work, women are not only actively engaged, but information about their experiences and how they are treated is directly relevant to the international community in building sustainable peace.

As discussed in Chapter 2, a focus on women leads to attention to others. Women are at the front lines of conflicts, literally and metaphorically. They are the first to experience extremism and the closing down of moderate space. The spikes in violence they experience in homes and communities are often the precursor to broader communal violence. Women are also at the front lines of peacemaking, as discussed in Chapter 3. Their courage and ability to reach out to erstwhile enemies, to talk, and to call for negotiated solutions often come years before the political class takes up the message, and long after violence has wreaked havoc. They bring the voices of victims to the peace table and broaden the agenda to tackle the economic, social, and cultural roots of conflict.

They are relevant to the business of disarmament, particularly the reintegration of fighters. As civilians, they bear the burden of reintegration and long-term rehabilitation. As fighters, they not only have a right to equal treatment and benefits, but also in many instances can be influential voices of peace within their own movements. In armed groups in which women fighters are respected and bearing weapons is a means of protection and empowerment, women may have the most to lose from DDR programming. Paying attention to their needs and alleviating their fears of marginalization can be key to sustaining the process. In instances in which women and girls provide the basic services to sustain armed groups, including them in DDR can be an effective means of weakening the structure and capacity of the movements.

Women's presence in governance structures can help set the stage for longer-term transformation. It widens the agenda of issues to be addressed, touching the lives of a more representative cross section of the population. Across the world, women are proving to be more amenable to working cooperatively, bridging political or ideological divides. That in many instances women are "trusted" more and perceived to be less corrupt, more dedicated to addressing people's needs, is in and of itself an important aspect of governance in the aftermath of violent conflict.

Their involvement in transitional justice processes opens new vistas for reconciliation. Their experiences give new meaning to "the whole truth" and notions of justice. Punishment of perpetrators and resources dedicated to that purpose seem somewhat inadequate when the victim has survived but is maimed, likely to be living with HIV/AIDS, or is a child born of rape. Their needs are in the future, and the justice they need must address this fact.

I am not suggesting that the international system ignores women entirely. As mentioned earlier, there has been support in a number of instances. Afghanistan was a watershed in terms of the attention given to women. There is ongoing work within the UN system and outside. The nascent UN Peacebuilding Commission has immense potential. Bilateral donors and regional institutions are making more concerted efforts to integrate the needs and perspectives of women into their programming. But the efforts under way are still largely ad hoc, too often dependent on a few committed individuals or small-scale units. Women are still an afterthought in many instances—the whole egg in the baked cake or the feel-good project to make donors and diplomats look good. A box to be ticked, a meeting to be had, a paragraph to be written: that is not enough.

Women have a right to protection and a right to equal say about the future of their countries. They also have a commitment to making that future as peaceful and just as possible and proving that it can be done. The international community must uphold these rights and live up to its commitments. It cannot be done through pilot projects and limited earmarked funding, the occasional speech, action plans, and recommendations that live on paper alone. Women must be considered and included at every stage and juncture: from analysis to practice, in the early planning and stages of any peace process, in the talks about the talks about the talks. This responsibility cannot be left to a lone gender adviser. Rather, consideration of the differing situations and needs of women and men (i.e., gendered perspectives) must become an integral part of every facet of work by governments and international actors, be it peacekeeping, elections and governance support, economic assistance, or advice on security issues. There needs to be accountability and transparency, a means of monitoring efforts, incentives, and penalties, from the leadership of every institution down to the proverbial trenches.

Women bring alternative perspectives and approaches; they can be strong allies in spreading the message of peace, but they also have needs. Attending to them may mean a reallocation of priorities and resources. It may demand expertise in new areas (sexual violence or family law, to help stem pervasive discrimination). It may also mean more cost-effective practices. To engage women directly, to implement the word and spirit of Resolution 1325, requires systemic change. It cannot be left to a handful of international NGOs with precarious funding or the small units dedicated to women across major agencies, with limited power to bring about that change.

In examining what women do for peace, I have sought to provide a balanced picture, neither overstated nor understated. It is easy to celebrate every initiative and believe that they are making *the* difference. That is rarely the case. To be true to them and their efforts, their achievements have to be qualified and contextualized because they rarely turn the tides completely. They cannot and do not purport to build peace alone. They work alongside others, making *a* contribution, *a* difference, sometimes affecting aspects of a process—say, peace negotiations or justice mechanism—other times giving a chance of life and dignity back to those in their communities through their reintegration and reconciliation efforts. They can be the deal makers, as in West Africa, but they are rarely the deal breakers. Therein lies the challenge. They are not typically the spoilers, the first to take up arms or revert to violence. So we tend to ignore them, but we do so at our own peril. It takes profound courage to speak of peace or reject arms in the midst of violence. Entering cantonment sites unarmed to disarm erstwhile fighters takes immense bravery. Even in the worst circumstances, as abducted children turned fighters and survivors, many are turning their victimhood into agency. Their commitment to peace far outweighs that of international actors. They are humanitarian workers and human rights activists, peacemakers and reconcilers before and after international actors weigh in. Thus, if overstating women's impact in peace and security is too much like advocacy, ignoring or understating their contributions is also taking a position.

Not all women are peacemakers; many are victimized into passivity. Others support war and violence. But they should not overshadow the countless thousands who do struggle for peace. Women's peace activism is not limited to any region, class, race, or religion. It is a global phenomenon that is growing every year and with every conflict. Within and among their organizations, people are not always collaborative or "sisterly." Ideologies, competition over scarce resources, egos, and the stress of working in war zones get in the way. They do not always adopt the best strategies and may not feel comfortable with the language and systems of the international actors or governmental counterparts. They may not have the means, time, or confidence to follow every political development and engage in every debate. They are not trained politicians and diplomats.

For the most part they are, for want of a better word, ordinary women who in the face of war have opted to take action. It is their ordinariness that makes them extraordinary. In the most adverse and seemingly intransigent conditions—Palestine, Iraq, Sudan, Somalia, Liberia, and elsewhere—they carry on, with hope and a vision of what is possible.

Their message is typically one of communication and negotiation, acknowledging that the conflict and its fallout are joint problems that must be solved together. They walk that talk. They also roll up their sleeves and get on with the arduous business of recovery—be it helping the displaced, caring for ex-soldiers and orphans, running a business, or entering politics. They are committed because it is their own lives; the political is deeply personal. They have no exit strategy. Time and again, women prove the invaluable contributions they can make, and their willingness to work for peace. As Liberian Leymah Gbowee says, "We showed our commitment through our peace advocacy. We showed it when we went into the cantonments to disarm the boys. We said it through the election of President Johnson-Sirleaf. We say it on behalf of women everywhere. We are capable. Hold on to our hands, and let us walk this walk together."[1]

The inclusion and empowerment of women in conflict prevention and peace processes is not simply idealism in the midst of international realpolitik. It is a necessary and infinitely pragmatic antidote to politics and business as usual, if the objective is sustainable peace.

Note

1. Leymah Gbowee, speaking at a public event, "Liberia's Priorities for Reconstruction" (Washington, DC: Woodrow Wilson Center for International Scholars, February 14, 2007).

Selected Bibliography

Anderlini, Sanam Naraghi. *Mainstreaming Gender in Conflict Analysis: Issues and Recommendations.* Social Development Papers No. 33, February 2006. Washington, DC: World Bank, 2006.
———. *Negotiating the Transition to Democracy and Reforming the Security Sector: The Vital Contributions of South African Women.* Washington, DC: Hunt Alternatives Fund, 2004, http://www.huntalternatives.org/pages/32 _case_studies.cfm.
———. *Women at the Peace Table: Making a Difference.* New York: UNIFEM, 2000.
Anderlini, Sanam Naraghi, Rita Manchanda, and Shireen Kermali (eds). *Women and Violent Conflict: Global Perspectives Conference Report.* London: International Alert, 1999.
Anderson, Mary B. *Do No Harm: How Aid Can Support Peace or War.* Boulder, CO: Lynne Rienner, 1999.
Anderson, Shelley. "My Only Clan Is Womanhood: Building Women's Peace Identities." International Fellowship on Reconciliation, Alkmaar, Netherlands, May 2005.
Annan, Kofi. *In Larger Freedom, Towards Security, Development, and Human Rights for All.* New York: UN, 2005.
Armstrong, Sally. *Veiled Threat: The Hidden Power of Afghan Women.* New York: Four Walls, Eight Windows, 2002.
Association of 1,000 Women for the Nobel Peace Prize 2005. *1000 PeaceWomen Across the Globe.* Zurich: Scalo, 2005.
Axworthy, Lloyd. *Human Security: Safety for People in a Changing World.* Ottawa: Canadian Ministry of Foreign Affairs, 1999.
Bannon, Ian, and Maria C. Correia. *The Other Half of Gender: Men's Issues in Development.* Washington, DC: World Bank, 2006.
Baron-Cohen, Simon. *The Essential Difference: The Truth About the Male and Female Brains.* New York: Basic Books, 2003.
Bennet, Olivia, Jo Bexley, and Kitty Warnock (eds.). *Arms to Fight, Arms to Protect: Women Speak Out About Conflict.* London: Panos, 1995.

Bloomfield, David, Martina Fischer, and Beatrix Schmelzle (eds.). *Berghof Handbook for Conflict Transformation*. Berlin: Berghof Research Center for Constructive Conflict Management, 2004, www.berghof-handbook.net.

Bouta, Tsjeard, Georg Frerks, and Ian Bannon. *Gender, Conflict, and Development*. Washington, DC: World Bank, 2005.

Boutros-Ghali, Boutros. *An Agenda for Peace: Preventive Diplomacy, Peacemaking, and Peacekeeping*. New York: UN, 1992, http://www.un.org/docs/SG/agpeace.html.

Chinkin, Christine. "Peace Agreements as a Means for Promoting Gender Equality and Ensuring Participation of Women." Expert Group Meeting Report. New York: United Nations Division for the Advancement of Women, 2003, http://www.peacewomen.org/resources/Peace_Negotiations/EGMChinkin.pdf.

Chitapi, Norman. "Too Many Cooks Could Spoil Mediation Process," *Africa Report,* June 6, 2007. London: Institute of War and Peace Reporting.

Cobban, Helena. "UNU Conference on Transitional Justice." *Just World News,* January 30, 2005, http://justworldnews.org/archives/001104.html.

Cock, Jacklyn. *Women and War in South Africa*. Cleveland, OH: Pilgrim Press, 1993.

Cockburn, Cynthia. Publications and ongoing research available at www.cynthia cockburn.org.

Collin Marks, Susan. *Watching the Wind: Conflict Resolution During South Africa's Transition to Democracy*. Washington, DC: United States Institute of Peace, 2000.

Deng, Francis. *Human Security and the Global Challenge of Displacement*. Speech, Ministerial Meeting on Human Security, May 11, 2000.

Deng, Francis, and Roberta Cohen. *Masses in Flight: The Global Crisis of Internal Displacement*. Washington, DC: Brookings Institution, 1998.

Dollar, David, Raymond Fisman, and Roberta Gatti. *Are Women Really the "Fairer" Sex? Corruption and Women in Government*. Policy Research Report on Gender and Development, Working Paper Series No. 4. Washington, DC: World Bank, 1999.

Enloe, Cynthia. *Bananas, Beaches, and Bases: Making Feminist Sense of International Politics*. London: Pandora Press, HarperCollins, 1989.

Farr, Vanessa. "Gendering Demilitarization as a Peacebuilding Tool." BICC Paper 20. Bonn, Germany: Bonn International Center for Conversion, 2002, http://www.bicc.de/general/paper20/content.html.

———. "The Importance of a Gender Perspective to Successful Disarmament, Demobilization, and Reintegration Processes." *Disarmament Forum* 4, 2003.

Fearon, Kate. *Women's Work: The Story of the Northern Ireland Coalition*. Belfast: Blackstaff Press, 1999.

Galtung, Johan. *Peace by Peaceful Means: Peace and Conflict, Development and Civilization*. Oslo: International Peace Research Institute, 1996.

Gobodo-Madikezela, Pumla. *Women's Contributions to the South African Truth and Reconciliation Commission*. Washington, DC: Hunt Alternatives Policy Commission, 2005.

Greenberg, Marcia, and Andrea Zuckerman. "The Gender Dimensions of Post-Conflict Reconstruction: An Analytical Framework." *Gender and Development:*

An Oxfam Journal 12, no. 3 (2004), http://www.genderaction.org/images /ez-mg%20oxfam%20g&d%20gender-pcr.pdf.

Hill, Felicity. "Engendering Early Warning Mechanisms for Effective Conflict Prevention: The Elusive Role of Women in Early Warning." *Conflict Trends,* no. 3 (October 2003). Durban, South Africa: African Centre for the Constructive Resolution of Disputes.

Humphreys, Macartan, and Jeremy Weinstein. *What the Fighters Say: A Survey of Ex-Combatants in Sierra Leone.* New York: Columbia University, 2004, http://www.columbia.edu/~mh2245/Report1_BW.pdf.

Hunt, Swanee. *This Was Not Our War: Bosnian Women Reclaiming the Peace.* Durham, NC: Duke University Press, 2004.

Initiative for Inclusive Security/International Alert. *Inclusive Security, Sustainable Peace: A Toolkit for Advocacy in Action.* Washington, DC, 2004, http:// www.huntalternatives.org/pages/87_inclusive_security_toolkit.cfm.

Initiative for Inclusive Security/Women Waging Peace. *Women's Rights and Democracy: Peaceful Transformation in Iran.* Washington, DC: Hunt Alternatives Fund, 2005.

Jacobs, Susie, Ruth Jacobson, and Jen Marchbank (eds.). *States of Conflict: Gender, Violence, and Resistance.* London: Zed Books, 2000.

Johnson Sirleaf, Ellen, and Elizabeth Rehn. *Women, War, and Peace: The Independent Experts' Assessment of the Impact of Armed Conflict on Women and Women's Role in Peace-building.* New York: UNIFEM, 2002.

Karami, Nader. "Grand Ayatollah Endorses End to Gender Discrimination." *Roozonline,* June 5, 2007, available at http://www.roozonline.com/english.

Kumar, Chetan. "United Nations Catalytic Processes for Peace-building." What Really Works in Preventing and Rebuilding Failed States, Occasional Paper Series, issue 2, December 2006. Washington, DC: Woodrow Wilson Center for International Scholars.

Kumar, Krishna (ed.). *Women and Civil War: Impact, Organizations, and Action.* Boulder, CO: Lynne Rienner, 2001.

Manchanda, Rita. *Naga Women Making a Difference: Peacebuilding in Northeastern India.* Washington, DC: Hunt Alternatives Fund, 2005.

———. *Women, War, and Peace in South Asia: Beyond Victimhood to Agency.* New Delhi: Sage Publications, 2001.

Mazurana, Dyan. "Women in Armed Opposition Groups in Africa and the Promotion of International Humanitarian Law and Human Rights." Report of a workshop organized in November 2005 in Addis Ababa by Geneva Call and the Program for the Study of International Organization(s), Geneva, 2006.

Mazurana, Dyan, and Kristopher Carlson. *From Combat to Community.* Washington, DC: Hunt Alternatives Fund, 2004.

Mazurana, Dyan, and Susan McKay. *Women and Peacebuilding: Essays on Human Rights and Development 8.* Montreal, Canada: International Center for Human Rights and Democratic Development, 1999.

McGrew, Laura, Kate Frieson, and Sambath Chan. *Good Governance from the Ground Up: Women's Roles in Post-Conflict Cambodia.* Washington, DC: Hunt Alternatives Fund, 2004.

Meintjes, Sheila, Anu Pillay, and Meredith Turshen. *The Aftermath: Women in Post-Conflict Transformation.* London: Zed Books, 2001.

Mertus, Julie. *War's Offensive on Women: The Humanitarian Challenge in Bos-nia, Kosovo, and Afghanistan.* Bloomfield, CT: Kumarian Press, 2000.
———. *Women's Participation in the International Tribunal for the Former Yugoslavia (ICTY): Transitional Justice for Bosnia and Herzegovina.* Washington, DC: Hunt Alternatives Fund, 2004.
Mertus, Julie, et al. (eds.). *The Suitcase: Refugee Voices from Bosnia and Croa-tia.* Berkeley: University of California Press, 1997.
Miall, Hugh. "Conflict Transformation: A Multi-Dimensional Task." In *Berghof Handbook for Conflict Transformation,* David Bloomfield, Martina Fis-cher, Beatrix Schmelzle (eds.). Wiesbaden, Germany: Berghof Research Center for Constructive Conflict Management, 2004, http://www.berghof-handbook.net.
Moser, Annalise. *Monitoring Peace and Conflict in the Solomon Islands.* Re-port No. 2. New York: UNIFEM, 2005.
Moser, Caroline. *Victims, Perpetrators, or Actors? Gender, Armed Conflict, and Political Violence.* London: Zed Books, 2001.
Nesiah, Vasuki. *Gender and Truth Commission Mandates.* New York: Interna-tional Center for Transitional Justice, 2005.
Newburger, Emily. "The Bus Driver's Daughter." *Harvard Law Bulletin* (Spring 2006), http://www.law.harvard.edu/alumni/bulletin/2006/spring/feature_3.php.
Nowrojee, Binaifer. "Making the Invisible War Crime Visible: Postconflict Jus-tice for Sierra Leone's Rape Victims." *Harvard Journal of Human Rights* 18 (Spring 2005).
Pampell Conaway, Camille, and Salomé Martinez. *Adding Value: Women's Contributions to Reintegration and Reconstruction in El Salvador.* Wash-ington, DC: Hunt Alternatives Fund, January 2004.
Paris, Roland. *At War's End: Building Peace After Civil Conflict.* Cambridge, UK: Cambridge University Press, 2004.
Paulson, Joshua. "Mothers of the Plaza de Mayo, Argentina, 1977–1983." In *Waging Nonviolent Struggle,* Gene Sharp (ed.). Boston: Extending Horizon Books, 2005.
Pires, Milena. *Enhancing Women's Participation in Electoral Processes Post-conflict: The Case of East Timor.* January 2004, UN Office of the Special Adviser on Gender Issues and the Advancement of Women, Experts Group Meeting, EGM/ELEC/2004/EP.6, http://www.un.org/womenwatch/osagi/meetings/2004/EGMelectoral/EP6-Pires.pdf.
Piza-Lopez, Eugenia, and Susanne Schmeidl. *Gender and Conflict Early Warn-ing: A Framework for Action.* London and Geneva: International Alert and Swiss Peace Foundation, 2002.
Potter, Antonia. "We the Women: Why Conflict Mediation Is Not Just a Job for Men." *Opinion,* October 2005. Geneva: Centre for Humanitarian Dialogue.
Powley, Elizabeth. *Strengthening Governance: The Role of Women in Rwanda's Transition.* Washington, DC: Hunt Alternatives Fund, 2004.
Reardon, Betty. *Women and Peace: Feminist Visions of Global Security.* Albany: SUNY Press, 1993.
Richards, Paul, et al. "Community Cohesion in Liberia: A Post-War Rapid Social Assessment." World Bank, Social Development Papers 31443, no. 21, Jan-uary 2005.

Rojas, Catalina. *In the Midst of War: Women's Contribution to Peace in Colombia.* Washington, DC: Hunt Alternatives Fund, 2004.

Ross, Amy. "Catch-22 in Uganda: The LRA, the ICC, and the Peace Process." *The Jurist,* July 17, 2006.

Ross, Fiona. *Bearing Witness: Women and the Truth and Reconciliation Commission in South Africa.* London: Pluto Press, 2003.

Sharoni, Simona. *Gender and the Israeli-Palestinian Conflict: The Politics of Women's Resistance.* Syracuse, NY: Syracuse University Press, 1994.

Shoemaker, Jolynn (ed.). *Conflict Prevention and Transformation: Women's Vital Contributions.* Washington, DC: Hunt Alternatives Fund, 2005.

Slim, Hugo. "A Response to Peter Uvin, Making Moral Low Ground: Rights as a Struggle for Justice and Abolition of Development." *PRAXIS, Fletcher Journal of Development Studies* 17 (2002).

Sultan, Masuda. *From Rhetoric to Reality: Afghan Women on the Agenda for Peace.* Washington, DC: Hunt Alternatives Fund, 2004.

Tait, Robert. "President's Future in Crisis as MPs Rebel and Economic Crisis Grows." *Guardian Unlimited,* January 16, 2007, http://www.guardian.co .uk/iran/story/0,,1991316,00.html.

Theidon, Kimberly. "Justice in Transition: The Micropolitics of Reconciliation in Postwar Peru." *Journal of Conflict Resolution* 50, no. 3 (June 2006).

Tickner, J. Ann. *Gender in International Relations: Feminist Perspectives on Achieving Global Security.* New York: Columbia University Press, 1992.

Turshen, Meredith, and Clotilde Twagiramariya (eds.). *What Women Do in Wartime: Gender and Conflict in Africa.* London: Zed Books, 1998.

United Nations Development Fund for Women. *Getting It Right, Doing It Right: Gender and Disarmament, Demobilization and Reintegration.* New York, 2004.

———. *Securing the Peace: Guiding the International Community Towards Women's Effective Participation Throughout Peace Processes.* New York: UNIFEM, October 2005.

United Nations Development Programme. "Evaluation of Gender Mainstreaming in UNDP." New York, 2006.

———. "Women: The Untapped Resource." *Essentials 11,* 2003.

United Nations Inter-Agency Standing Committee. *Women, Girls, Boys and Men, Different Needs, Equal Opportunities: A Gender Handbook for Humanitarian Action.* New York, December 2006.

United Nations Security Council. *Resolution 1325 on Women, Peace, and Security.* New York, 2000.

Victor, Barbara. *Army of Roses: Inside the World of Palestinian Suicide Bombers.* Rodale Press, 2003.

Vlachovà, Marie, and Lea Biason (eds.). *Women in an Insecure World: Violence Against Women: Facts, Figures and Analysis.* Geneva: Geneva Centre for the Democratic Control of Armed Forces, 2005.

Whitworth, Sandra. *Men, Militarism, and UN Peacekeeping.* Boulder, CO: Lynne Rienner, 2005.

Wolpe, Howard, et al. "Rebuilding Peace and State Capacity in War-Torn Burundi." *Round Table* 93, no. 375 (July 2004).

Women in International Security/Stanley Foundation. *United Nations Reform:*

Improving Peace Operations by Advancing the Role of Women. Washington, DC: WIIS, 2007.

Women's Commission for Refugee Women and Children. *Room to Maneuver: Lessons from Gender Mainstreaming in the UN's Department of Peacekeeping.* New York: WCRWC, 2007.

Woodrow Wilson Center for International Scholars. "United Nations Catalytic Processes for Peace-building: What Really Works in Preventing and Rebuilding Failed States." Occasional Paper Series, issue 2, December 2006. Washington, DC: WWIC.

Index

About the Book

How and why do women's contributions matter in peace and security processes? Why should women's activities in this sphere be explored separately from peacebuilding efforts in general? Decisively answering these questions, Sanam Naraghi Anderlini offers a comprehensive, cross-regional analysis of women's contributions to conflict prevention, resolution, and reconstruction around the world.

Anderlini also traces the evolution of international policies in this arena and highlights the endemic problems that stunt progress. Her astute analysis, based on extensive research and field experience, demonstrates how gender sensitivity in programming can be a catalytic component in the complex task of building sustainable peace—and she provides concrete examples of how to draw on and strengthen women's untapped potential.

Sanam Naraghi Anderlini is a research affiliate of the MIT Center for International Studies. For over a decade she has worked with the UN, NGOs, and bilateral donors as an advocate, researcher, trainer, and writer on issues relating to women's participation in peace and security. Her publications include *Civil Wars, Civil Peace: An Introduction to Conflict Resolution* (with Kumar Rupesinghe) and *Inclusive Security, Sustainable Peace: A Toolkit for Advocacy and Action.*